P9-CME-550

THE UNBANKING OF AMERICA

THE
UNBANKING
OF
AMER★CA

How the New Middle Class Survives

LISA
SERVON

HOUGHTON MIFFLIN HARCOURT
BOSTON —— NEW YORK
2017

Copyright © 2017 by Lisa Servon

ALL RIGHTS RESERVED

For information about permission to reproduce selections from this book,
write to trade.permissions@hmhco.com or to Permissions,
Houghton Mifflin Harcourt Publishing Company, 3 Park Avenue,
19th Floor, New York, New York 10016.

WWW.HMHCO.COM

Library of Congress Cataloging-in-Publication Data is available.
ISBN 978-0-544-60231-1

BOOK DESIGN BY MARK R. ROBINSON

Printed in the United States of America
DOC 10 9 8 7 6 5 4 3 2 1

For C.C. and Milo

CONTENTS

Not everything that counts can be counted,
and not everything that can be counted counts.

— WILLIAM BRUCE CAMERON

Introduction:

WE'RE ALL UNDERBANKED

GROWING UP IN SOUTH RIVER, NEW JERSEY, IN THE LATE 1960s and early 70s, I went to our local bank, Pulaski Savings and Loan, with my father as part of his Saturday errand ritual. We'd start out at the post office to mail the bills, stop in at Mike the butcher's shop to buy meat for the week, and then head to Pulaski Savings and Loan to deposit my father's check and take out some cash. I also went to the bank with my mother on the way home from school on Friday afternoons, sitting in the passenger seat of our 1976 Ford Elite while she cashed her teacher's paycheck at the drive-through. She deposited most of her pay, which my father would draw on to take care of the bills, and kept an envelope with a small amount of cash that she used to pick up milk and bread and pay for school field trips and the occasional treat until the next payday.

My parents opened my first savings account for me when I was seven. The teller gave me a green Pulaski passbook with gold lettering. It made me feel important, like I'd crossed some threshold and joined a club that bigger kids and grownups got to be a part of. I brought the passbook to the bank to deposit birthday checks from my grandparents and, later, babysitting money.

Growing up, I watched my parents write checks to pay the bills and use cash to buy groceries, clothes, and the infrequent meal out. I now realize that they were training me to become a particular kind of financial consumer. Their role modeling was critical, as were their expectation that I would go to college and their assumption that, by doing so, I'd get a job that would support me.

When I got my first job cleaning hotel rooms at the age of fourteen, I deposited my paychecks at Pulaski. Using the bank to manage my money still felt more like fulfilling an expectation than making a choice. In the early 1980s I moved away from home to go to college. I opened an account near campus without thinking much about it. That's what all my friends did. I didn't even know other options existed.

My parents didn't get a credit card until after I had left home, and I got my first — an American Express card — in 1987, the year after I graduated from college.

The world has changed. These days I do most of my banking online at odd hours. For my children, going to the bank means popping over to the nearest ATM to get cash. And on the rare occasion when I need to visit the teller window, I don't recognize any of the bank employees, and they don't know me. Today banks are bigger and more expensive to use, and their products are harder to understand. There's a lot more fine print than there used to be. In addition, all kinds of new financial products and services have become available. Many are coming not from banks, but from entrepreneurs who are harnessing technology, information, and the current moment in ways that are disrupting the entire financial-services industry.

The result? Banks are now catering more and more to the well-off, leaving the rest of us to pay too much at banks or to settle for imperfect alternatives such as check cashers and payday lenders. Check cashers enable people, for a fee, to cash checks, purchase money orders and prepaid debit cards, wire money, and pay bills. Payday lenders provide small short-term, high-cost loans.

• • •

As a university professor who studies financial services, I wanted to understand why people were leaving banks and using alternative financial-services providers when policymakers and consumer advocates were so convinced that this was a poor decision. I knew I could get only so far by reading policy reports and academic articles in my university office. So I got a job as a teller at RiteCheck, a check casher in the South Bronx, where I could get up close to people's decisions. Before working as a teller, I assumed that mainstream and alternative financial services were separate. Like a lot of policymakers, I thought educated, middle-class people like me used banks and that poor people used check cashers and payday lenders. I figured that people who didn't use banks aspired to having a bank account, that becoming "banked" was part of the well-traveled path of upward mobility. That was my path. And that's what the news accounts, policy reports, and research had led me to believe. I soon learned that the reality is much more complicated.

The consumer financial-services system — the large industry that consists of (1) mainstream banks, (2) alternative financial services (check cashers, payday lenders, pawnshops, and so on), and (3) informal practices such as saving in structured groups of friends or coworkers — is broken. Over the past four decades, most particularly since the financial crisis of 2008, banking itself has morphed into a system that no longer serves the needs of far too many Americans.

What caused this breakdown? First, banking has changed. Starting in the late 1970s, bank failures, policies that enabled consolidation, and aggressive marketing of credit to a larger and riskier group combined to transform banks. They got bigger and they focused less on consumers. Meanwhile, alternative financial-services providers, such as check cashers and payday lenders, expanded to fill the gap. Second, many more Americans are dealing with chronic financial instability. Declining wages, increased income volatility, and the erosion of benefits, along with increased costs for health care, childcare, and education, make it harder to make ends meet. The one-two punch of these trends has left Americans in a dire situation. We lack safe, affordable financial products and services when we need them most.

In 2012 the *Wall Street Journal* reported that a large number of Americans left banks in the wake of the 2008 financial crisis. For some, the departure was a way of protesting the role banks played in a crisis that left them and their neighbors jobless or behind on their mortgages. Others felt as though they got less value from banks than they did before. Still others found that they couldn't afford banks' rising fees. Between 2009 and 2013, the percentage of Americans with a checking account dropped from 92 percent to 88 percent, and the percentage with a savings account dropped from 72 percent to 68 percent.

A reader, responding to one of my articles, told the story of taking his young daughter to open a savings account. He was excited to begin her training as a saver and wanted to show her the magic of compound interest. (I remember the thrill of watching my own bank account grow — the money I earned just by leaving it there.) "We put in fifty dollars," my reader wrote, "and I had the idea that once a month we would go to the bank and make a deposit. Then we would watch the money grow, along with interest." His plan didn't pan out. "The next month we went back to make the next deposit, and lo and behold, there was only forty-five dollars in the account. Turned out that the bank was charging for low balances in savings accounts. End of lesson." The little girl was crestfallen and the father was angry. He got the bank to return the five dollars and closed her account—and his own.

Whether fed up with bank fees, like this reader, or lacking other options, many Americans have had it with banks. And the banks don't seem to care. If profits are your only concern, it doesn't make sense to provide savings accounts to children and other people who don't have much to save. It costs a lot for banks to collect small deposits. They're interested in providing these accounts only if they can cover their costs by charging fees. But the fees make it irrational for people to save. The result? A dearth of opportunities for people to save, a behavior considered important over the long term.

Meanwhile, the use of alternative financial services—check cashers, payday lenders, and the like—has exploded despite the perception that these businesses are "predatory," "sleazy," and part of the "poverty industry." Industry studies estimate that more than $58 billion in check-cashing transactions took place in 2010, up from $45 billion in 1990. Payday lending grew from $10 billion in 2001 to nearly $30 billion in 2012. Some people are attracted to what they perceive as the advantages offered by the alternatives: superior service, better product mix, and lower costs.

Many consumers are also using informal financial arrangements, such as rotating savings and credit associations (ROSCAs) and other systems worked out among family and friends, to substitute for or complement relationships with formal institutions. These consumers trust people they know more than they trust the banks.

While some have chosen to leave banks, others have been pushed out. Major banks and credit unions rely on private-sector databases such as ChexSystems, which keep data on how consumers handle their deposit accounts at banking institutions. This is how these databases work. Banks report bounced checks, negative balances, and other "irregularities" to ChexSystems, which then passes on the information to banks. A ChexSystems report that includes negative information about your account is the equivalent of blacklisting—even after a minor incident like a forty-dollar overdraft, you may be unable to open an account elsewhere for several years, despite having resolved all issues related to balance. Banks have closed the accounts of approximately 6 percent of Americans, without their consent, after receiving such information. More than one million people with low incomes have been deemed ineligible for bank accounts because of ChexSystems.

A graduate student recently wrote me the following note expressing his frustration with trying to become "banked":

> I've been attempting to maintain a bank account with TD Bank for the past year with little success. When I had a student account with TD, I wasn't required to maintain a monthly minimum . . . I currently work two jobs and yet still have a hard time actually keeping a healthy positive balance. I've had my account . . . closed three times and have pretty much given up (at least temporarily) on the idea of maintaining a checking account. Additionally, in response to the claim that the maintenance of a bank account is a sign of stability, I say this: In a labor market such as ours, where the college diploma has been wholly devalued, where median wages have remained stagnant for far too long, and where firms dispense of people as if they were unnecessary appendages, to what degree is financial stability actually attainable? And at what cost?

While people try to adapt to these changing situations, policymakers' view of personal finance has remained static. The Federal Deposit and Insurance Corporation (FDIC) conducts the biannual "National Survey of Unbanked and Underbanked Households." The survey classifies respondents as "banked" (they use only banks and credit unions), "unbanked" (they have no bank account), or "underbanked" (they have bank accounts but continue to rely on alternative financial services). As of 2013, the year of the FDIC's most recent survey, approximately 8 percent of Americans were unbanked and another 20 percent were underbanked. The picture looks far worse for people of color. One in five African American households and nearly 18 percent of Latino households are unbanked.

Policymakers, alarmed by these statistics, have been working hard to enfranchise the unbanked and underbanked. They insist that a formal relationship with a mainstream financial institution will improve these people's lives. Convinced that having a bank account enables one to move up the economic ladder, they paint banks as the good guys and alternatives as the bad guys. This simplistic view reflects unstated value judgments. Labeling people as *un-* or *under-* implies that they are somehow deficient, that they've made the wrong choices.

Julie Menin, commissioner for the Department of Consumer Affairs in New York City, writes that "mainstream banking services are associated with increased financial stability." This may be true, but there's a chicken-and-egg problem here — do banks make financial security possible for their customers, or is it the other way around? Do people with financial security make banks possible? From the evidence I've gathered, mainstream banks aren't doing a whole lot for people who aren't financially stable already. Right now, alternative and informal practices do a better job of serving many people's financial needs, especially among the many Americans who lack savings or a stable source of income.

My time working as a teller taught me that this reality is truly complex. Many people — and not just the poor — move in and out of the banking system. They don't necessarily "graduate" from alternative to mainstream. Is the term "alternative" still meaning-ful when many people use check cashers as a matter of course and may have no desire to get a bank account?

My months at RiteCheck answered some of my questions and raised new ones. I went on to work as a teller and loan collector at Check Center, a payday lender in Oakland, California. I staffed a hotline for payday-loan borrowers who were mired in debt and couldn't pay off their loans. I interviewed students who had made difficult decisions to take on debt in order to get the jobs they wanted, though they felt that they were placing other goals — such as buying a home or having a family — at risk. I got to know peo-ple who save, lend, and borrow money informally in their commu-nities and workplaces — strategies completely invisible to most of us. I spoke to people who work for credit unions, big banks, and small mission-oriented banks, to get their perspectives. I met with high-ranking government officials — some of whom understand our complex current reality and others whose bank-centered view of economic stability is completely outdated. And I talked to pas-sionate entrepreneurs who are creating new products, services, and infrastructure to make the consumer financial-services sys-tem work better for all of us.

Though my work began in a poor neighborhood in the South Bronx, I quickly realized that the problem was more widespread than I had thought. I discovered that chronic financial insecu-rity is growing among the middle class. In his book *The Great Risk Shift,* Jacob Hacker writes that "economic insecurity is not a prob-lem faced by a small vulnerable segment of the population. It is a problem faced by a wide swath of Americans ... Problems once confined to the working poor ... have crept up the income ladder to become an increasingly normal part of middle-class life." A re-cent study conducted by the Center for Financial Services Innova-tion found that 57 percent of Americans — 138 million people — are struggling financially, more than double the number of adults the FDIC categorized as unbanked or underbanked in its most recent survey.

I also learned that categorizing people as banked or unbanked seems largely irrelevant outside the financial-services industry. Not a single person I met when I worked as a teller thought of herself in those terms. Most of the people I met used mainstream, informal, and alternative financial products and services at different points in life, depending on what they needed and the resources available to them. What they all had in common was trying to figure out the best way to manage finances, in order to meet today's needs and plan for the future. To do this, people need to be able to trust the financial institutions they patronize and the products and services they use. Yet fewer people today are willing to put their trust in banks.

It's time to launch a movement that will pressure the public and private sectors to reform the consumer financial-services industry, in a way that makes financial health attainable and sustainable for all Americans. We need an industry that keeps people's money safe, provides high-quality, affordable products and services, aligns with our democratic values, and truly *serves* people, in the best sense of that word.

Right now we're all underbanked, but not in the way Washington believes us to be. We're underbanked because the banks that hold most of our assets do a lousy job of serving us. Mainstream banking especially doesn't make sense for many people who are financially insecure. To figure out what current banking trends mean for them, I entered the belly of the beast — a small check-cashing store in the South Bronx.

THE UNBANKING OF AMERICA

1

WHERE EVERYBODY KNOWS YOUR NAME

THE SKY IS INKY BLACK WHEN MY ALARM CLOCK GONGS AT 5:30 a.m. By the time I've showered and left the house, it's 6:20, and I hunch my shoulders against January's cold, hurrying the two blocks from my still-quiet house in Brooklyn to the 7th Avenue F train stop. The bright light of the station is a shock against the dark, sleepy street. I find a seat easily and settle in for the ride to Manhattan, where I'll change to the 6 train, which will take me to the South Bronx. The other passengers are mostly dressed in pastel-hued hospital scrubs, well-worn steel-toe boots, fast-food-worker and security-guard uniforms. These are the people who make the city work, who toil for little money and even less financial security.

My down coat conceals my own check casher's uniform, but my jeans and sneakers blend right in. Not fully awake yet, I try to re-create the feeling of being back home in my warm bed by retreating under my hood and closing my eyes.

I emerge from the subway at 138th Street and Alexander in the Mott Haven neighborhood of the South Bronx, next to the police precinct and across from Mitchel Houses, a ten-building high-rise public-housing project completed in the mid-1960s. Commenters on a Foursquare site dedicated to Mitchel Houses warn readers about this area: "Keep to yourself and you'll survive" and "Don't come here after dark. Hide your kids. Hide your wife." I stop at the Dunkin' Donuts on the corner of 138th and Willis for a large tea and a microwaved egg sandwich that will harden into a hockey puck if I wait too long to eat it. Dunkin' Donuts is the only national chain on the three-block strip between the subway station and RiteCheck, the check casher where I work as a teller. The Bangladeshi cashier, who has commuted to the South Bronx from Queens along with everyone else who works here, recognizes me and offers me a free donut. I've become one of the regulars. It's 7:30. The trains have been good to me today, so I'm early for my 8:00 a.m. shift; I'm supposed to arrive at 7:45 for the shift transition. Sitting at the counter and eating my sandwich, I lose myself in *El Diario,* the newspaper of Spanish-speaking New York. They don't sell the *New York Times* and the *Wall Street Journal* in these parts.

"You see that? White people coming in here now."

Slowly I tune in to the conversation behind me and realize that the woman who spoke these words is talking about me. Indeed, I am the only white person in the store.

The neighborhood is awake now — mothers with children in uniforms head to school, people stop into bodegas for a quick *café con leche,* others, equipped with briefcases or tool belts, hurry to the train. Marta, my favorite tamale lady, is virtually hidden beneath layers of sweatshirts and jackets, the scarf around her neck keeping her hood in place and nearly obscuring her face. Only her dark eyes are visible as she greets me while ladling steaming *arroz con leche* from an enormous orange insulated container into a cup for a customer. I can smell the milky sweetness, the pungent *canela,* from where I stand. Reaching into her granny cart, Marta hands me my usual — two *pollo con salsa verde* tamales. I have my money ready in my gloved hand and place it on her cart as she bags my lunch. She smiles and then turns to the next customer.

The South Bronx is Exhibit A of what researchers call a "geography of financial exclusion," where people tend to use mainstream financial services like banks less than people do in more affluent places. Its population of 500,000, including many immigrants and minorities, has only one bank per 20,000 residents. In Manhattan, one bank serves every 3,000 residents. More than half of the residents of Bronx Community Board 1, which includes Mott Haven, have no bank account; that figure is less than one in ten nationwide.

South Bronx households show evidence of severe financial distress. Almost three-quarters of Bronx residents have no money left over after paying the bills — that means fewer trips to Dunkin' Donuts, or to the toy store, or even to the supermarket. What money these residents do have often moves through informal channels and check cashers like RiteCheck rather than banks.

The South Bronx, encompassed within New York's 15th Congressional District, consists of the Hunts Point, Morrisania, Melrose, Tremont, Mott Haven, and Highbridge neighborhoods. Gentrification may be on its way; a recent article in the *New York Times* real-estate section proclaimed that Mott Haven can no longer be defined by old stereotypes like those perpetuated by the Foursquare site. "It is going through a gradual reinvention," writes the author, "with restaurants opening, scruffy buildings getting spiffed up, and apartments being built on gap-toothed lots." But the South Bronx is still the poorest area in the United States. Forty percent of its residents live below the poverty line, and nearly half used food stamps in the year 2010. The federal government's Home Owners' Loan Corporation triggered massive white flight from the area when it gave vast sections of the area its lowest rating — a D — in 1937.

Home to waves of Polish, Russian, Italian, German, and Irish immigrants through the 1940s, the area flipped from being two-thirds non-Latino white in 1950 to being two-thirds black or Puerto Rican in 1960. In 1969 the New York City welfare department was accused of "dumping" poor black and Puerto Rican families into public housing complexes like Mitchel Houses in the South Bronx, and in that same year the New York City Master Plan deemed 25 percent of the Bronx's rental units to be "dilapidated or deteriorating." An arson epidemic swept through the area in the 1970s; in 1974 there were 34,465 fires in the South Bronx. Urban legend has it that during Game One of the 1977 World Series, with the Yankees competing against the Los Angeles Dodgers, the overhead camera panned out to the neighborhood beyond the stadium as Howard Cosell announced, "There it is, ladies and gentlemen. The Bronx is burning." Cosell never said those words, but the phrase became a lasting descriptor of the borough during that era.

President Carter's 1977 appearance on a burned-out tract on Charlotte Street to "demonstrate a commitment to cities" was met with shouts of "Give us money!" and "We want jobs!" During his presidential campaign in 1980, Ronald Reagan returned to the same site to make the point that Carter had not made good on his promise. President Clinton visited twice, in 1995 and again in 2007. By then, Charlotte Street had been transformed into a well-maintained strip of single-family homes. Politicians pointed to Charlotte Street as an urban-policy success even though the statistics for the South Bronx hadn't changed all that much.

RiteCheck 12 sits in the middle of the block it shares with two barbershops, a bodega, a store selling medical supplies, and a large 99 Cent store run by a Chinese family. Most of the two- to seven-story buildings house apartments above the shops. RiteCheck's crisp blue-and-white awning looks fresher than those of the other businesses, and a sign on the door advertises the 24/7 hours. My sneakers squeak on the lobby's white tile floor as I pass between the two ATMs that flank the space. Posters of happy-looking people cover the walls. One announces a program for trading in unwanted gift cards for cash. Another advertises a way to send money to friends or family members who are doing time in jail. Along the right-hand wall sit a coin-counting machine and a copier, along with a counter holding wire-transfer forms for MoneyGram, which enables customers to send money to people in other countries and within the United States, and receive it too.

Balancing my tea and tamales in one hand, I rap on the bullet-proof glass of the teller window and wave to Tiffany, who is finishing up the night shift. She buzzes me through the first door and, when it closes safely behind me, opens the second door, which lets me into the room where we work all day, cashing people's checks, paying their bills, and selling stamps, MetroCards, and scratch-off tickets with promising names like "Lucky Dog" and "Black Pearls." I clock in and take off my coat, put my lunch in the refrigerator, and set down my tea and purse.

"Morning, Tiffany. How was the night?"

"Slow, slow, slow."

I notice the economics textbook peeking out of her bag. "At least you got some time to study."

"Mmmm hmmm."

Cristina, the senior teller on my shift, sits next to Tiffany. She is seven months pregnant, her posture perfectly erect as she works at the back computer, checking the overnight stats.

I find "my" drawer in one of the two gray metal safes along the wall. The safe is nearly my height and stocked with wrapped bundles of singles, fives, tens, twenties, fifties, and hundreds. One of last night's tellers left the drawer there after closing out; it is full of bills and change, with a stack of neatly rubber-banded Metro-Cards, stamps, and scratch-off tickets balanced on top. I count everything, making sure my tallies match those of the receipt in one of the drawer's compartments.

I set up my station, arranging the drawer in a file cabinet next to me. I turn on my MoneyGram machine and log into TellerMet-rix, the software program we use most often. I remove the NEXT WINDOW PLEASE sign from the bulletproof glass that separates me from the lobby and wave my first customer forward.

Several years ago I met Joe Coleman, president of RiteCheck, a small chain of check-cashing stores operating in the South Bronx and Harlem. A mutual friend had recommended him as a guest speaker for a course I was teaching. That week, my students had read critiques of check cashers that were as negative as they were predictable: this "shadow" banking system preyed on the most vulnerable, charging usurious interest rates and high fees. I had levied those criticisms myself. Even though I had never set foot in a check-cashing store, I looked forward to calling Joe Coleman to account.

He arrived at my classroom door in a slightly rumpled gray suit, his blue eyes bright behind metal-framed glasses. The twenty-three students in my class eyed him warily as he sat down next to me at the long seminar table and greeted them. Coleman began to speak persuasively about the services RiteCheck provides to the people who live in communities where his stores are located. "These people don't have any real alternatives," he told us. "The banks don't work for them. And to tell you the truth, the banks don't want them." Surprisingly, his presentation eventually disarmed us; he was not the calculating shark we had expected.

Coleman doesn't like the words "alternative" and "fringe" that people use to describe the check-cashing industry. He prefers the word "transactional" because that's how check cashers make their money—more transactions lead to bigger profits. "Let me tell you something about banks and check cashers, about their business models," he explained. "Banks want one customer with a million dollars. Check cashers like us want a million customers with one dollar." People who use check cashers come to the physical store frequently — once a week or more. Each individual transaction doesn't cost the customer very much — $1.50 to pay a bill, 89¢ to buy a money order — but these sums add up, which is one reason why people often denounce check-cashing businesses. Check cashers make their money by paying a lot of bills, selling a lot of money orders, cashing a lot of checks.

When my students asked Coleman about the fees customers pay to cash their checks, he told us his customers would rather pay a flat fee that they understand than get hit with unexpected charges and overdraft fees at a bank. He explained that people trust his tellers and continue to come back week after week, month after month, and year after year because they find RiteCheck to be less expensive than the local bank, and because they value the transparency, the convenience, and the service they receive. "Let's say a customer gets paid on Friday. If he brings his check to us, he gets his money immediately. He can pay his bills right away, go food shopping over the weekend. If he goes to the bank, his check won't clear until sometime the next week. He'll be late on his bills. And if he writes a check and it hits his account before the check he deposited clears, he'll be hit with an overdraft fee for more than thirty dollars — much more than the fee he would have paid us."

Coleman's visit raised more questions than it answered. Policymakers and consumer advocates claim that banks are safer and less expensive than check cashers. So why weren't Coleman's customers going to banks?

Conflict between residents and financial-services providers has a long history in the Bronx. In 1975, Congress passed the Home Mortgage Disclosure Act (HMDA), which required lending institutions to report loan data publicly. The community development expert Bill Frey used HMDA data that same year to determine that the number of mortgages made in the Bronx over the previous decade had dropped severely—just when the neighborhood was transitioning from a white population to black and Latino. Frey also found that the area's largest savings banks "had collected hundreds of millions of dollars in deposits from Bronx residents but issued only a tiny fraction of this amount in mortgages to them." In 1980, organizers and residents used the Community Reinvestment Act of 1977 as leverage to get local banks to pledge funds to underwrite two hundred new building projects and announce the availability of loans. This history could easily have driven some residents away from banks completely. But why did so many people who had maintained checking and savings accounts in traditional banks also continue to frequent alternative financial-services providers? What did the people who worked in check-cashing stores know that so many analysts failed to see?

Some time after Joe Coleman's guest lecture, I called him and asked if he would hire me as a teller. I wanted to understand firsthand the differences between check cashers, payday lenders, and banks. Even though Joe's presentation in my class had been convincing, a part of me still believed that this type of business had something to hide. My gut told me I needed to talk to people about how they made financial decisions rather than try to make sense of it from the comfort of my West Village office. I didn't expect Coleman's enthusiastic reaction to my proposal. I couldn't believe that anyone in the industry would want a professor getting that close to what happens on the other side of the teller window.

Before I could start my new job, I had to report to a nondescript office in the West Thirties of Manhattan. Tony, the armed ex-cop who handled my job screening, handed me an application on a clipboard. I wasn't going undercover, but as I read the questions on the forms—"How much money did you make at your last job?" and "Highest level of education?"—I realized how odd my responses would look. I waited anxiously as Tony perused my application. He merely told me he knew a couple of people who had gone to my New Jersey high school. Then he fingerprinted me and swabbed the inside of my cheek to test me for drug use. My credit score was analyzed, and I answered a hundred yes/no questions on a test designed to evaluate my honesty and integrity. Virtually every question was some form of this one: "Is it okay to steal from your employer?"

Next I attended an orientation at RiteCheck headquarters, a cramped floor above one of the stores, staffed by a team of smart, capable women. Six of us had made it through the initial screening, all Latino women except for me, all younger than me. Some were chatting and seemed to know one another. All were thrilled to have landed their jobs. Gigi Guerrero, who ran the orientation, showed us a PowerPoint presentation that detailed RiteCheck's policies, benefits, and perks. Some slides featured photos of staff members, and a couple of the new tellers recognized people in the photos. "That's my cousin!" one said, as a slide taken at the holiday party appeared. RiteCheck prides itself on being a family business and, indeed, new teller positions often go to the cousins, siblings, and friends of current tellers. Many of the managers and office staff began as tellers.

On my first day, I arrived at my assigned store in my royal-blue RiteCheck polo shirt, nervous about how things would go. It was late November, and the store was decorated with a turquoise-and-fuchsia Christmas tree. Matching tinsel and ornaments adorned the teller windows. Ana Paula, the manager for the branch, was speaking Spanish to the two tellers. She quickly switched to English after buzzing me through the doors. They all seemed apprehensive — I could imagine how news of my imminent arrival had gone down when Joe told folks I'd be working the window at their store. Ana Paula shook my hand and introduced me to Cristina and Joana, the two other tellers on my shift.

I hesitated to respond in Spanish because chances were good that their English was better than my Spanish. But I figured I could at least make an attempt: *"Bueno, podemos hablar en español si ustedes prefieren."*

"You speak Spanish?" Ana Paula seemed surprised. "They told me you only spoke English!"

Although my Spanish is far from perfect—and in fact became the subject of many jokes over the ensuing months—it helped break the ice.

I was itching to wait on customers, but I first had to pass a battery of online courses lasting a couple of hours, on topics ranging from how to use the "Z method" of spotting a bad check to how to identify "smurfing"—laundering money by breaking down a large transaction into smaller ones, to avoid tipping off the regulators. (The term comes from the comic-book characters known as Smurfs, a large group with many small members.) I spent my first two days on the job sitting at a computer and working my way through the modules. Although I passed the courses easily, the information clogged my brain, and I became convinced that a rogue gang would hoodwink me, targeting me as an easy mark.

Once I completed my studies, I shadowed Cristina for a couple of shifts to learn the software programs tellers use to pay bills and to send money to places like Guatemala, Kazakhstan, and Rikers Island. I then worked Cristina's window while she hovered behind me, helping me with what to do next, guiding me through the more complex and infrequent transactions that I had not yet observed. Several weeks passed before I got my own drawer at my own station, right next to Cristina, so that she could lend a hand when I needed it, which was a lot.

I had expected check cashing to be something like working the register at a store, but it was much more complicated. In addition to mastering the various software programs, I also had to remember the sequence of steps necessary to cash a check (I was forever forgetting to put the check through the scanner at the proper moment). I routinely dealt with hundreds or thousands of dollars and constantly felt anxious that I would screw up the count.

The worst part of the day was counting out my drawer at the end of the shift. While my fellow tellers would be humming to whatever was playing on 97.9 "La Mega" and talking about their plans for the evening as they easily squared the contents of their drawers with what the computer system told them they should have, I would be frowning, hunched over my drawer. I ran my enormous stack of cash through the bill counter over and over and never got the same total twice. We were supposed to close our tills about twenty minutes before the end of our shift, so that we could leave on time, but it always took me longer — sometimes much longer — to reconcile my tallies.

One day several weeks after I started, I counted out and held my breath while Cristina checked the computer to see how far off I was. My drawer came out exactly even, not a penny over or under. I was elated beyond reason. Cristina and Joana high-fived me and pronounced that I had now "graduated."

That day was more of a blip than the plateau point of my learning curve. The very next week I was more than two hundred dollars short. When one of us was short by such a large amount, we counted and re-counted everything; we scoured every single transaction conducted over the course of the eight-hour shift. Usually we figured it out, but not always. I didn't find out what I'd done wrong until the next week. A customer who had come in to take more than two hundred dollars in cash from her Electronic Benefits Transfer (EBT) card didn't have enough money in her account. When a customer asks for this kind of transaction, we look her up in the system, swipe her card through a special scanner, punch in the amount she wants taken out, and then ask the customer to enter her PIN. The system processes the information and then spits out a receipt with one of two messages: "approved" or "insufficient funds." Apparently I didn't read the "insufficient funds" message correctly, or at all. So much for my big "graduation."

"*Que va pasar ahora?*" I asked Cristina uneasily. "*Van a despedir me? Puedo pagar doscientos dólares.*" I thought I'd be fired. I offered to pay the money.

Cristina laughed. "They don't do that here," she reassured me. "Maybe if it keeps happening, yes, but you haven't been on the job that long. Everyone makes mistakes. They understand."

"We've all been there," Joana chimed in, reassuring me that my error was no big deal.

I did a mental tally of how much I'd been paid for that eight-hour shift — and figured that between the two hundred dollars I had given away plus my wages, I probably hadn't made much money for RiteCheck that day. I'd been trying to work as quickly as my colleagues, both of whom were veteran tellers. I envied them their lightning-fast bill-counting skills, their ability to move between monitor screens so quickly I could barely keep up even if I was just watching. My slow pace felt like a liability. I glanced up at the growing line of customers and felt I wasn't pulling my weight.

"Don't worry about fast," Joana told me. "Take your time and get it right."

So I slowed down. My drawer never came out exactly even again, but I never was short by a large amount.

Joe Coleman's former father-in-law, Howard Stein, got into the check-cashing business in 1949 after returning from Japan following World War II. A friend told him about his new financial business in Harlem and invited Stein to become a partner. Stein eventually bought out the partner and turned that first store on the corner of Striver's Row in Harlem into the chain of thirteen Rite-Check stores that now dot Harlem and the South Bronx.

New York began to regulate check-cashing businesses in 1944. At that time, policymakers approved of these businesses as a safe place for servicemen to cash their checks. "They would leave the Navy Yard," Stein told me, "and the bartenders would cash their checks if they bought a drink, but then they'd end up going home drunk with no money."

Back when he was growing the business, Stein did everything from working the window to balancing the books. He has lived the history of the check-cashing industry. At ninety-two, Stein is known around the office as "Papí" — a Latino term of endearment. Most of his stores are located in Latino neighborhoods. He told the story of the Harlem riots that followed the 1968 assassination of Dr. Martin Luther King Jr. "Someone called to tell me what was happening," Stein recounted, "and I got to the store as quickly as I could. When I arrived, many of the stores had broken windows, but one of our customers had parked a car with its front facing my store and the headlights on to try and keep the store safe." Stein exuded pride as he said, "People have always liked us — we're part of the community here."

Until recently, Stein came to the office every day. During the time I worked at RiteCheck, he went on safari to Africa and tripped outside his hotel room, breaking a leg. It took a long time to come back from that injury. Although he's moving a bit more slowly these days, Stein still comes to the office three days a week, shuffling down the hall with his walker. "I want to keep my hands in it," he said, his eyes sparkling. "I want to know what's going on."

Joe Coleman worked for Citibank before marrying Stein's daughter and moving to RiteCheck; they're divorced now, but

Coleman still runs the business under Howard Stein's watchful eye. Coleman is a well-respected figure in the alternative financial-services industry. When Stein started the business, check cashers were as generic as laundromats. It was Coleman who introduced the idea of branding, creating the RiteCheck name and its red, white, and blue color scheme. "Back then you didn't have a name," Stein told me. "We were just the currency exchange."

Coleman is also known among his peers as an intellectual, someone who is apt to quote Hegel and whose politics are more liberal than the typical check casher's. When I called him recently to get his response to some new legislation, he had just returned from an eight-day silent-meditation retreat.

Coleman has written an essay called "Let Them Have Bank Accounts," in which he questions the fixed notion that the answer to poor people's financial problems is to get them all to open bank accounts. "This assumption fails to frame the problem from the bottom up rather than the top down," Coleman says. "It's like providing pots and pans as the solution to hunger."

I hypothesized that I would see things at the RiteCheck teller window, working closely with customers, that I couldn't glean from the data sets that policymakers use to understand how and why people use "alternative" financial services. My hypothesis was correct.

Take Carlos, a local contractor who came to RiteCheck frequently to cash checks of several hundred to a few thousand dollars for his small business. One Thursday afternoon he came through the door, dressed in work boots and paint-splattered pants. He smiled at me and waved to Cristina as he approached my window and passed me a check for $5,000.

I input Carlos's RiteCheck keytag number into my computer. I took his photo with the small camera attached to my counter by a flexible metal neck, ran his check through the scanner, and counted out his money, checking the fat stack of bills by running them through the bill counter on the table behind me. I slid $4,902.50 through the window. The $97.50 fee — 1.95 percent of the face value of the check — is regulated by state law. Carlos slid a ten-dollar bill back to me — my tip — and waved and smiled as he turned to walk to the door.

I placed the ten on top of a small stack of bills on the shelf near my window and watched as he left the store. I thought about what Carlos could have done with that $97.50. Put it in a retirement account or in a savings account for his children's education? Bought some new tools for his business? Taken his wife out for a couple of nice dinners? I turned to Cristina again. *"Carlos — Porque paga casi cien dólares para cambiar su cheque aqui? Seguro que tiene cuenta de banco,"* I asked. Why would Carlos pay nearly a hundred dollars to cash his check here when he must have a bank account?

Cristina studied me for a moment and then began to explain in her patient, matter-of-fact way. "Today is Thursday, which means tomorrow is Friday, so Carlos probably has to pay his workers tomorrow." If Carlos is like many small contractors operating in New York City, he relies at least in part on undocumented workers, who are unlikely to have bank accounts. If Carlos deposited his check in a bank, it would take a few days to clear — too late to deliver cash on payday. Or maybe the check was a deposit for a job he had just been contracted to do, and he needed supplies to get started. If he couldn't start right away, he risked losing the job to another contractor.

Weeks later, we had had a leak in our ceiling at home in Brooklyn and the next morning our contractor, Tom, came by to check it out. Still thinking about Carlos, I asked him if contractors commonly use check cashers.

"I mean, you don't use one, do you, Tom?"

He laughed. "I got accounts at three, Lisa. Everyone does."

"But why?" Tom has a pretty big business — several renovation projects going at once, trucks painted with his firm's logo.

"The insurance, the taxes, the workers' comp — it's killing us. Some guys try to hide as much of their income as they can — they got two-million-dollar businesses and they report half a mil. I'm telling you — it's impossible to stay afloat if you don't do some of that. You can't run a business like this in New York City and be 100 percent legit."

The Bank Secrecy Act mandates that cash payments and checks over ten thousand dollars must be reported to the IRS, whether those payments happen through a bank or a check casher. Checks under ten thousand dollars will appear on your bank statement, but they're more difficult to trace if they are cashed at a check casher. Transactions are recorded and archived at the check casher, as they are at banks, but the IRS is unlikely to mount the cumbersome process of auditing and cross-referencing those records. How much a customer relies on check cashers to conceal his income depends on his conscience and his appetite for risk.

Consumers who overdraft their bank accounts look a lot like those who use alternative financial services. A twenty-five-year-old is 133 percent more likely to pay an overdraft fee than a sixty-five-year-old, and nearly 11 percent of consumers between the ages of eighteen and twenty-five have more than ten overdrafts per year. No wonder millennials envision a future without banks.

RiteCheck customers told me clearly that bank fees were an important factor in their decision to patronize check cashers. Zeke, a RiteCheck regular in his early thirties, told me he used to have a bank account, but closed it soon after he lost his job as an assistant chef at John F. Kennedy International Airport. Zeke now works as a janitor and hopes he can one day go to college; he uses a loan shark when he's short on cash. "I'd like to go back to the bank, but I can't afford the monthly charges," he told me. Maria, another regular customer, left her bank for the same reason. "It was like I just kept paying more and more," she said.

Beginning in 2010, the Federal Reserve mandated that banks allow customers to "opt in" to overdraft protection — that is, allow transactions to go through and get charged a fee when funds in the account are inadequate, or "opt out" and have transactions declined for nonsufficient funds (NSF). Consumers who have opted in pay an average of $21.61 in overdraft fees monthly, while those who opted out pay $2.98. Both categories of consumers pay more in overdraft and NSF fees than for all other types of fees.

Some banks don't charge an overdraft fee if an account is overdrawn by only a small amount, and some have placed a cap on the maximum amount that can be charged daily. Huntington Bank initiated a twenty-four-hour grace period on overdrafts and renewed its commitment to free checking, just when rivals had started pulling back on such accounts. But for most banks, overdrafts remain a significant source of revenue.

Despite this new regulation, both the Consumer Banking Project at the Pew Charitable Trusts and the Consumer Financial Protection Bureau (CFPB) have found that the opt in/opt out process is confusing, and many customers don't know whether they have opted in or out. More than half of the consumers surveyed for a Pew study don't recall opting in to their bank's overdraft service. Both Pew and the CFPB found that consumers would rather have their transactions declined than pay the overdraft fees.

Many independent contractors are willing to pay the fees charged by alternative financial-services providers to "stay afloat," as my contractor Tom puts it. But others simply need their money as soon as they can get it. Customer after customer told me that they couldn't afford to have the bank hold their check, waiting for it to clear. They needed that money right away to put food in the cupboard, avoid late fees on bills, or keep the electricity from being cut off.

Customers like Michelle come to RiteCheck to withdraw money from Electronic Benefits Transfer (EBT) cards, the vehicle by which the New York State Office of Temporary and Disability Assistance delivers cash and Supplemental Nutrition Assistance Program (SNAP) benefits to those who are eligible. Cash and SNAP benefits are deposited into electronic benefit accounts, which can be accessed by swiping the EBT card at an ATM or a terminal like the one on my counter at RiteCheck. Michelle came in one day and asked me to take ten dollars from her account. I swiped Michelle's card, she punched in her PIN, and I waited for the message: "approved" or "insufficient funds." RiteCheck charges a flat two-dollar fee for each transaction, even where neighborhood ATMs allow people to make two free withdrawals per month. When Michelle's request was approved, I gave her eight dollars; she paid what amounts to a 20 percent fee. Puzzled, I completed the transaction and turned to Cristina again.

"Bueno, Lisa, no puede sacar ocho dólares, o veintisiete dólares, de la ATM," she told me. You can't take eight dollars, or twenty-seven dollars, out of the ATM. Most let you withdraw amounts only in multiples of twenty, and these customers need every dollar they can get as soon as it becomes available. They pay the two dollars to get the eight dollars now because they can't wait until their account builds up to twenty dollars.

This is logical, albeit expensive, behavior. Yes, it's expensive to be poor. I can save money in ways that Michelle can't. I buy thirty rolls of toilet paper at a time at Costco instead of paying for the costly four-pack at my corner store. A steady job with good pay, a car, and space to store bulk goods allow me to spend two hundred dollars to stock up toilet paper and groceries, saving me money over the long term. Michelle has to focus on the short term.

Another reason people gave for choosing check cashers over banks is that they've found check cashers to be more transparent. Customers can find it difficult to predict when banks will charge them a fee (they sometimes change the timing) and what the amount of the fee will be; this lack of clarity can be costly, especially when budgets are tight. And checking-account disclosure statements, which are meant to clearly articulate the terms and conditions of the account, are anything but transparent. I had never looked at mine prior to doing the research for this book. So I did a little digging and found that the median length of these disclosure statements is forty-four pages, in fine print and highly technical language, excluding addenda and supplementary information. Customers who don't have time to parse forty-four pages and can't afford to guess when the checks they deposit will clear appreciate the security, even with a fee, offered by check cashers.

The physical design of bank branches also contributes to this lack of transparency. Picture the interior of your bank. Now imagine for a moment that you are a new immigrant. Is information prominently posted to tell you what products are on offer and how much they cost? Now imagine the interior of a check casher — or visit one. It resembles a fast-food restaurant more than a bank. Posters tell you what products are sold, and large signs above the teller windows list every product, along with its price — at Rite-Check, it's clear that a money order costs 89¢ (less than the $1.20 that the post office charges), you need $1.50 to pay a bill, and to cash a check, you'll pay 1.95 percent of its face value.

Working at RiteCheck, I quickly observed another difference between banks and alternative financial-services providers: personal relationships. The person-to-person connections I witnessed and experienced as a teller resembled those I had enjoyed as a child at Pulaski Savings and Loan with my dad. It's not what I find today at the big banks. The last time I visited the nearest branch of my current bank, a well-dressed employee offered to help me with the ATM "so I wouldn't have to wait in line to see a teller." Never mind that I couldn't get what I needed at the ATM — I got the message.

The customer-teller relationship at RiteCheck creates remarkable loyalty. Nina, who has spent most of her life in Mott Haven, told me that when her mother was very ill, the RiteCheck staff had called her at home to ask about her. "So we can be family," Nina explained. "We know all of them." This "family feeling" makes customers feel comfortable asking the tellers for small favors. Sometimes a Spanish-speaking customer would ask for help with translating an official letter she had received, and perhaps even for advice on how to deal with its contents. Brett King, the global finance expert, explains the contrasting ethic at many banks: "What a banker might call advice — the cross-sell and upsell — is not advice from a customer perspective. True, unsolicited advice that helps the customer without expectation of revenue is very rare because there is simply no metric in the system that allows for this."

Being a frequent customer at the check casher brings other more tangible benefits. Luz, a regular, came to my window one afternoon with a government-issued disability check to cash. When I input the number from her RiteCheck keytag into my computer, the screen indicated she owed RiteCheck twenty dollars from every check she cashed. I turned to Cristina for help and learned that Luz had cashed a bad check a while back. RiteCheck had worked out an arrangement whereby she pays back what she owes in twenty-dollar installments.

"Pero no tengo los veinte pesos hoy," Luz explained. She could not pay the twenty dollars today — she needed her entire check to

cover an unexpected expense. I called Cristina over and she assessed the situation.

"No te preocupes, mami— la próxima vez." Cristina knew that Luz would repay her debt and that accommodating her was good for business. Management had also empowered Cristina, who had years of experience working directly with customers, to decide how to handle this type of situation. At RiteCheck, the tellers treated the customers as individuals and went the extra mile to serve them, just as a neighborhood grocer might allow a trusted customer to run a monthly tab.

Like the more experienced waitresses I worked with at a diner during summer breaks from college, Cristina often knew what her customers needed before they reached her window. Jorge, a grizzled, wheelchair-bound man, came in every morning, greeting the tellers by name and steering himself to Cristina's station. He bestowed a wide, toothless smile on her as she checked the previous day's winning Lotto numbers and slipped the printout under the bulletproof glass window without his having to ask for it. Jorge gave Cristina a slip of paper with the pencil-scrawled numbers he wanted to play that day, and she entered them quickly into the Lotto machine. *"¡Suerte!"* she called after him as he wheeled his way out the door.

Our busiest days occurred at the beginning and the end of the month, when customers came for their government benefits checks. Scores of customers paid RiteCheck $2.50 each month to have their monthly Supplemental Security Income checks sent directly to the store—because the checks would arrive at RiteCheck electronically a day or two before the mail would have delivered them to their homes. (I observed this in the spring of 2012, shortly before the federal government stopped issuing paper checks in favor of direct deposit, a cost-saving measure that required aid recipients to open a bank account.)

At RiteCheck we never knew exactly when the checks would arrive, and the phones rang incessantly a day or two beforehand. Some callers didn't even bother to say hello — "Are they there yet?" was their greeting. Once the checks appeared, word spread like wildfire, and within the hour our lobby would be crowded. On days like these, tellers skipped lunch and coffee breaks in order to keep the wait times down. Ana Paula, our manager, often joined us at the window. The customer always came first.

This level of affability wasn't accidental; it was baked into the culture of the business. Check cashers depend on customer loyalty. As Joe Coleman had explained to my class, the business model requires a high volume of transactions; one of the best ways to ensure this outcome is to encourage customers to keep coming back. To select its tellers, RiteCheck used some of the same criteria Apple uses when hiring staff for its stores: friendliness, patience, and a service orientation.

Our customers clearly valued this level of service. It was not unusual for a customer to bring us coffee in the morning. RiteCheck customers often tipped us, as Carlos did; for tellers who had been working at the store for a long time, those tips could add up to an extra forty or fifty dollars a day. When Cristina, who was very pregnant when I started, had her baby, customers asked after her and dropped off gifts.

When consumers choose between a bank and a check casher, business atmosphere and staff attitudes are not the only criteria considered. But they are important. As the theme song of the old TV show *Cheers* puts it, "You want to go where everybody knows your name."

RiteCheck meets the specific, immediate needs of people who believe they cannot save right now, who have been burned by banks, who are focused on figuring out what to do today in a way that makes planning for the future challenging. If banks want to attract the customers who tend to choose check cashers (and it's not clear that they do), banks should remember their identity as a service industry involved in one of society's most important basic relationships. Why don't they do this now? The answer is complicated and involves policy, business models, and acceptable business practice. I had to go to Washington, DC, to begin to piece this puzzle together.

2

BANKONOMICS, OR HOW BANKING CHANGED AND MOST OF US LOST OUT

DEBATES ABOUT THE PERILS ASSOCIATED WITH OVERLY large banks have been going on since the founding of our nation. Thomas Jefferson, Woodrow Wilson, and Supreme Court Justice Louis Brandeis all warned about dangers stemming from the growth of banks and from bankers' self-interested business practices. Sometimes their arguments were heeded and sometimes not: the pendulum has swung both ways as to whether government should require banks to do more to serve all of us equally well in exchange for the economic benefits they get from the public sector. The FDIC, for example, insures all of the money we keep at banks. If banks fail, as they did in 1929, we won't lose our money.

Over the past few decades, regulation has favored the banks. During this most recent period, small, locally based banks like Pulaski Savings and Loan have morphed into large multinational organizations that often have little connection to the communities where they operate or the customers they serve. These supersized institutions are growing bigger, lending less, and increasingly serving only the wealthiest customers.

A reader who happens to be an expert on money and banking recently sent me an email that's worth quoting in its entirety:

My wife and I use [a major bank] and get good service. We have five accounts there, including free checking, free safety deposit box, and free stock trading in the Merrill Lynch account linked to my accounts. If we have a question, we call a special dedicated line for preferred customers and get immediate detailed responses to our questions from knowledgeable staff. We have additional valuable perks as well. In return, they modestly ask that the asset balances in our accounts exceed $1,000,000 and our checking account balance stay above $50,000. They even pay interest on the checking balance.

Free stock trading saves us a bundle but it's really not free. They execute our stock orders in their dark pool and feed us to high-frequency traders—including their in-house staff of thieves—who front-run our orders and steal a penny or two from each share traded whenever they can ... When we sell stocks, it takes forever for our orders to clear, and they hold the proceeds for an additional day; we get charged very quickly when we buy stocks. Thus, free trading means they steal around $200 a year from us through front-running and fraudulent clearing of trades. I've priced it out and it's cheaper than using a discount broker (most of them steal too). Welcome to modern banking.

Banks got big for two main reasons. First, they were allowed to do more than just maintain depository accounts. After the Great Crash of 1929, Congress passed the Glass-Steagall Act, which prevented banks from engaging in both investment banking (what Wall Street does) and commercial banking (what smaller, more local banks that take deposits typically do). Risky investment had led to the crash, and the law was designed to minimize banks' ability to take such risks. Seventy years later, in 1999, Congress passed the Gramm-Leach-Bliley Act, permitting banks once again to engage in both commercial and investment activities. This legislation effectively nullified Glass-Steagall. It allowed commercial banks, investment banks, securities firms, and insurance companies to merge and grow, and the industry became increasingly consolidated. Individual depositors are protected by deposit insurance, which was created in 1933. But as the recent crisis has shown, the consequences of banks' high-risk investment strategies can affect consumers in many different ways.

The second reason banks got so big is that they are no longer extremely restricted in terms of where they can do business. Walking the streets of any major city, where outlets of the largest banks seem to populate virtually every corner, you might find it hard to imagine a time when banks weren't allowed to open branches. But nearly all states restricted branching in the late nineteenth and early twentieth centuries to protect consumers from monopolies. Most of these laws remained in place until the early 1980s. Once banks were allowed to branch, they expanded by opening in new locations and, like giant Pac-Man characters, by gobbling up small banks.

Everyone who worked at Pulaski Savings and Loan lived in South River. The bankers and their customers were connected in all kinds of ways: their children went to school together, they ran into one another at the grocery store, they attended the same places of worship. The proximity of bank and customer enabled the kind of relationships that check-casher customers value so highly today. Many people I spoke with while researching this book told me how their small local banks had changed names and ownership four or five times since they had opened their accounts, leaving them with no connection to the current business.

Banks like Pulaski still exist but have dwindled in number: very small banks (those with less than $100 million in assets) decreased by 85 percent between 1985 and 2013, while the number of very

large banks (those with more than $10 billion in assets) nearly tri-
pled. Local banking is now the exception rather than the norm it
was when I opened my first account in 1971.

Trying to figure out what had motivated these changes and led to
the consumer financial-services industry we have today, I put together an eleven-page, five-column table that listed and described
every piece of bank legislation that had been passed and every policy event that occurred since 1900. Despite months of research and
reading, I couldn't discern a story that would link the boxes in my
table. I sent the table to Ellen Seidman, a bank-policy expert I had
met at a conference, and asked if she would look it over. I met with
Seidman the following week at her office at the Urban Institute, a
DC think tank, where she is a senior fellow. A lawyer by training,
Seidman has spent most of her long career in the public and nonprofit sectors, including directing the Office of Thrift Supervision,
serving as special assistant for economic policy to President Clinton, and holding senior positions at Fannie Mae, the Department
of Transportation, and the Treasury.

Seidman was on the phone when I reached her office. She
smiled and motioned me to sit, and I noticed my eleven pages sitting on her desk, covered in notes. "Damn," I thought. "I knew I
should have worked on that more before I sent it." Seidman ended
her phone call and jumped right in, correcting my misperceptions
and providing me with insight and information that added meat to
the bones of my skeletal outline. I left her office with a list of people I needed to interview and a longer reading list. I talked with
Seidman's contacts, kept reading, and circled back to her several
times, until the story finally came together.

I learned that as banks grew and became more removed from
the day-to-day needs of their customers, their business models
also changed. Over time, they made more and more of their money

from fees instead of interest. The larger banks also became more complex. Historically, banks made their money by borrowing and lending, which generated interest income. But events like the savings and loan crisis in the late 1980s and early 1990s, when so many banks failed, illustrated how disastrous that model could be. In order to make banks less vulnerable to volatile interest rates, bank examiners encouraged them to find other ways to make a profit. That's when banks discovered fees — the fees that anger and frustrate nearly everyone I've spoken with.

JoAnn Barefoot was one of the first people on Seidman's list. Barefoot's career includes stops at the US Department of Housing and Urban Development, the Federal Housing Administration, the Federal Home Loan Bank Board, and a time as deputy controller of the currency. Her long, center-parted hair and slim build give her more than a passing resemblance to Gloria Steinem. Barefoot had brought along her colleague Lyn Farrell, a managing director at the bank advisory firm Treliant, where she leads the firm's consumer compliance group. Farrell was excited about my project and eager to join our conversation.

Farrell explained how and why banks began to charge so many fees. "It used to be that banks offered overdraft protection to customers as a courtesy. Until the mid-1990s, bankers hated overdraft protection. They didn't charge much for it, and it just generated more paperwork," she said. "They only did it for people who had a lot of money in the bank, whom they trusted."

But then consulting firms and vendors like Haberfeld Associates and Strunk and Associates helped banks figure out how to turn services like overdraft protection and ATMs into cash cows. Once these consulting firms showed bankers how little they would lose compared to the money they could make from new fees, the change spread quickly.

Some banks, particularly those with close ties to their communities, resisted charging these new fees for as long as they could. Among smaller and more mission-driven banks, the "culture of 'high overdraft fees are bad' was very strong," Farrell said. "I had this CEO of the First National Bank of Eagle Lake, Texas, tell me that he wasn't going to charge overdraft fees. He thought it was unconscionable to charge a thirty-dollar overdraft fee when the overdraft doesn't cost the bank that much." She paused. "I mean, that was his view, but he couldn't make it in the big city either." It became difficult for "banks with a conscience" to compete with banks that valued profits over customers.

Once bankers experienced this new way to profit from over-drafts, it was impossible to go back. Farrell said that one bank CEO told her, "It's like a drug. Once people get this, it's like a drug." Barefoot concurred: "I've heard people say it's like crack cocaine." In a *Bank Director* magazine article published in 2011, a Haberfeld executive boasted that banks working with his firm generate 86 percent of their fee revenue from overdraft and other new fees, which the firm calls the "gold mine of checking."

And it wasn't just overdraft fees. Seidman explained that so-called free checking, the ability to overdraw an account, and variable interest rates on credit cards initially seemed to be good for consumers. But once banks began to see that these products and services could be profitable, she noted, "bad things started happening."

The average charge per overdraft went from $21.57 in 1998 to $31.26 in 2012. Similarly, average ATM fees more than doubled between 2001 and 2014. Some banks began to charge one or two dollars for paper statements and up to twenty-five dollars for a replacement debit card. The Financial Clinic, a New York City–based financial coaching nonprofit that works primarily with people with lower incomes, had considered "lower use of alternative financial services/increased use of banks" as a measure of success.

Not anymore. "When I sat down and looked at my clients' bank statements and saw that they had paid $110 in fees, I often ended up sending them to the check casher instead," said the clinic's executive director, Mae Watson Grote.

Many consumers became overly reliant on overdrafts. Some who lack other sources of funds use overdrafts like a short-term loan. Unfortunately, a single overdraft can result in cascading bad checks and hundreds of dollars in charges.

Let's take a look at exactly how this works: Say you have $100 in your account, and today you have an automatic student-loan payment of $110 scheduled. The automatic payment will result in a deficit of $10. The bank will charge a $34 overdraft fee, which is typical for big banks. You now have a deficit of $44. Imagine you also use your checking-account debit card that day to purchase $25 worth of groceries. That purchase will trigger another overdraft, and you will be charged another $34. For $135 worth of transactions, you have been charged $78. But it may not stop there. If the account balance remains overdrawn for five consecutive business days, the bank will charge an extended overdraft fee per item, typically between $15 and $35.

It's quite possible that the chain reaction started with a common miscalculation: you presumed that a check you'd deposited into your account would clear before the student-loan payment came due. But your check took a day longer than usual to clear. Banks depend on these miscalculations. In 2014, Americans paid nearly $32 billion in overdraft fees, and $6 billion of it went to the three biggest banks (Chase, Bank of America, and Wells Fargo). That's just one reason why more than twelve million Americans manage their money without a bank.

A sizable chunk of the consumers who began to depend on overdrafts couldn't pay them back. The banks eventually closed their accounts. The consumers then ended up in one of the databases, like ChexSystems, that banks use to screen new customers and decide whether they can open an account.

For years, regulators did nothing about banks' increasing generation of overdraft fees. Dodd-Frank, the 2010 legislation passed in the wake of the financial crisis, took a big bite out of banks' ability to generate overdraft and other fees, but banks have figured out how to get around it. In May 2014, Haberfeld Associates presented a webinar showing participants how overdraft protection could continue to function as an income stream for banks, even after Dodd-Frank required banks to get customers to opt in to the service. The paperwork for setting up an account is so opaque that nearly half of all consumers who overdrew their accounts didn't remember opting in to overdraft protection. That's because the paperwork is designed to be unclear. This lack of transparency is one of the primary reasons my check-casher customers didn't like going to the bank.

In February 2015, Adam Griesel, the current CEO of Haberfeld, wrote an article titled "Add Customers, Grow Profits," in which he advised banks to market free checking accounts to customers and then turn those customers into fee generators. Checking accounts, Griesel wrote, are the gateway to a range of other bank products — debit cards, paper checks, overdraft protection — that generate fee income. Having a checking account is typically a consumer's main reason for working with a bank. Sixty-four percent of consumers exclusively use a debit card from that account, and free-checking customers use an average of 4.75 products and services, all of which generate fee income.

Haberfeld Associates also instructed banks and credit unions on how to make money from debit cards. The firm found that customers with debit cards generated more fees annually, an average of $336, than other customers, who generated only $260. Banks charge merchants every time a debit card is swiped, and although those fees have dropped, banks are doing everything they can to increase the volume of use. To get customers to use their debit cards more frequently, Haberfeld recommended launching a onetime reward campaign — something like a ten-dollar reward for using the debit card ten times in a month. The idea is that a campaign like this will get the customer into the habit of using the card, which will generate more fee income over the long term. Such incentives aren't new to banks — I still have a well-functioning Black & Decker hand mixer that I got when I opened a bank account more than ten years ago. But that gift wasn't inspired by the kind of sophisticated behavioral research that underlies today's bank strategies.

Another big-bank practice is called "debit resequencing"; the bank processes the debits and credits to an account in a way that causes account balances to fall faster, thereby boosting potential overdraft fees. In February 2012, Chase settled a class-action suit accusing the bank of charging excessive overdraft fees. In November 2011, Bank of America was ordered to pay $410 million to customers for wrongfully charging excessive overdraft fees resulting from debit resequencing. Despite these two huge suits and subsequent regulatory action, 44 percent of banks included in a recent study still engage in this practice. The numbers are decreasing, but not enough.

Here's how debit resequencing works. Let's say that on a given date you send two checks — one to your credit card company for $150 and another to your local electric company for $75; the credit card company and the electric company try to get their money from your account on the same date. An automatic withdrawal you've set up to pay your rent also hits your account; your rent is $500. On the date that those three things hit your account, you have a balance of $100. The bank could clear the $75 charge first, resulting in two overdraft fees. Instead, many use software that reorders the transactions. This software presents the $500 charge first, then the $150 charge, and finally the $75 charge, and you end up paying three overdraft fees instead of two. Banks make this choice to maximize profit rather than to do right by their customers.

To make matters worse, it's becoming more difficult for consumers to resort to the kind of class-action lawsuits that led to settlements with Chase and Bank of America. More corporations are requiring that consumers waive their right to sue before gaining access to a product or service. Instead, plaintiffs must seek arbitration, pursuing their claims individually and privately. Research shows that if people cannot go to court as a group, they are likely to drop their claims completely, decreasing the chances that corporations will be held accountable for wrongdoing. This shift from lawsuits to arbitration means that law-enforcement officials "have lost an essential tool for uncovering patterns of corporate abuse," says Walter Hackett, a former banker turned consumer lawyer, quoted in the *New York Times*. Hackett links this shift to companies' fear that lawsuits will force them to "abandon lucrative billing practices... When banks make mistakes or do bad things," Hackett says, "they tend to do them many times and to many people."

Banks are not the only type of business to engage in practices that aren't in the best interest of consumers. In their book *Phishing for Phools,* the Nobel Prize–winning economists George Akerlof and Robert Shiller argue that the free market is set up to reward tricksters. Business people, they say, are under pressure to compete and to make the most profit possible. This environment leads them to engage in manipulation and deception. "The economic system," Akerloff and Shiller write, "is filled with trickery." Manipulation and deception, from opaque fees to unethical debt-collection practices, run through the entire consumer financial-services system. It is essential to pay special attention to this bad behavior for two main reasons. First, its consequences, as we saw in the subprime mortgage crisis, can be dire and widespread. And second, the financial sector is a key part of our economic infrastructure and, as such, receives a lot of benefits from the government. These benefits should come with an understanding that manipulation and deception will not be tolerated. But even after the severe lesson of the financial crisis of 2008, the relationship between the government and the financial sector is tilted too far in favor of the banks.

Banks deposit funds into customers' accounts only five days a week, but withdraw funds seven days a week. How can you plan when you don't know when you'll get access to your money? The lag between depositing checks and being able to access cash explains why so many working people who get paid at the end of the week go to the check casher — they need that money to buy food and to pay bills. They can't wait for their checks to clear.

With practices like overdraft fees and debit resequencing, it's hard to argue that banks are working in their customers' best interests. When I travel around the country talking about my work, people mob me, telling stories of how their banks have wronged them. Worn down by escalating fees, errors in their accounts, and endless hours on hold with customer "service" representatives, they've simply had it.

Cantwell Faulkner Muckenfuss III, who goes by "Chuck," recently retired from the global law firm Gibson Dunn. Bred in Montgomery, Alabama, and trained as a lawyer at Yale, Muckenfuss has had a long and varied career in financial policy and practice, which is why Seidman put him on the list of people I had to meet. Muckenfuss has been senior deputy controller for policy at the Office of the Comptroller of the Currency, special assistant to the director of the FDIC, and founder of City First Bank, a community development bank in DC. Lanky and relaxed, with blond hair gone white, Muckenfuss has a mischievous twinkle in his blue eyes and a penchant for straight talk.

On the day I visit him in his bright, spacious office in downtown Washington, he is in the process of moving to another office down the hall. Boxes of books and papers cover every surface. Muckenfuss paces up and down his office's plush carpet as I explain what I'm doing and what I hope to learn from him. When I ask about his take on bank practices during this period of escalating fees, he stops and looks me right in the eye. "In the words of one of my Texas clients," he says, "consumer finance got to be about tricking people — getting them to engage in behavior that's not in their interest."

As the biggest banks have grown larger and larger, they've gained more and more influence on government, and the economy has grown overly dependent on their success. It's become easier for big banks to make demands on government instead of the other way around. "Public interest" — the kind that Woodrow Wilson and Louis Brandeis once argued for — used to mean working for the benefit of the public. But somewhere along the way it's been redefined to mean efficiency and profitability for the banks.

The idea that banks have become "too big to fail" has a longer history than many of us realize. The Connecticut congressman Stewart McKinney coined that term in 1984, justifying the government bailout of Continental Illinois, the nation's seventh-largest bank, twenty-four years before the recent financial crisis that made it a common catchphrase.

The situation has only worsened since then. When Washington Mutual went under during the financial crisis in 2008, the bank was seven times larger than Continental Illinois had been. But because banks know they're "too big to fail" and that the government will bail them out, they continue to engage in risky behavior with "other people's money" — our money. The potential for high profits is incredibly seductive. Some call the relationship between banks and government a "doom loop," a "virtue-less cycle in which banks take ever greater risks to boost returns . . . and governments are forced to break their promises 'never again' to bankroll losses."

Today, the four largest banks — Chase, Bank of America, Wells Fargo, and Citigroup — collectively hold about half of all US bank assets, a total of $6.8 trillion, while the remaining 6,395 banks share the other half. The smallest banks — those with less than $100 million in assets and more likely to be closely tied to their communities — declined by 85 percent from 1985 to 2013. The dramatic drop in the number of banks over the past few decades gives individual consumers fewer choices and banks less incentive to compete to serve customers best. As banks have grown larger and their overall numbers have dwindled, they've become less responsive to the needs of consumers. They've focused so single-mindedly on profit that they've sacrificed the well-being of their customers.

Smaller banks, credit unions, and, sometimes, check cashers often do a better job of serving their customers because service is either critical to their business model, part of their mission, or both. Unfortunately, most of these smaller institutions lack the reach and the resources of the big banks.

The extraordinary size of the largest banks also makes it harder for the government to keep tabs on them. As Seidman told me, "I don't think you'll find a bank regulator who thinks they are governable or possible to regulate." That's a problem.

When banks or other financial institutions misbehave, grow too large, or both, it's tempting to say we need more regulation, or better regulation. Regulation is supposed to keep banks in line and protect consumers. For several decades following the Great Crash, bankers and regulators acted cautiously and people began using banks in greater numbers again, opening checking accounts in order to make purchases and payments. In a post-crisis column titled "Making Banking Boring," the Nobel Prize–winning economist Paul Krugman wrote that "the banking industry that emerged from [the Depression] was tightly regulated, far less colorful than it had been before the Depression, and far less lucrative for those who ran it." These were the years when my parents were buying their first home, starting to have children, and beginning to put money away for retirement.

That period became known as the "3-6-3 era" of banking: pay 3 percent on deposits, charge 6 percent on loans, and get to the golf course by 3 p.m. I witnessed this firsthand: Mr. Konopacki, the president of Pulaski Savings and Loan, lived across the street from us in South River. His shiny black car pulled out of the driveway every day shortly before 9 a.m., and Mrs. Konopacki, a homemaker who cared for their five children, had dinner on the table every day at exactly 5:15. Mr. Konopacki's workday was over.

Starting in the late 1970s, banking policy leaned toward *deregulation* — making banks less accountable to government. The spirit of deregulation explains the massive move away from policy that protected consumers and smaller banks, launching the Wild West attitude that gained momentum over the next two decades. The repeal of laws like Glass-Steagall and the lax regulatory environment opened the door for banks to mislead customers in classic "phishing for phools" fashion.

Fast-forward to 2008. We all know what happened next. In September, Lehman Brothers collapsed, sending panic through the stock market and threatening to bring down the world's financial system. The financial crisis mobilized policymakers in Washington. Senator Christopher Dodd (D-CT), who became one of the lead architects of the ensuing legislation, called it the economic equivalent of 9/11. Chris Cox, chairman of the Securities and Exchange Commission, labeled it "a save-your-country moment."

In July 2010, President Obama signed the Dodd-Frank Wall Street Reform and Consumer Protection Act, known as Dodd-Frank, into law. Developed through the leadership of Senator Christopher Dodd and Congressman Barney Frank (D-MA) in response to the 2008 crisis, the act aimed to prevent future financial crises and to protect consumers from the risky behaviors and practices of banks. This was an extraordinary moment in the history of consumer finance.

Dodd-Frank mandated the creation of the Consumer Financial Protection Bureau (CFPB) in 2011 in order to "make markets for consumer financial products and services work for Americans." Elizabeth Warren had conceived of this idea in 2007, before the crisis. A Harvard Law School professor at the time, she wrote an article titled "Unsafe at Any Rate," a reference to Ralph Nader's 1965 book *Unsafe at Any Speed*. Warren argued for a government consumer-financial-protection agency akin to the Consumer Product Safety Commission created under President Nixon in 1972.

To make her point, she likened credit cards and mortgages to toasters and microwaves:

> It is impossible to buy a toaster that has a one-in-five chance of bursting into flames and burning down your house. But it is possible to refinance an existing home with a mortgage that has the same one-in-five chance of putting the family out on the street —and the mortgage won't even carry a disclosure of that fact to the homeowner. Similarly, it's impossible to change the price on a toaster once it has been purchased. But long after the papers have been signed, it is possible to triple the price of the credit used to finance the purchase of that appliance, even if the customer meets all the credit terms, in full and on time. Why are consumers safe when they purchase tangible consumer prod-

ucts with cash, but when they sign up for routine financial products like mortgages and credit cards they are left at the mercy of their creditors?

The financial crisis of 2008 was the perfect moment for Warren's idea to take hold. It grabbed the attention of policymakers such as the presidential hopefuls John Edwards and Hillary Clinton. Those who wholeheartedly supported the creation of the CFPB skillfully used the crisis to pass legislation they thought was long overdue. Others, who never would have dreamed of supporting it prior to the crisis, knew they had to show their constituents that they were doing something to punish the banks. Consumers felt that banks were robbing them, and public-opinion polls showed that voters wanted policymakers to take action.

Before the CFPB, four federal agencies played different roles in regulating the financial-services industry. Was yet another regulatory body needed when regulation was already so complicated and opaque? Yes—because not a single one of these agencies had consumer protection as its core mission. Simply put, the CFPB focuses on people. In a speech introducing the idea of the new agency, President Obama decreed that the CFPB would be "a new and powerful agency charged with just one job: looking out for ordinary consumers." If you haven't spent much of your life knee-deep in bank regulation, this may not seem like such a big deal. But nearly every industry insider I spoke with called this moment profound. As Seidman put it, "Until we got the CFPB, the consumers were always second-class citizens as far as bank regulators were concerned."

Everyone I spoke with in DC—including former regulators—told me that regulation is a mess, partly because it has been created incrementally, over decades. As Muckenfuss put it, "I would do away with all retail finance regulation if I could somehow apply the following test: Would the CEO let his or her parent or child use the product?"

It even got to the point where regulators "competed with each other for 'customers,' and banks shopped for the regulator they thought would be most congenial." And despite the existence of what Seidman calls "a lot of crap that never worked anyway," policymakers didn't do away with old laws and regulations — they just kept adding more and more. There's no incentive or political will to create a blank slate and start again, even though that might seem the best option. As any good cook knows, once a pot of soup is overspiced, it's impossible to correct it. You just have to toss it out and start from scratch. But when it comes to regulation, that's easier said than done.

Each agency with a role in financial-services regulation is its own fiefdom; its ability to regulate gives it power. It may seem logical, from the outside looking in, to argue that regulation should be streamlined and simplified. But in Washington, it's simply not rational to give up power willingly.

All banks have compliance departments, people who work to ensure that banks aren't breaking any rules. Some experts worry that banks have to be so careful, they've retreated even more from serving the people who are most in need of safe, affordable financial products. "The regulators are causing the opposite of the desired effect by making it so dangerous now to serve a lower-income segment," Barefoot said. In short, banks have retreated from the subprime market partly for rational reasons. But, as usual, it's the people living on the margins who suffer the most.

For most of our nation's history, banks practiced "financial exclusion," and policy backed them up. The Home Owners' Loan Corporation (HOLC), part of FDR's New Deal, rated neighborhoods on a scale of A to D. HOLC used the racial and socioeconomic characteristics of residents to determine whether a neighborhood was a safe investment. Predominantly white neighborhoods were consistently rated A, an acceptable credit risk. Predominantly black areas were labeled D, or unsuitable for investing. Banks and the federal government "redlined" entire neighborhoods, literally drawing red lines on maps to indicate locations where they wouldn't lend. The residents of these redlined neighborhoods were poor and often people of color and immigrants.

Banks have a history of discriminating against both people and places. In 1961, the US Commission on Civil Rights found that African American borrowers were often required to make higher down payments on homes and other major credit-based purchases, and to pay off loans faster than whites had to. In so-called "changing neighborhoods," even people with steady incomes struggled to get access to credit, as savings and loan banks denied mortgage applications. In 1971, the president of Chicago's National Security Bank told a group of community organizers why it denied loans to potential borrowers in a particular area. "Well, of course we don't make loans in this neighborhood," he said. "Have you looked around? It's a slum."

Research on discrimination in the mortgage market shows that it has primarily been based on race. The Equal Credit Opportunity Act and the Fair Housing Act make it unlawful for lenders to discriminate against credit applicants based on race, color, sex, national origin, or other personal attributes; the housing act applies these protections for credit as part of housing transactions. But discrimination continues. As recently as 2014, the US Department of Justice settled a complaint with Countrywide Financial Corporation for engaging in a widespread pattern of charging African American and Latino borrowers higher fees and interest rates than it charged other clientele. And in March 2015 the *Atlanta Blackstar* reported on eight major banks caught discriminating against

African Americans and Latinos. Financial discrimination may be more subtle than it used to be, but it's still present.

Women also faced discrimination when trying to access financial services. I interviewed a woman with decades of banking and government experience who relayed the story of sitting on a bank board a few years before the Equal Credit Opportunity Act was passed in 1974. "A resolution was brought to the board members on the adoption of non-discrimination standards for women," she told me. "And a board member said, 'I'm not going to vote for that. Women get pregnant and they should have their husbands and fathers have to cosign for their loans.' And . . . that was a very respectable point of view."

In urban neighborhoods across the country, activists organized "bank-ins" to protest credit discrimination and put pressure on government to ensure that financial services would be available to everyone. Over twenty civil rights reforms aimed at declaring and implementing citizens' right to bank without discrimination were passed between 1968 and 1988. These provisions included banking laws mandating greater transparency on the part of banks and made discrimination explicitly illegal.

One of the most important of these was the 1974 Community Reinvestment Act (CRA), which pushed banks to end redlining and to serve all communities in the area where they operated. Banks created community development offices and initiatives to deal with all of this new legislation, but enforcement was spotty. CRA didn't have very sharp teeth: prior to its amendment in 1989, 97 percent of banks received one of the two highest CRA ratings, and it wasn't because they were providing exemplary service. The struggle to make banks accountable to diverse communities continues. As recently as 2015, a federal judge struck down the New York City Responsible Banking Act of 2012, which required banks to reveal how well they were serving communities of color. The judge deemed it unconstitutional because it gave the city too much regulatory power.

The Home Mortgage Disclosure Act (HMDA), passed in 1975, required financial institutions to make public detailed information about mortgages. HMDA provided proof of discrimination in key neighborhoods and among certain groups; it powerfully strengthened CRA.

Even with today's stringent laws that guard against discrimination, African Americans, Latinos, and women pay more for credit. The Department of Justice has sued mortgage lenders for violating fair-lending laws after discovering patterns of charging African American women higher broker fees than those charged to white males in the same situation. Research conducted by the Federal Reserve showed that African American and Latino applicants are more likely to be offered higher-priced mortgage loans, even after controlling for borrower and loan characteristics. Studies of the 2008 financial crisis show that 63 percent of those who were offered subprime mortgages qualified for prime. After controlling for individual, credit, and housing characteristics, research showed that African American females were five times more likely to get a subprime mortgage than comparable white male applicants were. And even though New York City's recently created ID card was intended to help people access critical services, large banks, including Bank of America, JP Morgan Chase, and Citigroup, refuse to accept it as a primary form of identification, denying banking services to a group that is more likely to be unbanked or underbanked. At a recent convention on financial inclusion at the Ford Foundation, I asked a banker from Citibank why his bank did not take the ID. He claimed that federal officials had not approved it. But smaller, more mission-oriented banks like Amalgamated were accepting the ID, apparently without problems.

Discrimination and its legacy have contributed to the lack of trust in banks, particularly among groups more likely to be "un-banked" or "financially excluded." Given the history of banks' poor service to particular groups, it should be no surprise that they find it hard to swallow the idea that opening a bank account is the best financial move to make. Decades of poor service to whole communities must be acknowledged and corrected before trust in the banking system can take root. One improvement would be to stop citing the ignorance of the unbanked and the excluded as the heart of the problem. In reality, they've never been served well.

It seems easier to get away with the manipulation and deception Akerloff and Shiller describe when disempowered groups are the target. But as the effects of long-term economic and policy trends and the 2008 financial crisis have converged, a much wider range of people find themselves at a disadvantage and feel real financial pain. When I discovered just how many Americans are living in a state of financial insecurity, I set out to learn as much as I could about them. They're the new middle class.

3

THE NEW MIDDLE CLASS

JUST READ THE HEADLINES: "MIDDLE-CLASS BETRAYAL? Why Working Hard Is No Longer Enough in America" and "Dear Middle Class: Welcome to Poverty." These ominous tidings appear in the media with increasing regularity. The middle class is "shrinking," "screwed," "doing worse than you think," and "turning proletarian." The economist Guy Standing labels this new group "the precariat, an emerging class characterized by chronic insecurity" and calls what has been happening to its members "unnecessary and amoral."

At the same time that the banking industry has reneged on its responsibilities to ordinary consumers, the larger economic context in which we make financial decisions has changed in ways that make the American Dream an unattainable fantasy for far too many people. Rising inequality, declining wages, a threadbare social safety net, decreased benefits for workers, and increases in the cost of living all play a role in how we got here. It's not just the consumer financial-services industry that got us into this mess.

The term "middle class" used to connote stability and security. Not anymore.

Jasmine is a thirty-three-year-old wife, student, and mother of three. She describes her family's financial situation as "fairly stable," but says it's still precarious. "If one thing goes wrong, we'll be in trouble," she says. Five years ago, her husband's job became less secure. His employer put him on furlough during the recession, reducing the family's already modest income. In Jasmine's words, "When they talk about cities needing to cut back, it seems the first place they start is their employees' pockets." Jasmine says that period was extremely stressful. Despite trying to work within a budget, she worried constantly about having enough money for rent or even to make it through the next week.

Jasmine decided to go back to school to get a teaching degree after losing her previous job as an apartment manager, which had provided a decent salary, free rent, and discounted utilities. She was laid off when the building was sold and the new owners brought in an outside management company. Jasmine hopes her teaching degree will allow her to get a better job.

More and more of us, like Jasmine, belong to the new middle class, a group that lives in a state of perpetual financial uncertainty. Nearly half of Americans now live paycheck to paycheck. Nearly half could not come up with two thousand dollars in the event of an emergency. Instability is the new normal.

Nearly three-fifths of respondents to a 2013 Heartland Monitor Poll worry about falling into a lower economic class. They believe the middle class today "enjoys less opportunity, job security, and disposable income than earlier generations did." The same poll finds that the term "middle class" has been "redefined to mean not falling behind, rather than material goods or upward mobility." The prescriptions typically recommended for achieving economic security and upward mobility—a good education and financial planning—are now seen as luxuries that only the upper classes can afford. This group wants economic security more than anything else.

A few years ago, Tim Ranney, president of Clarity Services, a subprime credit bureau, began noticing a change in the profiles of consumers who populate his database. There was growth in the proportion of consumers with subprime credit scores who had relatively high incomes, held college degrees, and owned their homes — in other words, people we would normally consider middle class. A credit score is a number that is supposed to reflect how creditworthy a person is. Scores below about 620 are considered subprime; those above are considered prime. Consumers with lower scores are deemed less able to take on and repay debt. They are riskier. As a result, they pay more for credit. Businesses contact Clarity to pull a credit report on potential customers who are seeking a loan or a service. The firm receives between 400,000 and 800,000 of these requests every day.

Ranney is on a crusade to correct misconceptions about subprime consumers and their need for credit, and he chose me as a beneficiary of his enormous database, which includes data on more than fifty-five million consumers. Out of curiosity, I flew to Clearwater, Florida. Before Ranney's office called me, I didn't know that separate credit bureaus existed for subprime consumers. The taxi dropped me in the middle of a nondescript office park, and it took several minutes of wandering around in the blinding sun to figure out where Clarity's offices were.

Ranney greeted me in the quiet reception area. An amply built man in jeans, a neatly pressed untucked shirt, and spotless white sneakers, Ranney has the open demeanor of his golden lab, Jack, who settled in for a snooze under Ranney's desk as he talked about the changes he is witnessing through the unique lens of Clarity's database. Ability to pay, intent to pay, and stability, Ranney says, are the three keys to understanding the riskiness of potential borrowers. "Other credit bureaus tend to look only at ability to pay," Ranney says, "but intent to pay and stability are even bigger issues." Seven years ago, the people in Clarity's database experienced a "destabilizing event," such as loss of a job, a medical issue, or a car breakdown, every eighty-seven days. Now it's every thirty

days. "There is a much larger group of people experiencing destabilizing events much more often," he says. Ranney believes that
policymakers need to understand the differences among different
types of borrowers, and that a one-size-fits-all policy agenda won't
work.

Ranney calls this new and growing group the "new non-prime,"
and they belong to the same group I've labeled the new middle class. Upon noticing this group's increase in numbers, Ranney and his team analyzed their data and found that "in the eighteen-month period between February 2010 and August 2011, there
was a substantial shift in the types of consumers who request payday loans. The more stable, higher-earner segment that is the new
non-prime increased by over 500 percent."

A 2015 study using updated Clarity data found that more than
20 percent of small-dollar borrowers had a net income of over
$50,000, 43 percent had a college degree, and over a third owned
their homes. This is not the picture that comes to mind when we
think of someone suffering from financial insecurity. Also, more
than 70 percent of respondents had prime (650 or higher) credit
at some point, with more than 21 percent having lost their prime
score within the past twelve months.

The decoupling of the terms "middle class" and "economic stability" is closely connected to the retraction of the public and private safety nets. It used to be that government and the private
sector helped people manage risk by providing health care, unemployment insurance, and pensions. Those benefits have been
eroded, leaving individuals to cope with the unexpected and un-
fortunate events that happen to all of us. As Jacob Hacker, author
of *The Great Risk Shift,* argues, "More and more economic risk has
been offloaded by government and corporations onto the increasingly fragile balance sheets of workers and their families."

Rising inequality also plays a role. The Occupy movement, with its slogan "We are the 99 percent," drew attention to this inequality in the wake of the financial crisis. Worldwide, people took to the streets to protest corporate greed and broken social contracts. The New York City incarnation of the movement, Occupy Wall Street, placed the financial sector at the center of the problem. In 2015, there is more income inequality in the United States than in any other "developed" democratic country. The financial implications of this inequality are enormous for all of us.

How has this happened? A disturbing part of the answer is that our tolerance for inequality has risen. Timothy Noah writes that as recently as the mid-twentieth century, "mainstream American opinion ... considered the prospect of growing income inequality to be unacceptably antidemocratic." It wasn't only radicals outside the mainstream of American culture who supported the idea of setting limits on income inequality; it was widely considered a reasonable viewpoint. Noah reports that President Franklin Roosevelt "wanted to raise the marginal tax on people making more than today's equivalent (after inflation) of about $345,000 to 100 percent [and to] bookend the minimum wage he'd created a decade earlier with a new maximum wage." (The marginal tax is the amount someone pays on the next dollar of income. The marginal tax rate rises as income rises.) Today these policy ideas seem extreme.

Declining wages compound income inequality. Controlling for inflation, wages have been declining since 1972. That's a forty-five-year downtrend.

Not everyone has had to make do with less. Productivity has actually risen during this same forty-five-year period. Historically, when productivity goes up (our economy becomes more efficient, the cost of inputs declines), we all share in the increased wealth that's generated. Between the mid-1940s and the 1970s, productivity and wages grew together. As the economy prospered, most of us did better. But for the past few decades, US productivity has increased significantly while wages have remained flat or declined. That gap between productivity and compensation growth has been larger in the "lost decade" since the early 2000s than at any point in the post–World War II period.

The fruits of that productivity haven't been distributed equally. In certain sectors, like finance, the rich have gotten richer. Much richer. Since the 1970s, the CEO-to-worker compensation ratio has increased from 30:1 in 1978 to 296:1 in 2013. In the same time period, CEO compensation has increased by 937 percent while worker compensation has increased by just over 10 percent. The story that growth is good for all of us has become a myth, one that we continue to cling to even as evidence to the contrary mounts.

Income has also become less predictable. Income volatility has doubled over the past thirty years. Asked whether "financial stability" or "moving up the income ladder" was more important to them, 77 percent of respondents to a recent survey chose financial stability. This same study, conducted by the Financial Diaries project, showed that families' monthly income fluctuated significantly over the course of the year, that jobs often provided irregular income and didn't last long, and that more than half of those who participated worked more than one job during the period of the study.

Income volatility is particularly problematic for the self-employed, whose businesses may be cyclical or seasonal. David, a self-employed financial adviser, falls into this group. David's earnings are based on commission, so they fluctuate over the course of the year. These changes are fairly predictable. But the financial advising business has taken two substantial hits over the past fifteen years: first, when the dot-com bubble burst in the early 2000s, and then when the 2008 financial crisis occurred. David couldn't foresee these shocks, and his earnings dipped both times, leaving him unprepared and unable to manage his expenses until business picked up again.

A key factor in this increase in income volatility is the rise in part-time work and tenuous "independent contractor" arrangements. Twenty percent of employed individuals are working part-time, the highest part-time rate since 1983, and their predicaments are often painfully difficult, and sometimes tragic. In August 2014, a woman named Maria Fernandes died in her car while taking a nap between shifts at her four part-time jobs. She succumbed to asphyxiation from fumes coming from a gas can that had spilled in her back seat. According to her friends, Fernandes kept the can in her car to avoid running out of gas while traveling between jobs. Fernandes was one of an estimated 7.5 million people currently working multiple jobs after losing full-time employment during the Great Recession, the economic downturn that began in 2007 and, following the financial crisis of 2008, continued through 2009.

Part-time jobs boomed after the financial crisis, as companies restructured staffing practices. Part-time workers typically get fewer if any benefits and have less bargaining power to negotiate higher wages. In 2015, the *Wall Street Journal* reported that about 2.4 million part-time workers (defined as people working less than thirty-five hours a week) said that the reason they were working part-time was that they could find only a part-time job; this number has not changed since the recession.

Some, like Elizabeth from Florida, could not meet the demands of full-time work and raising a family. Elizabeth is married and has three children — two teenagers and a seven-year-old. She currently works two part-time retail jobs (one at a clothing store and one at a shoe store); her goal is to work thirty hours per week between the two. Previously, she worked full-time as a manager at a clothing store, but full-time meant sixty to seventy hours per week. Those hours didn't allow Elizabeth enough time with her children, who needed her. However, she wasn't fully prepared for the drop in income. Before she knew it, she had accumulated debt she couldn't repay.

When your income fluctuates from week to week, as it does for more and more people, or when you work for minimum wage, it becomes impossible to budget and plan for the future. The tendency is to click into a present-focused survival mode that changes the way we function. The psychologist Eldar Shafir and the economist Sendhil Mullainathan call this the "scarcity mindset." This way of thinking, they argue, costs us. "We neglect other concerns, and we become less effective in the rest of our lives."

Consider what it means when so many people experience this struggle to survive. Aside from the potential impact on health, serious financial concerns allow less time to be a good parent and a helpful neighbor, cutting off many resources that make society function well. When many people are forced to focus on short-term survival, their own well-being and the vitality of their community suffer.

Many part-time workers earn the minimum wage, and that minimum-wage worker is no longer the teenage kid who lives on your block. Pay attention next time you grab a quick cup of coffee at Dunkin' Donuts or pop into Barnes & Noble to buy a book. The person serving you is likely a couple of decades out of high school. Only 12 percent of minimum-wage workers were teenagers in 2013, compared to 27 percent in 1979. Today more than half are women, and 28 percent support children.

The gap between the minimum wage and the average hourly wage is the largest it has ever been. Furthermore, low-wage workers are much more highly educated than they used to be — and that education has not earned them a place at the middle-class table. Seventy-nine percent had a high school degree in 2012, compared to only 48 percent in 1968. Their wages, however, have declined — by 23 percent, to be exact — even after you account for inflation.

In recent years, movements across the country have sought to raise both the minimum wage and public awareness about the plight of people who earn it. Yet many businesses appear unfazed by the difficulties their low-wage employees face. The fast-food giant McDonald's came under fire for the budgeting tool it designed, in conjunction with Visa, to help its minimum-wage employees plan their finances. The mock budget provided to these workers revealed remarkable insensitivity to the reality of their lives: it presumed that workers would hold two jobs, that health insurance would cost them twenty dollars per month, and that their monthly rent or mortgage payment would be about six hundred dollars. The budget entirely failed to factor in childcare, groceries, clothing, or gas.

Many who managed to hold on to their jobs in the wake of the 2008 financial crisis found that several employers had peeled back benefits. As job security declined, "fewer employers provided health coverage, and employers shifted away from offering guaranteed pensions or any retirement plan at all." This occurred after the government had already rolled back public benefits, hitting many families hard.

Teresa has two children and understands what a drop in benefits can mean. Her first child is ten years old, and the entire first pregnancy cost her thirty dollars out of pocket; her insurance covered the rest. But her second pregnancy was high-risk, and she needed to see a specialist, a service that wasn't covered. Her insurance had changed — it now required a deductible of fifteen hundred dollars and stipulated a maximum out-of-pocket expense of thirty-five hundred dollars, so she was responsible for paying thirty-five hundred dollars before her coverage kicked in. Even when both parents work, the cost of insurance and medical costs not covered by insurance can break the budget. The widespread rollback in benefits can cause severe financial stress for working families.

The fact that many educated working people are unable to make ends meet signals widespread financial instability. More than three-quarters of Americans are struggling, and younger families (those headed by someone younger than forty) have been hit particularly hard — this demographic got whomped in the Great Recession surrounding the financial crisis of 2008. Over-investment in home ownership, increased reliance on student loans, and bad luck have combined to make these families particularly vulnerable. During the recession, younger families lost much more of their wealth — nearly 44 percent — than their older counterparts did; they lost 17 percent. A similar dynamic held true for African American and Latino families, who lost much more than white families did.

Older workers are also feeling the pinch. Many baby boomers who lost their jobs during the recession have been able to find only part-time work. This has happened in part because many workplaces openly discriminate against older people. For example, in early 2015, the Equal Employment Opportunity Commission filed a lawsuit against Darden Restaurants, claiming that its upscale grill and wine-bar chain Seasons 52 had disproportionately denied jobs to applicants age forty and older because it wanted its restaurants to main a youthful image, thereby violating the federal Age Discrimination in Employment Act.

In 2013, the *New York Times* reported that just one in six older workers laid off during the recession had found another job, and half of that group had accepted pay cuts. Because of these losses, many older Americans will have to continue working far past retirement age in order to make ends meet. Mavis, in her seventies, drives one and a half hours each way, to work selling ads for the Yellow Pages. She was laid off from her previous job in 2011 after the company she worked for was bought out. Her income fluctuates a great deal because her pay is based on commission. She and her husband, who is disabled, are barely scraping by. Mavis would love to retire and start her own business, but she can't afford to leave the formal workforce. Asked what she would need in order to retire, she replied, "I'd have to win the lottery."

Tony spent much of his career as a high school administrator, where he earned enough to cover his expenses and even accrued a small retirement fund. It wasn't enough, so after he retired, Tony found a job as a security guard, staffing the gatehouse of a gated community nearby. He worked in the same position for seven years, and during that time his superiors regularly complimented him on his performance. But he was abruptly terminated when the security company decided to replace him with three part-time workers. The sudden drop in income left Tony unable to keep up with his bills.

Some of the older workers and retirees I interviewed are also coping with the stress of supporting their adult children. This phenomenon tends to be underreported because surveys typically ask respondents only about children living at home who are minors. But it appears that a surprising number of parents are supporting their adult children. Sometimes these children return home, and two generations struggle to make ends meet in the same household.

Rose, a retiree, is supporting her two adult sons, ages thirty-two and thirty-eight. Both are living at home. Rose covers the rent and utilities and buys food for the household. She also pays sixteen dollars each day for her younger son's public transportation to architecture school, and she helps with gas money. Though they are adults, Rose feels responsible for her sons. "What are you going to do?" Rose says. "It's your child. They're still living in the house that I rent, so I'm paying the majority of the bills."

Rose knows that things aren't as easy for her sons as they were for her. After graduating from a good university, she got a job that paid well and provided benefits. But things are different now "unless you're in the computer industry," she says. Her sons' experiences have shown her that the same opportunities just don't exist, and the cost of living in California is high and continues to rise.

Tom is seventy-three and works as the CFO of a utility company, netting $11,000 per month. Tom currently has eight payday loans — small short-term loans with relatively high fees — in addition to loans from his mother, his sister, and two friends. He realizes that his combination of high income and high indebtedness is "not typical." Tom uses all of his available money to assist his two adult sons. One is trying to revive a faltering business while keeping up mortgage payments; this son has six children. The other lost his job and is also struggling. "I have a pretty good income and I use it all to help my kids, my family, my grown children and grandchildren and my former daughter-in-law," he said. "They're the low-income people; I'm not low-income." Tom would do anything to help his family.

Still, Tom is anxious about his finances. He takes a piece of paper out of his pocket and unfolds it, revealing a complex table that documents every loan, bill, and account Tom has, when each payment is due, and what action he will take and when. He updates and prints it every day. Though he keeps careful track of his financial position, this doesn't make life easier. "I'm still really on the financial edge," he said. "I'm just really stressed about money." His data on ChexSystems means that he cannot get a new bank account or a credit card.

Wages, after factoring in inflation, have been flat or stagnant for most of us for the past thirty years. Families with incomes less than $75,000 have been hit the hardest, and not just at the very low end: more than half of families with incomes between $30,000 and $75,000 say they are falling behind, as their cost of living increases faster than their income.

Medical expenses constitute a big piece of the problem. Nearly one in five consumers has medical debt that has gone to a collection agency for nonpayment. That medical debt makes up over half of overdue debt mentioned on credit reports. Although some consumers do owe tens of thousands of dollars, the average unpaid medical debt in collections is $579. That may sound manageable, but in fact almost half of all Americans have to struggle to pay off a $400 emergency medical expense.

Mavis, who works for the Yellow Pages, has rheumatoid arthritis, but it's her disabled husband's medical bills that are hardest to pay. Even though he has medical insurance, he sees four or five doctors each month, each requiring a thirty-five-dollar copay. His medications, which cost three to four hundred dollars every month, add to the financial burden.

Although the job market has made a slow recovery from the financial crash, the housing market has bounced back; its growth exceeds pre-crisis levels. This sounds like good news on the surface, but when housing costs outpace wage growth, the middle class becomes squeezed even harder. In July 2015, the US Department of Labor reported that housing prices went up by more than 3 percent from a year prior and were expected to continue rising over the coming months. Housing costs across the United States have grown by about 18 percent since 1995, and while growth dipped in the early 2000s, prices have grown by 10 percent since 2011.

The proportion of renters who spent more than 30 percent of their income on housing increased from 37 percent in 2003 to 50 percent just ten years later. According to the US Department of Housing and Urban Development, families that devote more than 30 percent of earnings to cover housing costs are considered "cost burdened."

Childcare costs have also soared: the Economic Policy Institute (EPI) reports that "in thirty-three states and the District of Columbia, infant care costs exceed the average cost of in-state college tuition at public, four-year institutions." That constitutes a kind of double whammy for many parents who are still paying off their own student loans as they start families. Childcare costs exceeded rent in 500 of the 618 "family budget areas" the EPI studied.

The US Department of Health and Human Services has established that in order to be affordable, childcare costs should not constitute more than 10 percent of a family's income. In all but a few of the EPI's family budget areas, childcare costs were more than the recommended percentage of family budget.

Many blame government for the current state of affairs. Seventy-two percent of respondents to a 2015 Pew Research Center study said that government policies "have done little or nothing to help middle-class people" since the recession.

An overwhelming sense of financial insecurity tears at the very fabric of society. When people feel safe, they take productive risks — they invest in the future, they encourage their children to go to college and graduate school, they start businesses. They trust that if they work hard enough, they can devote themselves to raising a family rather than working two jobs just to put food on the table. Our culture no longer supports this kind of risk taking. Having no slack financially also means that when times get tough, as they do for all of us, there's no buffer to soften the blow. Which is why so many people have turned to credit. And at the same moment, credit markets expanded to accommodate the growing need.

4

THE CREDIT TRAP: "BAD DEBT" AND REAL LIFE

THE POPULAR FINANCIAL GURU SUZE ORMAN EXPLAINS THE difference between good and bad debt by using a clever simile: "Debt is like cholesterol," Orman wrote in one of her columns. "Good debt is money you borrow to purchase an asset, such as a home you can afford ... Bad debt is money you borrow to purchase a depreciating asset or to finance a 'want' rather than a 'need.'" But what happens when what you need — but can't afford — is food, or medication, necessities that will not appreciate over time? The new middle class is facing this situation, and often they take on debt to pay for basic needs. How many Americans do this? More than half.

As Americans find themselves facing financial insecurity, many rely more and more on credit — and so-called "bad debt" in particular. The credit card industry has been more than happy to cooperate by providing credit to a growing group of consumers and using deceptive practices to increase their own profits. When the government began to crack down on these practices, credit all but disappeared for the financially vulnerable, leaving them with no good options.

Currently, 40 percent of Americans report that income shortfalls cause them to spend more than they earn — a virtually unprecedented situation. This often leads them to take desperate measures. They borrow from family and friends, withdraw money from retirement accounts, or take equity out of their homes. They sell assets like jewelry or cars. They cash in life insurance policies. And when they deplete their assets, they turn to credit: credit cards, pawnshops, loan sharks, and payday lenders. A 2012 survey of credit card users showed that among those experiencing unemployment, 86 percent had to take on credit card debt. But borrowing makes sense only if you can repay. For the growing numbers who cannot, a short-term solution becomes a long-term problem. The average household carries $129,579 in debt—$15,355 of it on credit cards.

How did we come to be so dependent on debt? The change has been rapid, within the span of a generation. My parents used cash and checks to pay for everything, but my children are much more accustomed to seeing plastic in my wallet. Credit itself is not the issue—using credit to fill gaps in wages or to finance the purchase of goods goes back thousands of years. But the way we use credit has changed a great deal, as have the rules and social norms associated with credit and the role it plays in our larger economy.

The practice of charging interest, and the upward creep in interest rates, hasn't always been a given. "Usury," a word that has come to mean exorbitant or predatory interest rates, originally referred to the practice of charging any interest at all. The medieval Catholic thinker Thomas Aquinas believed it was wrong to make money from the lending of money, that doing so went against "moral and natural law" and led to inequality. And in *Inferno,* the Italian poet Dante put usurers on the lowest ledge of the seventh circle of hell —lower even than murderers.

Times have changed. Arguments now focus not on whether it's okay to charge interest, but what interest rate is acceptable.

But ethics and morality continue to enter the debate. A 2013 report from the National Consumer Law Center put it well: "Interest caps are more than numbers: they are reflections of society's collective judgment about moral and ethical behavior, as well as business and personal responsibility. Interest rates embody fundamental values."

Until the 1920s, employers and "salary lenders" met the need for small amounts of short-term credit by making loans to workers who needed advances on their paychecks. These salary lenders charged very high interest rates and went to great lengths to hide from borrowers the true cost of the illegal loans. Uniform Small Loan Laws, the first of which was introduced in 1914 in New Jersey, proposed an interest rate of 36 to 42 percent per year — higher than the current usury rate but much lower than what salary lenders charged. Between 1945 and 1979, all states capped interest rates for these small loans at 36 percent.

Lending, like banking in general, used to be much more personal than it is today. Credit, both from banks and from less formal sources, was based on lenders' personal knowledge of borrowers' financial situations. Once banks started making loans in the 1920s, they dealt with only the well-to-do and the well-connected. This "relationship lending" was good for some but less so for others.

The credit system in the United States has always been stratified. A person's gender, race, social class, or a combination of these factors determined which lenders would offer credit, and on what terms. Until the Equal Credit Opportunity Act (ECOA) was passed in 1974, women faced many obstacles in acquiring credit. For married women, a husband's financial standing and his wishes concerning his wife's application for credit determined the outcome. A husband could control his wife's spending by asking the credit card issuer to impose certain limits or revoke credit entirely if, in his opinion, she was spending too much. For single women, many banks required that a man cosign the application for credit. Businesswomen could be issued credit cards only under the auspices of a corporate employer. Even with ECOA, banks and other card issuers made it hard for women to get a credit card. Applications commonly asked intrusive personal questions about marital status and motherhood, and banks often discounted a woman's income by 50 percent when evaluating her application. As recently as 2012, the Financial Industry Regulation Authority reported that women continue to pay more than men for credit cards.

Obtaining and using credit have been problematic for African Americans too. Historically they have faced discrimination when attempting to use their charge cards. Many businesses have entirely refused to serve African Americans; others demanded to be paid in cash. This stratified credit system constrained opportunities for African Americans and other minority groups, limiting their ability to purchase homes and grow businesses. It still does.

From the 1920s through the 1960s, the use of credit became an indispensable part of American life. Mass production made an enormous range of relatively low-cost consumer goods available. Credit markets developed and expanded to help people buy these products. And the distinctions between "wants" and "needs" began to blur as it became easier and more acceptable to buy on credit. Manufacturers, and then finance companies, offered installment credit to consumers to finance these purchases.

Finance companies appeared in the 1920s as the first formalization of small-dollar credit, loans that banks deemed too small to be profitable, and financial advising. In the postwar boom era, consumerism grew as household income and wealth increased, driving demand for financial products and services. Finance companies provided financing services to previously excluded social groups, allowing more people to get mortgages, purchase homes, and invest in low-cost portfolios. These expansions in the number and type of products and the share of the population with access to them gave American consumers unprecedented financial flexibility. (Today, the term "small dollar credit" generally refers to loans of less than $5,000.) At the end of World War II, nearly all payment activity was paper-based — cash, checks, and money orders.

The Diners Club card, introduced in 1949, revolutionized the credit market, becoming the first card issuer that didn't offer the goods or services being purchased. The introduction of BankAmericard by Bank of America in 1958 and Master Charge by Chase Manhattan Bank in 1966 heralded the expansion of the bank card industry. The use of credit grew steadily through the 1960s and 70s.

Then the deregulation period of the 1970s and 80s allowed banks to merge and engage in riskier forms of business. Many states eviscerated their usury caps. Six states currently have none; other states have loopholes that enable lenders to get around the caps. This dramatic change paved the way for payday and other small-dollar, high-priced lenders to enter the scene. During the period between the Uniform Small Loan Laws and deregulation, such loans were virtually unavailable except through informal and illegal lenders.

As credit cards proliferated, notions of what made someone a good credit risk changed in ways that opened up new markets for credit card issuers. Until credit scores began to be widely used in the 1980s, perceptions of creditworthiness tended to be highly subjective and skewed along the lines of gender, race, and the location of a potential borrower's home.

The shift from "character lending" to credit scores was positive for some. It enabled truly creditworthy individuals who had faced discrimination to gain access to credit, albeit often at a higher price. But credit scores are far from perfect measures of creditworthiness, especially for certain groups. The data used to compute the scores are limited and often inaccurate. And they're based on a relatively narrow definition of what "creditworthy" means. Just as having too much debt can make it harder to get a loan, so can having no debt at all. The industry uses the terms "thin file" and "no file" to label people who have few or no credit records, and these people tend to get worse terms.

Credit scores are now being used more broadly. Landlords and employers often screen the credit scores of prospective renters and employees. Mavis, whom we met in the previous chapter, was turned down for a position at a furniture store close to home, which would have eliminated her burdensome commute. "They feel that if your credit score isn't A1, ipsy-pipsy, over 650, you're gonna steal. Yes, my credit score has held me back."

As the connection between card issuers and cardholders became more remote in the 1970s, credit cards transitioned from being a courtesy offered by retailers to moneymaking endeavors in their own right. The cost of using credit cards rose, and policy has abetted this trend. Consumer debt grew concurrently with deregulation of the credit card industry, beginning with the 1978 Supreme Court ruling of *Marquette v. First Omaha Savings Corp.*, which virtually eliminated caps on interest rates for credit cards. In 1996, the *Smiley v. Citibank* decision did the same for credit card fees, allowing them to be determined by the lender's home state. Prior to this decision, the average late-payment fee was sixteen dollars. By 2009, it had climbed to as much as thirty-nine dollars.

Although it's become more acceptable to use credit for all kinds of purposes, borrowers often face public judgment about their need to borrow. Google the term "money shame" and then peruse the 458 million results that pop up on your screen. You'll find confessions from people who for decades have felt humiliated about their relationship with money, a financial therapist who has started a "conscious money movement" to "bring money out of the shadows and into the light," an author who claims that her book can help you overcome money shame and "flip your rich switch." Bankruptcy and indebtedness for the "wrong reasons" are highly stigmatized in the United States. We look down on those who are mired in credit card debt or who use payday lenders and loan sharks. We judge them without understanding their stories.

In this culture of shame, people blame themselves for being unable to manage situations beyond their control, such as medical problems, layoffs, and inconsistent work hours. Many of the people I interviewed were so ashamed of their debt that they hid it even from those closest to them. Julie, a Dallas resident in her early thirties, put it this way: "It doesn't make me feel comfortable. It's just always like a pride hit. It's a little embarrassing, you know? I'd rather go and take care of it on my own and let no one else know about it." Kyle, who is in his forties and lives in San Francisco, broke down as he described how he felt: "It's very tough. It's embarrassing. I talk to very few people about it because people are very judgmental."

During her earlier career as a law professor, Senator Elizabeth Warren sought to understand the rise in bankruptcy filings that began in the late 1970s and continued through the late 1990s. Warren expected to uncover stories of appalling irresponsibility: consumers seeking protection from their debts after years of reckless spending. Instead she found that most people who filed for bankruptcy were from middle-class families affected by economic volatility — job loss, a serious medical problem, or a divorce that left one partner economically vulnerable.

When Congress debated bankruptcy reform legislation in 2005, those in favor of reform aimed to cut down on abusive and fraudulent use of the bankruptcy system, which they believed was rampant. But consumer advocates, bolstered by Warren's study, argued that claims about bankruptcy fraud were overblown. Most people filed for bankrupty legitimately as a response to hardship, rather than an escape from paying up for their lavish overspending. They felt stuck and could see no other way out.

Low interest rates and easy access to credit made credit cards a simple option for people experiencing financial stress, and credit card companies did everything they could to entice new categories of customers. In 1983, only 43 percent of US households had a MasterCard, Visa, or other general-purpose credit card. By 1995, that number had risen to 66 percent. In 2005, credit card companies sent nearly six billion solicitations to consumers, or twenty solicitations for every man, woman, and child in the United States.

Over time the endless quest for profit and growth led many card issuers to offer cards to people whose creditworthiness was questionable. In 2014, the credit-reporting firm TransUnion found that 16.5 percent of new credit cards were being opened by subprime customers (defined as having credit scores below 601).

Courting these customers may seem a questionable risk, but for credit card companies, subprime customers are actually more profitable than super-prime customers, who tend to pay on time and in full, and therefore have lower interest rates. Subprime customers build balances and pay high interest rates, often making only the minimum payment due.

As credit card issuers expanded into new markets, the mix of cardholders changed. In contrast to typical cardholders in 1989, their counterparts in 1995 were more likely to be single, to rent instead of owning a home, and to hold a position at work with less seniority. Certain factors made these new borrowers riskier than traditional ones. Newer cardholders had a substantially higher debt-to-income ratio, so even small drops in income could lead to financial distress. New borrowers were also more likely to hold unskilled jobs with wages dependent on the business cycle. Card companies began offering these customers more credit, and they went out and spent that money. But they didn't pay it all back: in just six years, between 1989 and 1995, the median outstanding credit card balance rose by more than 50 percent. Only a few hundred years after Thomas Aquinas called lending with interest immoral, we had a fully legal system in which firms routinely charged double- and triple-digit interest rates. The median available credit per card increased by about $900, or about one-third, and the median outstanding balance rose from $1,100 in 1989 to about $1,700 in 1995.

Credit card companies also sought to attract younger customers, who almost always rank as "thin file" or "no file." These firms set up tables along campus walkways, using free T-shirts and two-pound bags of M&Ms to entice first-year college students into opening a credit card account. Many quickly racked up debt that they had no ability to repay.

David, a twenty-eight-year-old from Dallas, got his credit card when he was eighteen. "I thought, 'Cool, all right. Now I have the flexibility in case I need to use it.' It didn't quite work out that way. Soon as my girlfriend found out I had a credit card: 'Oh, we're going shopping, baby.' Three days later that sucker was maxed out. And I was figuring out how in the H am I going to pay this back? Let's open up another credit card. So it was an endless cycle of doing that, paying minimums, charging it back, for about eight years after that. Except then as you get more history, people are willing to give you more credit cards. Credit was plentiful. They didn't care, you know?"

Things only got worse. In 2005, Visa launched its pink-and-white Hello Kitty credit card aimed at ten- to fourteen-year-olds. Although corporate officials proclaimed that the card would help kids develop money-management skills, the website marketing the card urged young shoppers to "shop 'til you drop!"

The Credit Card Accountability, Responsibility, and Disclosure Act (the CARD Act) of 2009, also known as "the credit card holders' bill of rights," is perhaps the most important piece of credit card legislation ever passed. It banned a range of deceptive practices that had become common in the credit card industry — raising interest rates and levying new fees without notifying customers, changing payment dates from month to month, increasing interest rates retroactively. Card issuers were no longer permitted to offer tangible enticements — like those T-shirts and M&Ms — to people under the age of twenty-one as an incentive to sign up for a card. Fees had to be "reasonable and proportional." Subprime cards — those targeted at people with lower credit scores or without much credit history — could charge account holders no more than 25 percent of the credit limit. And the CARD Act mandated that credit card issuers determine cardholders' ability to pay before issuing or increasing credit limits. Before passage of the CARD Act, Americans were paying $15 billion in penalty fees every year.

We hear all the time about how predatory payday lenders are. What's less well known is just how unscrupulous credit card companies can be, engaging in deceptive practices designed to generate revenue in ways that don't serve consumers. Despite legislation like the CARD Act, these practices persist. As recently as July 2015, the CFPB ordered Citibank to refund $700 million to consumers and pay $70 million in fines for illegal and deceptive credit card practices. Citibank had sold its customers bogus services, such as identity theft protection and credit monitoring, that it did not actually provide.

Together, the CARD Act and the financial crisis led credit card providers to cut way back on the amount of credit they would extend, for both new and existing cardholders. People who were approved for credit cards in 2011 were offered only half the amount offered to those approved in 2005. So a person who would have gotten a card with a $10,000 credit limit in 2005 was offered a card with a $5,000 limit in 2011. The "most risky" applicants experienced even greater declines: their credit limits fell by fully two-thirds, to $500.*

These cutbacks hit people exactly when they were looking for credit — as their incomes decreased or they lost their jobs. Credit cards weren't the best way to deal with these challenges, but for many they were the only way.

Government programs offered some relief, but not enough. In a context of declining wages and reductions in the social safety net, people had already begun to use credit cards as a "plastic safety net." In 2012, 40 percent of Americans were using their cards to pay for the kinds of things Suze Orman would surely label "bad debt" — basic expenses such as food, rent, and utilities.

Even though nearly half of households cut spending they would have normally charged to a credit card, their incomes still didn't cover their needs. Nearly half of households carried medical debt averaging almost $1,700 on their credit cards. As credit card issuers decreased the amount of credit they were willing to issue people, those who were suffering had to look elsewhere for loans.

African Americans were hit harder by the financial crisis of 2008 than any other group, experiencing the highest unemployment rates and the biggest drops in annual income. Over half of African American middle-class households underwent the cancellation of

---

* IT'S POSSIBLE THAT SOME OF THIS DROP IN CREDIT LIMITS RESULTED FROM THE DIMINISHMENT OF CREDITWORTHINESS THAT PEOPLE EXPERIENCED DURING THE FINANCIAL CRISIS.

a credit card, a lowering of credit limits, or a denial of application for credit. Only 66 percent report having a credit score of over 620, compared with 85 percent of white middle-class households.

African Americans had fewer resources to deal with these financial challenges — fewer savings, investments, and friends and family members with money to spare. African Americans own just one dollar in assets for every twenty dollars owned by whites, and Latinos are not much better off. They own one dollar for every eighteen dollars of white wealth. More than half of the wealth African Americans could claim came in the form of their homes, which lost more value than whites' homes did when the housing bubble burst. Not surprisingly, African Americans were three times more likely to turn to loan sharks, pawnshops, and payday lenders, and to be charged higher rates, than whites were. Likewise, African Americans were four times more likely to cash out their life insurance policies.

On the positive side, credit card balances have fallen since the financial crisis: the average credit card debt declined from $9,887 to $7,145 between 2008 and 2012. But that didn't happen because the need for credit declined. It's more likely the result of cards being canceled, borrowers' credit limits being reduced, or applicants being denied credit. Among those who had less credit available to them, nearly 10 percent took out a loan from a bank or credit union, 13 percent sold a car or other valuable, 36 percent worked extra hours or found another job, 8 percent used loans from alternative financial-services providers, and 1 percent used funds from informal lending circles.

While the CARD Act introduced some much-needed protection, it likely created some unintended negative consequences as well. A primary factor in your credit score is how much credit you're using with respect to how much is available to you. So if your credit card maximum is $1,000 and you've used $250 of that, you're using a quarter of what's available. If your credit card issuer suddenly lowers your maximum to $500 — as many did upon passage of the CARD Act — you're using half of your available credit, and your credit score is likely to drop as a result.

Tim Ranney, president of the subprime credit bureau Clarity Services, says the CARD Act helps explain why many relatively financially stable people have appeared in his database of subprime borrowers over the past several years. "It happened to me," Ranney said. "I have two Bank of America Visa cards, and I've been banking with B of A for years. One day I got two letters from B of A telling me they were lowering my credit limits significantly. My credit score dropped by fifty points. I have a great credit score, so it didn't really matter, but imagine what that did for people who were just marginally prime."

Credit makes up about two-thirds of the resources the average household has to spend on immediate needs. During the financial crisis, commercial banks reduced credit limits by 25 percent overall and cut off many consumers completely. The Federal Reserve's quarterly survey of senior loan officers in October 2008 found that 60 percent of banks had reduced credit card limits for subprime borrowers, and 25 percent had reduced limits for prime borrowers. For example, in the last quarter of 2008, one-fifth of credit card holders had at least one credit card account closed, including consumers with the best credit scores, and overall credit limits fell by a quarter from 2008 to 2009. And, as of 2012, people were paying higher interest rates — 16 percent on average, and a quarter of all Americans were paying more than 20 percent interest on their credit card debt. In 2014, the national average interest rate on a credit card was just over 15 percent, with much higher interest rates for instant-approval cards (28 percent) and cards for "bad credit" consumers (22.7 percent).

With credit from conventional sources becoming harder to obtain, many people were forced to turn elsewhere when they didn't have enough cash. And alternative lenders — payday lenders, pawnshops, and auto-title lenders (who make somewhat larger loans, $2,500 to $7,500, using the borrower's car as collateral) — were suddenly thriving. With an introduction from Joe Coleman verifying that I wasn't on a witch hunt, I prepared for a cross-country trip to embed myself in the industry once again, this time at a payday lender.

5

PAYDAY LOANS:
MAKING THE BEST OF POOR OPTIONS

IT'S LATE OCTOBER, AND ARIANE AND I ARE TAKING OUR AF-ternoon break on the steps outside the back door of Check Center, the payday lender in downtown Oakland, California, where I've taken my second job as a teller. Payday loans are illegal in New York and thirteen other states, including the District of Columbia, but they are at the center of policy debates about predatory lending, and usage has increased dramatically over the past twenty years: growing from a $10 billion industry in 2001 to $48 billion in 2011. Given that they're such a big part of the alternative financial-services landscape, I wanted the firsthand experience with a payday lender that I got at RiteCheck.

The store sits in the middle of a small commercial strip that hosts a bar, a Subway shop, a laundromat, and two banks. Rodney, our young security guard, stands watch over the small gated parking lot. He's slight and he's unarmed; with his wide smile and baggy uniform, he looks more like a greeter than a guard. Rodney is new — the last guy quit after one of the drug dealers who hang out in front of the building pulled a gun on him.

I drive to work because my coworkers don't think it's safe for me to walk the half-mile from the Lake Merritt BART stop. Today, on our break, Ariane and I are talking about how my teller training is going. Just that morning, I had a customer who wanted a three-hundred-dollar payday loan but qualified for only seventy-five. He became angry when I refused to budge, so I called Ariane over. The daughter of an Indonesian mother and an African American father, she grew up in Oakland and was raised by her mother. Though just twenty-two and short of stature, with glossy black hair pulled back in a girlish ponytail, she can be imposing when she needs to be. She quickly scanned the customer's application, stood erect as she looked him in the eye. After a polite greeting, Ariane ticked off the reasons for his denial. "Number one, you haven't been employed at your job for long enough. Number two, we can't verify that your paychecks are being deposited into your checking account. And number three, your income is too low for you to qualify for the larger loan. Would you like the seventy-five-dollar loan today?" His intimidation tactics having failed, the customer took the smaller amount and left.

Hours later Ariane is still shaking her head. "He was hella rude!" she says. "No one deserves to be talked to like that!"

Ariane takes a long sip of her coffee and we're silent for a moment, savoring the warmth of the northern California sun on our faces. Then she turns to me. "You know, Lisa, if you really want to learn about payday lending, you should know what happened to me."

When I arrived at Check Center, I told my new colleagues that I had spent the past year learning about how and why people use check cashers, payday lenders, and other alternative financial-services providers. They were curious about how things worked in other places and shocked to learn that payday loans were illegal in the state of New York. In fact, most storefront payday lenders also do everything check cashers do. The primary difference is that check cashers don't make loans. But the clientele of each differs somewhat as well. Many check-casher customers have no bank account, whereas all payday borrowers must have a bank account and a steady income — either from a job or from the government, as in the form of a regular social security check.

A payday loan is a small unsecured loan — generally less than five hundred dollars — that is due in full on the date of the borrower's paycheck, typically two to four weeks from the date when the loan was taken out. The terms vary from state to state, but a typical fee for these loans is fifteen dollars for every hundred dollars borrowed. Payday lenders do little to no underwriting (meaning they take on financial responsibility themselves), making these loans more risky than those that require a thorough credit check. The borrower gives the lender the right to take the loan amount directly out of a certain bank account on the day the loan is due.

I found Ariane to be particularly insightful about her part of the business. We talked regularly about what I was learning and how it squared with her experience. She asked to see what I was writing, and she was a thoughtful reader, adding dimension to my observations. And now she was trusting me with her own story.

Ariane told me that five months earlier, her car broke down. A young single mother, she took the bus for a few weeks, but her changing work hours made it impossible to take her child to daycare and then get herself to work on time.

Her daughter, Camille, who's nearly three, attends a publicly subsidized daycare center that they both like. Ariane can't afford to give it up, and Camille's father is absent. Some days Ariane has to get to work by 7:30 a.m. to open the store. Other days she comes in later and stays later. Ultimately she decided she had to repair her car or risk losing her job. She has never had a credit card and didn't think she would qualify for one. Ariane's mother helps with childcare but has no money to spare; she also had plans to move back to Indonesia, leaving Ariane to care for Camille on her own. Lacking other options, Ariane took out five loans from five different payday lenders, ranging from $55 to $300 each. The loans cost

$15 for every $100 borrowed, and all were due on the date of her next paycheck.

In addition to financial concerns about her car, food, childcare, and health care, Ariane worries about losing her home through inability to pay the rent: $800 per month to live in what she calls "the best apartment I've ever had," even though it's within the ten-block area where 70 percent of Oakland's murders occurred last year.

"If you think this is bad," she said, gesturing at the bullet holes that pierce the Check Center storefront, "you should see where I live. It makes this place look like Beverly Hills." Besides continuing engine trouble, her car's back window no longer goes up, and it's starting to get chilly. "I just pile, like, six blankets on Camille when we leave in the morning," Ariane said. "But I don't know what I'll do in January when it starts raining."

When Ariane took out the loans, she knew that they wouldn't solve all her problems. She needed every dollar of her paycheck to pay the rent and the utilities and to buy food. So she paid the loans back and immediately took out others, paying a new set of fees and effectively extending the length of the loans. She found that one payday loan often leads to another. Then, when the lenders tried to withdraw what she owed from her checking account, her account didn't have enough money, and she was hit with overdraft fees that quickly mounted to $300. Almost overnight, Ariane—responsible, frugal, and hardworking—found herself buried in debt.

Months after Ariane took out the loans, she was still filled with angst about what felt like a perpetual state of financial instability. "What if something happens one day and I get really sick?" she said. "I'll just have to go back for even more." Ariane used to have a bank account—she had to, in order to qualify for the payday loans she received—but she has since closed it because she can't afford to keep it open. She took on a second job, at a bar down the street from Check Center, working from 10 p.m. to 3 a.m. on Friday and Saturday, but soon quit because she never saw Camille. When we spoke, she was still paying back five dollars a month on her loans. (Most payday lenders will work out a payment plan with borrowers who fall behind.)

Check Center customers are drawn to Ariane — she knows their names and greets them by asking about their children or their jobs. She takes her work seriously and she does it well. But even though Check Center pays her more than minimum wage, it's not enough to absorb unexpected expenses like car repairs.

Payday loans are perhaps the most hotly debated topic in the area of consumer financial services. Consumer advocates vehemently oppose these loans; they object to what they see as a mismatch between the way loans are packaged and promoted and the way people actually use them. Though they are sold as "quick fixes" for a duration of two to four weeks, many people end up taking out loans, then rolling them over or renewing them. (Rollovers and renewals are ways to delay the repayment of a loan, and they require an additional fee.) Or borrowers take out another loan immediately, thereby staying in debt longer. Ability to pay, reformers argue, should be determined before a potential borrower is approved for a loan.

There are arguments too over the true interest rates of these loans. Consumer advocates believe that annual percentage rate (APR) is the right way to represent the cost of loans, given that so many borrowers take a long time to repay. But lenders maintain that a loan with a term of two to four weeks can't meaningfully be represented by an annual percentage rate. Most states nevertheless require lenders to post the APR for a payday loan in large print where it's easily visible to potential borrowers. Payday loan APRs range from 300 to 600 percent in the United States and up to 4,000 percent at similar lenders in other countries.

Consumer advocates also argue that payday lenders — and other purveyors of small-dollar credit such as pawnbrokers and auto-title lenders — take advantage of people like Ariane, trapping them at a vulnerable moment so that they must eventually repay much more than they borrowed. The Center for Responsible Lending (CRL), a leading consumer advocacy agency, maintains that these loans "catch borrowers in a turnstile of debt. Before long, payday's cycle of debt denies dollars for household budget items like child care, groceries or utilities." (This argument doesn't address the predicament of many borrowers — they don't have enough money to pay for these necessities in the first place.)

CRL is staunchly opposed to payday lending, full stop. Early in my research, I got into a debate about payday loans with a senior staff member of the Self Help Federal Credit Union, which is affiliated with CRL. He argued that payday loans were an easy choice for people, but not the best choice. "Imagine that you've been thrown out of a boat and you can't swim well," he said. "There's a float very near you and another one, farther away, that's tied to the boat. The easiest thing would be to grab onto the closest float, but that might take you farther and farther away from the boat, where you need to be. The smarter thing to do would be to get yourself over to that float that's attached to the boat." In this analogy the detached float nearby is the payday loan.

"I get that," I replied. "But what is the attached float in this story? What is the better choice for the payday borrower?"

"They need to save up," he said. "Or borrow from friends and family." These are great options if you have them. The problem is, most borrowers don't.

Even industry insiders admit that payday-loan rollovers are

troubling. One executive of a payday lending chain, who asked not to be identified, said, "It's wrong! There needs to be some kind of enforcement so that the good customers aren't paying for the bad ones. Sometimes these loans are being used as short-term loans, but more often they're being used long term. That's not the intention." Joe Coleman of RiteCheck (which does not make payday loans because they're illegal in New York) echoed this sentiment: "It's the repeated use, the overuse of rollovers — that's where I'm concerned." Still, payday insiders maintain that they are playing a crucial role as lenders-of-last-resort for borrowers with no other options. Rob Zweig, who has been Check Center's COO for the past eight years, told me, "We're in business to do our best by the customer. It makes good business sense to make these loans." He too acknowledged the downside: "I'm concerned about these loans being used as high-cost lines of credit, because they were designed to be short-term, intermittent loans."

When I asked Ariane whether she thought payday loans should be illegal in California, she replied, "No, I think they should still exist. You know it's undoable to take out five loans and be able to pay them back. But sometimes you have no choice. The reason I'm working so hard to pay these loans back is because I want to be in good standing, in case I ever need another one."

So where does the true problem lie? There's no denying that payday loans are expensive. The question that remains is whether expensive credit is better than no credit at all. Is Ariane better off by getting the loans to have her car repaired? She thinks so.

If lenders are to blame for the indebtedness of so many borrowers, the easy answer would be to shut them all down. But wiping each and every lender off the map would do nothing to quell the demand for these loans. What would Ariane have done if payday loans were unavailable?

· · ·

I met with John Weinstein, president of Check Center, months after I had worked in the Oakland branch store. I wanted to understand Weinstein's story and get his take on the industry. Weinstein leaves the day-to-day management of the business to Zweig and spends most of his time in Sonoma, where he lives. I drove north from San Francisco to meet him one overcast January day, winding along a narrow road through vineyards to his home. Weinstein stood out front and greeted me cheerfully as I pulled in. A slight man with white hair and an athletic build — he swims daily — he was wearing faded jeans and a hunter-green Oakland A's hoodie. Two dogs — an Australian blue heeler and a bassett hound/lab mix — jumped at him as he led me inside. John introduced the dogs as Chaz and Lucy.

John and I stood in the kitchen, making small talk as he prepared a plate of cheese and crackers. He was engaging and friendly. "Have you eaten? Shall I cut up an apple? I'll cut up an apple." He looked out the window to assess the weather. "Honestly, this is the first day it hasn't been sunny. Winter is here! I thought we'd sit outside in the gazebo, but maybe it's too cold for you?"

"It was twelve degrees when I left New York," I reassured him. "I'd love to sit outside."

We took a path that led to a gazebo affording a beautiful view of the surrounding countryside. Lucy, ecstatic to be outdoors, ran circles around us. We settled in, and I asked John to tell me how he got started in the payday business.

"My grandfather started a check-cashing business in Chicago during the Depression," John told me. "The banks were closing, and people needed a place to get their checks cashed. My grandfather was one of the first to start up."

The banks came back eventually, but they showed little interest in serving the market that check cashers had begun to target.

Weinstein's father grew the Ohio business in the 1960s. At that time, there were no branch banks on the south side of Chicago. "That was the heyday of check cashing in Illinois. The welfare business, government business was huge. The government sent AFDC checks and food stamps right to us, and we cashed 85 percent of them." (AFDC, or Aid for Families with Dependent Children, was that era's name for welfare.) Weinstein worked in the store as a kid but didn't really enjoy waiting on customers.

The check-cashing industry expanded to other states in the 1970s and, at some point, corruption entered the picture. "In Illinois the politicians always had their hands out," he explained. "The industry got in trouble going to Springfield, the capital, with paper bags full of unmarked bills. My father was involved but fortunately he had a good lawyer. He got immunity but he had to testify. Now the industry is almost gone." At the height of the industry, Weinstein's family had thirty stores in four states. Weinstein and his brother recently sold their last check-cashing store in Chicago.

"Most banks want to minimize their relationships with lower-income earners," Weinstein told me. "We see that as an opportunity. Because we've gained their trust, we have this market. They have financial needs and we want to fulfill them."

Weinstein set out on his own and, using the experience he had accumulated in Ohio, started the Check Center chain in the Bay Area in 1984. When payday lending became legal, Weinstein was incredulous. "I never thought anything like that would pass," he told me. "It just seemed so crazy to me. It was the easiest money we ever made." Check Center's first store was in downtown Berkeley, and the location turned out to be a good one. "It was like throwing darts at a board to find a good spot." Weinstein next opened a store in Fremont, a suburb that's slightly higher up the socioeconomic ladder. At the time, it felt like a risky move because Weinstein had been raised as a banker to the poor. "There was an auto factory there — they made Chevys back then — now they make Teslas. We didn't get a lot of checks from the auto factory, but it turned out that the area's check-cashing market was very good. Fremont opened my eyes," he continued. "I realized that I didn't need to be the welfare banker, so I started trying to focus more on the payroll community than the welfare community." People, in other words, with the kind of jobs that used to pay a living wage.

Which brings us to the demand part of the story. Real wages have declined, the welfare state has shrunk, and credit markets have contracted, creating a greater demand for payday loans. There are more payday lending stores than there are McDonald's restaurants and Starbucks shops combined. This statistic is even more impressive when you realize that payday lending is illegal in fourteen states, where plenty of burgers and coffee are sold.

The growth of payday lending isn't a coincidence. Just as the use of credit cards shifted from "needs" to "wants," people began to use payday loans to pay for basic expenses. Some are predictable, like rent, and others, like car repairs, are not.

Using the "good debt/bad debt" framework, how should we classify Ariane's debt? The money she borrowed to fix her car will not add much to its value, so the loans could not be called "good debt" by either historical or current thinking. But it would also be hard to label these loans as "bad debt" — a want and not a need. Ariane needed that money to make her life work, just as other payday borrowers I spoke with needed the food they bought or the rent they paid.

The contraction of credit, both from banks and from credit card issuers, also drives demand. It used to be that some people could walk into a bank and get a five-hundred-dollar loan with just a signature. Greg Fairchild, a professor of management at the University of Virginia, told me his father called those "white man's loans." The label comes from years of observation: Fairchild's father worked as a commercial lender, then as the head of community development at a bank that was acquired by Wachovia. Now, no matter what your race or gender, those days are gone.

Banks have retreated from small-dollar credit because they don't find it sufficiently profitable, and many borrowers don't qualify to begin with. Some banks, like Wells Fargo, offered payroll-advance loans for a while. But once the media reported that these loans were basically the same as payday loans, the banks stopped offering the products. The risk to their reputation was too great. Of course, banks do offer all of us a short-term loan. It's called an overdraft, and if it had a repayment period of seven days, the APR for a typical incident would be over 5,000 percent. Americans paid $38 billion in overdraft fees in 2011, more than they paid to payday lenders.

The shrinkage of credit has also caused people to juggle their available credit and use payday loans in ways that would seem counterintuitive without complete knowledge of individuals' situations. For example, some people who take out payday loans also have credit cards that are not maxed out. It would seem that they should use the credit cards before getting a payday loan, right? Not necessarily. Tim Ranney, president of Clarity Services, relayed a conversation he had with the head of risk for one of the country's largest credit card issuers, who asked him, "Why are people taking out loans instead of using their cards?" Ranney told me, "This guy was implying that these people weren't smart enough to make the 'right' decision. I laughed in his face. 'They're protecting the card!' I told him. People don't want to use their last available line of credit." In these cases, the credit card is the safety net. Whereas failure to repay a payday loan won't affect a consumer's credit score, failure to repay a credit card will.

Here are two possible answers as to whether the benefits of payday loans outweigh the costs: (1) it depends, and (2) the jury's still out.

One study found that these loans allowed victims of natural disasters in California to pay for hotel rooms and other necessities at a time when banks and other traditional financial institutions failed to provide the small-dollar loans that the displaced people needed. Another study found that payday loans helped borrowers manage their money in the event of a financial setback, such as an unexpected bill for dental care, a reduction in work hours, or auto repair. Oftentimes people use payday loans because, like Ariane, they find themselves with no other good option. Should they take out a payday loan or have their utilities shut off? Take out the loan or risk losing their job? Several studies find that the benefits of the loans can outweigh the costs in these circumstances. In other words, it depends.

Other research indicates that borrowers who use payday loans for unexpected emergencies are the exception rather than the norm. A 2012 study found that only 16 percent of first-time borrowers use the loan to cover unexpected or emergency expenses. But the same study found that 69 percent used their loans to cover other necessary expenses such as a utility bill, a credit card bill, rent, or food. Eighty-five percent of borrowers, in other words, don't have enough money to pay for everyday needs and the kind of unexpected costs we all incur from time to time. So: the jury's still out.

Leaders in the US Department of Defense have been particularly outspoken critics of the payday-loan industry; they argue that it undermines military readiness, hurts troop morale, and adds to the cost of fielding an all-volunteer military. Payday lending stores often locate just outside military bases, making these loans an easy fix for young men and women who find themselves in a financial bind. Defense leaders argue that high interest rates and fees contribute to cyclical borrowing and that marketing payday loans to young, inexperienced service members can have negative implications for their careers. Among navy personnel, financial issues are the cause of 80 percent of security clearance denials or revocations, but it's impossible to know whether these financial issues were caused by payday loans. As a result of advocacy in the defense sphere, payday-loan regulations differ for military personnel.

Researchers also look at what happens when consumers' access to payday loans is limited or cut off. Payday lending is regulated at the state level, rather than the federal. (That's about to change, as the Consumer Financial Protection Bureau rolls out federal rules that will apply to all lenders in all states.) Each state has different rules, different fee structures, and different maximum loan amounts. Some states have changed their rules recently, which has allowed researchers to conduct important "before and after" studies.

In 2004 and 2005, Georgia and North Carolina enacted legislation to close all payday lending stores within their states. A 2008 study examined changes in consumers' well-being after these laws were passed. Compared with other states where payday credit is available, households in Georgia have bounced more checks, filed more complaints with the Federal Trade Commission about lenders and debt collectors, and filed for Chapter 7 bankruptcy more often. The Dartmouth economist Jonathan Zinman examined what happened before and after Oregon passed legislation in 2007 that restricted access to expensive credit. He found that former payday borrowers shifted their behavior following the cap, using "plausibly inferior" alternatives such as checking account overdrafts.

Other states have placed restrictions on the payday industry — limiting the number of loans a borrower can have, requiring cooling-off periods, and allowing storefront but not online lending. In Florida, for example, borrowers can take out only one payday loan at a time; the loans are tracked through a statewide database. Colorado enacted legislation in 2010 that bans "lump sum" loans —those that must be repaid in full. Lenders are allowed to offer installment loans instead; these loans are structured to allow borrowers to repay in smaller amounts over longer periods of time. On average, payments in Colorado amount to only 4 percent of a borrower's paycheck. A study by the Pew Research Center found that after the legislation was passed in Colorado, the number of payday stores decreased from 505 in 2009 to 238 in 2013, and the number of payday-loan borrowers decreased by 15 percent. Each borrower spent about 42 percent less on payday-loan fees, and the number of renewals or rollover loans decreased by more than 50 percent. Pew is confident that Coloradans are better off with the current situation than they were before the ban on "lump sum" loans.

Research on payday lenders tends to lump them all together. But there are important differences among them. Rick Hackett, a retired Consumer Financial Protection Bureau (CFPB) official who now engages in consulting, told me that "there are people who operate licensed businesses, and those businesses are okay. Regulators need to do what has to be done to ensure that. And that's not easy to do. Hard cases with bad facts make bad law." When I asked Weinstein about the poor reputation of payday lenders, he acknowledged that there are good guys and bad guys in the business. "There are places where the only underwriting that's done is a breath test," he told me. "If you can fog up a mirror, you can get a loan." This is one reason why the CFPB has proposed regulation that would require lenders to determine a borrower's "ability to pay" before making a loan.

The wide range of findings from research on payday lending leaves policymakers in a tough spot. It seems that some borrowers benefit, in certain situations, if they get their loans from a lender who plays by the rules. But how to determine which borrowers and which lenders meet these criteria? One key characteristic of good policy is that it's easy to implement. It's difficult to make a practical policy that takes all of this variation into account. Pressure on policymakers to stem the perceived damage from these loans is strong, however, and the CFPB is responding, doing its best to implement policy that allows people in need, and with the ability to pay, to avail themselves of these loans.

The Check Center payday-loan application is short—one double-sided page with larger-than-average font size. There is no fine print. The fees and interest rates are posted on the wall next to the teller windows, also in very large print. At Check Center, at least, it would be hard to argue, as some do, that the loans have hidden fees or that they are designed to trick people. What's not disputable is that they are expensive compared to other kinds of credit available to those of us who enjoy greater financial stability. The Check Center borrowers we interviewed complained about the cost of the loans they took out, but they had no other place to turn when they needed quick cash.

Applicants provide name, address, phone numbers, name of workplace, amount of paycheck, and how often the paycheck is cut. The application also asks for the phone number of the prospective borrower's supervisor and one other person who can be called if Check Center is unable to reach the borrower. The application makes it clear that the borrower cannot be taken to court for nonpayment of the debt; payday lenders can do very little when a borrower fails to pay. Check Center's COO, Rob Zweig, emphasized this repeatedly during our many conversations. "We have no way to collect on the debt," he told me. "We have no leverage except the customer's conscience."

The debt collections department for the entire Check Center chain is housed at the back of the store in downtown Oakland where I worked as a teller. Four computer terminals sit at a long table in a small windowless room, each workstation differentiated by only the small personal items its occupant keeps there: small stuffed animals, a mini pumpkin (Halloween was approaching), a special coffee mug. On the wall behind the computers, a large whiteboard displays the current statistics on loans collected for each of Check Center's twenty stores, and goals for each month. The chart is updated each morning, so every collections agent knows exactly where she stands. Each is responsible for two or three of the chain's stores.

I worked in collections for only a week, but it was enough time to understand that calling up debtors hour after hour, day after day, is soul-killing work. I spent the first day shadowing Delia, a chipper young woman with long, straight hair and a can-do attitude. That morning she arrived shortly after I did, took off her jacket, and set down her purse — a bag shaped like a rubber chicken, replete with red comb and wattle — beside her terminal. "Ready?" she asked. She pulled up a file of clients that the computer system had generated — people whose checking accounts had been tapped the day before, when their loan payment was due, and whose accounts had insufficient funds. We called these customers first; if they paid back their loans on the first day after the bounce, Check Center waived the fifteen-dollar late fee.

Delia teaches me the protocol for which people we call, when we call them, and what the law allows us to say. We make calls only between 8 a.m. and 6:30 p.m. If we don't reach the person and have to leave a message, we are not allowed to say we're calling about a late loan. We say, "I am calling about an urgent business matter." The same holds true if we call the borrower's office or the other person whose name and number appear on the loan application. If a person asks us not to call before or after a certain time, or not to call at work, the Fair Debt Collection Practices Act (FDCPA), which I was required to read before working in collections, mandates that we respect the request. Many borrowers don't understand their rights, however; they've never heard of the FDCPA. Some lenders take advantage of this gap between the law and consumer awareness.

Delia thumbs through a small red notebook. "I wrote down the most aggressive thing I'm allowed to say," she tells me. Here it is: "I can no longer hold your file open." Check Center stops calling once the loan is sixty days overdue. After that, Zweig says, "The cost/benefit of investing more resources to collect on the loan is limited."

Most payday lenders do not report to the big three credit bureaus. This is a good thing if you haven't repaid your loan, because failure to pay is unlikely to affect your future ability to obtain credit anywhere but at Check Center. It's not so good if you do pay off the loan because those payments don't enable you to build your credit score.

Delia scans the list of calls and predicts that it will be a tough day. She's right. Most of the time we don't reach the people we call. Sometimes they simply don't answer, so we leave a message.

Sometimes the trail goes cold. We call several delinquent borrowers whose phone numbers don't work. In one instance, the reference we call claims she doesn't know the borrower, and the work supervisor listed tells us the borrower doesn't work there anymore.

But Delia tells me that a surprising number of people do respond. "They form relationships with the people here. They're lonely," she says. "And they realize that if they do pay, we'll stop calling them." It's clear from the conversations I'm hearing that she's right. Some of the people we call are downright chatty with Delia; others are deeply distressed and trust her to understand their plight. Of those who do talk to us, most tell us they want to repay their loans. We call a customer who promised in September that he would repay his loan on October 20. It's now October 23, and the borrower tells us he will come to the store to pay off the debt on October 28. Delia hangs up the phone and turns to me. "Highly unlikely," she says. "You can just hear it in the voice. But he could've dodged me and he didn't. I guess I should be happy I got to speak to an actual human being. Who knows — maybe he will pay!"

We call another customer who tells us she has lost her job and has health issues that are eating into her available funds. She asks us to call her back in two or three weeks. "I wish I could pay you," she says. "But right now I just have nothing."

Delia sighs. "I hate having to do that," she says. "At the beginning of the month we get the Supplemental Security Income folks, and I just feel so bad for them." Yet another customer tells us she had an emergency with her son. She can't repay the entire loan, but she'd like to set up a repayment plan, and we agree that she will pay twenty-five dollars twice each month until the loan is paid off. One proactive customer calls us, wanting to create a payment plan; she's having trouble with her job and isn't sure how much she'll be able to pay, but she wants to do something.

What happens when you can't pay back a payday loan when it comes due? The answer depends on the state you live in and the lender you use. "States are all over the map regarding whether lenders can sue borrowers," Rick Hackett said. "Most don't. They just sell off the loan for two cents on the dollar." There is a growing group of third-party debt collectors who buy this and other debt. They believe they can collect more than what they purchased the debt for, and some use aggressive tactics to recoup their investment.

At Check Center, a borrower has to pay off one loan before taking out another. But most of the people who came in paid off that first loan and immediately took out another, generally for the same amount or more. This situation amounts to pretty much the same thing as a rollover. If the borrower does not repay the loan, it goes to collections.

"We're pretty limited in what we can do," Delia tells me. These limitations made it challenging for her to meet the goals displayed on the wall chart, and she sometimes played with the edge of what she was legally allowed to do. Once, as I observed her during a call, she put her hand over the phone's mouthpiece and pretended to be talking to someone else in the office. "Yes, we're going to have to move this one along to the next stage," she said, implying perhaps that Check Center would somehow step up its efforts to collect.

I quickly realized that the tellers and collections agents I worked with at Check Center were not too different from their customers in terms of financial stability. Most were either single, or married with kids. Ariane, as a single mother, was an outlier, and the fact that she and her daughter had to survive on her Check

Center paycheck likely explains why she couldn't absorb the financial shock of her car breaking down. Flor, who worked full-time at Check Center, was married to a janitor at McDonald's. Terry worked a second job at Target. At another Check Center store, one teller worked both at Check Center and at a RadioShack in the same strip mall. She simply changed from one shirt uniform to the other and walked the short distance between the two shops — that is, when she could manage to coordinate her hours at both businesses.

The tellers brought their lunches or bought the cheapest food they could find at the supermarket across the street. One day when I offered to pick up coffee for Ariane and the other teller on my shift, they asked if it was okay if they got expensive, "fancy" coffees. The extent of their gratitude when I returned with the whipped cream–topped treats made me uncomfortable; these were clearly rare delicacies.

The tellers and the collections agents talked constantly about finding a different, better job, although in this economy the quest seemed the equivalent of searching for the Holy Grail. "Are you coming to the mall with me after work?" Delia asked another agent one afternoon. "I want to apply at Victoria's Secret; you get free bras when they get new styles." Delia was working full-time at Check Center, part-time at a bar, and picking up seasonal work with a wedding caterer. "The health insurance is the only reason I stay here," she told me.

I knew my experience at Check Center might not be representative of the larger payday-loan industry. I had heard so many negative stories about payday lenders, and I wanted exposure to a broad range of lenders and borrowers. So I called Dana Wiggins, who runs the Predatory Loan Help Hotline out of the Virginia Poverty Law Center for Virginia residents who are having trouble with their payday loans. I told Dana about my interest in payday lending and asked her if I could volunteer on the hotline. She thought it was a great idea, so I scheduled a trip to Richmond to learn the ropes.

When Dana first mentioned the hotline, I imagined a room filled with computer terminals and headsets like those on the Jerry Lewis Telethon. It turned out that the hotline was no more than an extension on Dana's office phone. She answered it when she was in the office. When she wasn't, callers left a message on her voicemail and she called them back. I wanted to answer a lot of calls, and I wouldn't be staying in Richmond, so Dana bought a cheap mobile phone and had the hotline number ring to it. For the next month, I *was* the hotline. I carried the mobile around with me. I could be working in my office or eating dinner with my family when the phone rang. "Predatory Loan Help Hotline. This is Lisa, how can I help you?" I'd answer, grabbing my notebook to document the call.

I listened to story after story from people who could not extricate themselves from payday debt, who were getting calls from loan collectors they didn't recognize, and who thought they were making the best — or only — decision they could when they had taken out their loans. I heard the distress and the panic in their voices as they told me of their predicaments. Tanya had taken out five Internet loans. "I'm not blaming nobody but me," she told me, "but they've been taking so much out of my checking account. I've been paying a year and a half and they're still telling me I owe more." Online lenders are the fastest-growing part of the industry. In states where payday loans are legal, some borrowers prefer the convenience and anonymity of the online option. People who live in states like New York, where payday lending is illegal, can in fact access this kind of credit. It's extremely difficult for regulators to stop this illegal lending.

Marjorie's lender called her repeatedly, threatening to sue her for nonpayment of her loan. Karen had taken out eight loans from eight different lenders, ranging from $200 to $1,250, to pay for her father's assisted living facility. She had a stable government job but couldn't make the payments. The lenders kept trying to get money from her bank account, and the bank fees for nonsufficient funds mounted. Karen didn't know what to do. "I'll suffer before I let my father suffer," she said. "Wouldn't you?"

Tanya, Marjorie, and Karen had taken out Internet loans. Fortunately for them, these loans are illegal in Virginia (storefront loans are legal). Most of the Internet borrowers who called the hotline did not know this. I was able to tell these three women — and many others like them — that because the loans themselves were illegal, they were not obligated to repay them.

I talked each caller through the long process of extricating herself from the debt and then sent each an email outlining the steps needed to clear up their situations. First, they needed to send a letter to their bank and to the lenders, informing them that they were no longer authorizing the bank and the lender to withdraw money from their account (I sent sample letters to the callers). Next the caller was to send another letter to the bank's customer service department, informing it about the first letter and attaching a copy. Both of these steps were necessary but not sufficient to keep the banks from debiting an account. Some banks and credit unions charged customers for a "stop payment" — in short, a lot of hassle and money for something that often didn't work.

The letters and forms were often insufficient. Many callers found that their banks continued to debit their accounts, in which case I recommended that they file a complaint with the CFPB. I also suggested that they open a new account at a new institution and move their direct deposit to that account. If they simply opened a new account at the same bank, it would likely be debited. Opening a new account could be difficult if the existing account was overdrawn. In that case, they needed to make the existing account "deposit only" and bring it to a zero balance. If they did not, they could be barred from opening a new account for several years, excluding them from the mainstream financial-services system.

Even though borrowers were not technically required to pay back Internet loans, I encouraged them to repay the principal. Most hotline callers I spoke with had already done this, and often had also paid hundreds of dollars in interest and overdraft fees.

For callers who had taken out storefront loans (those available only at brick-and-mortar stores) or auto-title loans (loans of $2,500 to $7,500 that use the borrower's car as collateral), the outlook was much less rosy. I counseled them on their rights under the Fair Debt Collection Practices Act and instructed them to ask the people who called them who they were, whom they worked for, and where they were located, and to request that collectors send documentation on the loans and what was owed. Loan collectors frequently refused to provide borrowers with this basic information. I told borrowers to get in writing any proposal that was being offered and not to agree to anything immediately on the phone. Loan collectors — both legitimate and not — often try to get borrowers to make payments over the phone. Sometimes these payments are not recorded anywhere, and the debt remains. And I reassured borrowers that, despite what they had been told, they could not be criminally prosecuted for not paying back a payday loan.

I told hotline callers how and where to file complaints with the Consumer Finance Protection Bureau, the Internet Crimes Complaint Center, and the Federal Trade Commission (FTC). The FTC gets more complaints about problematic debt collecting than about any activity other than identity theft. Even though en-

couraging callers to file complaints made me feel that I was helping them do something proactive, I had little hope that the effort
would make a difference in the long run. In 2009, the FTC received 88,190 complaints about debt collectors but acted on only
one company. And even though the CFPB recently created smart
new rules to deal with these issues, the agency is unlikely to have
sufficient enforcement resources. As Jake Halpern, author of *Bad
Paper: Chasing Debt from Wall Street to the Underworld,* writes, the
CFPB's entire budget is equal to "just 2 percent of what JP Morgan
Chase set aside in reserves for its litigation expenses in 2013."

Even so, unlike the debt collection work I did at Check Center,
my time as a hotline operator was enormously satisfying. Much
of the time, I could actually do something to help people. Callers
were exceedingly grateful. But it was terrifically frustrating when
I had no good news, no easy answers. Getting that close to the
hopelessness of a person's situation changed me.

Hotline callers often didn't recognize the names of the loan
collectors who called them. That's because there is a huge market in third-party debt collection, and it's not only payday lenders
who use them. Banks, credit card companies, doctors' offices, and
phone companies all sell old debt to third-party collectors for pen-
nies on the dollar, a practice that became legal in the 1920s. One
hotline caller, who took out payday loans in an attempt to keep her
house from being foreclosed on, realized she was the victim of a
scam only after paying $495 to a firm that claimed she owed them
money. She closed her bank account after they continued to try to
get money from her bank. The company then demanded another
$399 in processing fees; she got nothing in return for the $495.

Things can get very murky when debt is sold and resold. The
original owners of the debt tend to include a standard line in their
contracts that says they are not responsible for the accuracy of the
information they sell. The new owners of the debt then attempt to

collect on that debt but have no relationship to the original borrower, and no responsibility for fixing the inevitable errors. After researching the debt-buying business for several months, Halpern concluded that "these mistakes aren't freak occurrences. They are the inevitable result of a haphazard system that transfers debt from one vendor to another — over and over — with minimal oversight or incentive to get it exactly right."

Computer files full of borrowers' personal information can be sold and resold many times. Halpern cites a source at the CFPB who told him that "as debts are sold from one buyer to another — and interest is added along the way — consumers will often receive calls from a collection agency they've never heard of, on behalf of a creditor that they've never done business with, over a balance they don't recognize." Operating the hotline, Wiggins sees this kind of thing a lot. "We've seen suspect lenders selling a person's information to one debt buyer, then selling to another debt buyer even after the loan has been paid," she said.

On one of my trips to California I visited Dan Leibsohn at Community Check Cashing (CCC) in Fruitvale, a low-income, mostly Latino neighborhood in Oakland. With his tweed jacket, wire-rimmed glasses, and white hair, Dan looks more like a professor than a check casher. Dan started CCC in 2009 in order to provide community members with services in a socially responsible way. To say that CCC is a shoestring operation is an understatement. The business does not break even, and Dan has had to let go of all but one employee. When we meet in January 2014 he tells me he doesn't think they'll be able to finish out the year unless they get an infusion of money. CCC cashes checks for 1 percent of face value, a rate that's significantly below the rate allowed by the state of California. They also offer payday loans, charging $7.50 per $100, half of the fee allowed by the state.

Leibsohn is clearly an advocate for consumers, but he believes his experience running a check casher/payday lender sets him apart from those who make their living from consumer advocacy. "It's jaw dropping," he said. "The consumer advocates don't understand the kind of pressures low-income people are under, the instability they face."

I found out about the stigma payday borrowers carry shortly after I published a magazine article about payday lending that included Ariane's story. My standard practice for my writing is to change the names of the people I work with and interview in order to keep their information confidential. Ariane insisted that I use her real name — she was not ashamed of what she had done and she wanted *her* story to be out there. But she ran into trouble shortly after the article was published. Ariane had landed a new job as a veterinary assistant — a job that paid well and came with benefits — and she was looking for a better apartment. She found one she liked and could afford, but the landlord Googled her, found my article, and told her she could no longer rent his apartment. He focused on the fact that she had taken out payday loans rather than recognizing her conscientiousness about repaying them. Even though she paid back every dime she owed, the fact that she needed the loans in the first place worked against her.

Society still judges borrowers like Ariane, despite her strong work ethic. In America, we're supposed to be able to make it on our own, without help. I next turned my lens to another group that's making hard choices about whether to take on debt in the face of bleak economic prospects — millennials.

6

LIVING IN THE MINUS:
THE MILLENNIAL PERSPECTIVE

THE RECESSION GENERATION. GENERATION DEBT. THE UN-
employables. The labels used to describe the group most commonly known as millennials are legion, and they tend to reflect the
financial instability these young adults face. There's even an acro-
nym that describes a large chunk of this group: NEETs, "not in education, employment, or training," and they make up 15 percent of
the population in rich countries like the United States.

Thinking about her future while coping with a very large student debt load, one woman summed it up this way: "You either get
to have a retirement account, or you can have a house. Or you can
have kids. I feel like you have to pick one. There's no 'you can have
all three.'"

Making up more than a quarter of the total US population, the
millennial generation, beginning with those born in 1980, the year
Ronald Reagan began to strip away the public safety net, totals
eighty-three million people and represents the largest generation
ever. Coming of age in an era defined by economic uncertainty and
financial insecurity has deeply affected how this generation thinks
about money. When asked to describe what money means to them,
42 percent of millennials chose the word "security" and 22 percent chose "stress."

The students and recent graduates I spoke with believe the American Dream their parents' generation pursued just isn't a viable option for them. Thirty-two-year-old Kendra served in the army for four years before returning to school. In the wake of the financial crisis, her house was foreclosed on. The mortgage payments were higher than her earnings. She lost her job and then moved out, in the hope that she could make the payments by renting out the house. But after four years of owning her home, she couldn't make it work any longer. "I actually managed to make my mortgage even when I was unemployed because I had renters in, and I was managing to come up with the extra. My credit score was the last thing I let go of. I lost everything else, but I had a 780. That was the very last thing that I let go of. Then when I let go of that, I was like, I don't have kids. I never plan on getting married. I never want to buy another house. I'm buying my next car with cash. So yeah, my parents had the American Dream. Good for them. Never going to be for me, and I don't want it anymore."

This generation dreams more modest dreams: paying off debt, obtaining financial stability, rising above the "gig economy" to find a job they enjoy and has some meaning for them. Their financial fears make it difficult — or painful — to look too far into the future. As Marisa, who was about to graduate with a master's degree in urban policy, put it, "I think at this point, looking forward to the next few years, it's less about being successful than can I even get out of this hole and get on an even foundation, to then maybe have some type of substantial savings? Or make a plan that means I do not live paycheck to paycheck?" Rachel echoed this sentiment, saying that because of the amount of money she owes, she has "lowered expectations. I don't even want to own anything. I just want to be able to not have to think about money, just not have to worry, because it takes up so much energy."

One young woman summed it up: "It's like we're all living in the minus."

There's increasing evidence that financial insecurity is placing a strain on millennials' personal networks. Some of the young people I spoke with became emotional when telling me they needed to move far from family and friends because they couldn't afford to live nearby. They're being forced to forgo the support that often comes from proximate relationships. Several expressed distress at having to miss out on important life events, like their friends' weddings. One twenty-six-year-old described her dilemma: "A lot of my friends are getting married and doing these things where I've had to say no. I feel really bad. I went on this bachelorette party, and now it's killing me. I feel like it's going to take me two months to pay off these two days of having fun. I was like, 'What a huge mistake I made.' But if I hadn't gone, it would be a huge schism in the relationship I have with my friend. It definitely is a stress that you want to just have a normal life, but you can't."

We all accumulate social capital as we move through life — it's a product of the family we're born into, the communities we're raised in, the relationships we make at school, summer camp, religious organizations, and work. We grow and maintain these relationships through contact and reciprocity. In this country, a large group of young people can't afford to participate in their own social networks. This isn't to say that the only way to build social capital is by spending money, but when you can't afford a train ticket to visit a sick friend or a flight home for Christmas, it puts a strain on the web of social capital.

The debt-related monikers given to this generation carry more than a hint of judgment. Headlines like "Why Millennials Are Spending More Than They Earn, and Parents Are Footing the Bill" foster perceptions that this generation is a bunch of fiscally irresponsible freeloaders. But research shows that millennials save more diligently, beginning at a younger age, than the generations that preceded them. A 2015 study found that 64 percent of millennials say they're more inclined to save than to spend, and more than half have set financial goals, compared with 38 percent of Americans age thirty-five and older. Millennials seem to have gotten the message that they'll get less help from their employers or from the government as they age.

But saving isn't easy. Kendra, the army veteran and former homeowner, has lost her faith in financial planning and her belief that she can save for retirement. "I've come to the realization that I will never have a retirement," she said. "I don't do savings. At eighteen I invested in a mutual fund, thinking that that was the responsible thing to do for an eighteen-year-old trying to think about the future. I think I had $5,000, and I now have $458 of that. So I lost all of that. That really made me very cynical about anything stock market related. Then of course watching the 2008 thing happen. I was like, I'll just shove my money in my mattress. That's literally my savings plan. I just don't see myself having a retirement plan, per se."

Kendra has all but given up on the notion that she *can* plan for her future. Other members of her generation are beset by worry: 39 percent of millennials say they worry once a week or more about their financial future, and women worry more than men. Only 2 percent of millennial women claim that they never worry about money, whereas 20 percent of men say they're worry-free. This is at least partially financial; while millennial women are making gains in closing the gender pay gap, they still earn about eighty-five cents to the millennial man's dollar. Most millennials have savings accounts but there's not much in them. They want to save but there's nothing left over after paying the bills. More than three-quarters of adults under the age of thirty worry that they aren't saving or investing enough.

Very often, college debt makes saving a distant goal. We've always been told that investment in assets like education is okay, assigning student loans to the category of "good debt." But since the 1980s, college tuition rates have risen faster than inflation, while the cost of living has increased and benefits — both public and private — have virtually disappeared. The college debt load increased by 400 percent in the fifteen years between 1987 and 2002. Americans currently have $1.2 trillion in student loan debt, more than the amount of credit card debt and the amount of auto debt. Millennials are more than twice as likely as the average American to have student loan debt.

As they try to understand these unstable circumstances, many millennials beat themselves up for educational decisions they made when they were too young to understand the long-term implications. They simply didn't know any better. Angela decided to attend an expensive liberal arts college. At the time, she had no idea she would be shouldering the debt burden she faces now. "When I chose my undergraduate institution, my parents weren't super-clear with me. My dad wanted me to understand exactly the commitment I was getting into. My mom wanted to protect me from that somehow, which, in retrospect, doesn't really make sense. But her parents had paid for her education, and she wanted to create that 'Don't worry about it, go where you want to go' for me. So I was kind of confused. I value my degree, but I think I could've made a better decision — gone to a state school or something like that — and gotten the same value for a lot less. And now I'm going to be paying for my education forever."

The assumption that investment in higher education will turn into a well-paying job with benefits no longer holds true. As of July 2014, more than a quarter of bachelor's degree holders under twenty-five years of age were unemployed. These students, already burdened by quantities of debt they can barely comprehend, quickly find that they can't get the jobs they want without a graduate degree. So what do they do? They keep on borrowing.

The jobs and wage crisis seems to have sent many members of this generation in search of alternative ways to make a living. Only 41 percent were employed full-time in 2010; another 24 percent were employed part-time. A 2014 survey found that for 35 percent of millennials with a bachelor's degree, their first postcollege full-time job did not require a college degree, and that 16 percent remained unemployed after six months in the job market. In May 2015, *Forbes* reported that 44 percent of college graduates in their twenties are stuck in low-wage, dead-end jobs.

Millennials were raised to believe they could find jobs that allowed them to pursue their passions, rather than simply work to make a living. What they've found is that the reality of "living the dream" is much scarier and more uncertain. Marielle traded a stable job she loathed in order to go back to school and become qualified for work that fulfills her: "I had a really well paying job for a twenty-three-year-old. I hated it. I was miserable. I just took a leap of faith and started working part-time so I could go to school. Now I work four part-time jobs. It's terrifying."

Six months after graduating, millennials find that they can no longer defer their undergraduate loans, and the impact of also paying off their new graduate degree hits home. Young people I spoke with were visibly distraught as they contemplated how they would manage the debt they had accumulated. Dina, a master's student in her early thirties, said, "I'm graduating this semester. I almost had a heart attack when I looked at my student loan calculator. I just got this new job, and it's a good job. It's a job in my field. It's the job that I wanted to get with this degree. But I'm still looking at these payments, and looking at my salary, and looking at other stuff I might want to do in the next ten years — like maybe go on a vacation or buy some shoes, take a bubble bath, you know what I mean? Even looking at the income-based repayment, it's like $750 a month. That's huge."

This debt, coupled with the increasing need for graduate education and the challenge of finding a good job, has hindered millennials' normal progression to adulthood and independence. In 2013, "The Clark University Poll of Parents of Emerging Adults" found that three in four "emerging adults" received some level of financial support from their parents. A full 30 percent got regular ongoing support to cover living expenses. As of 2012, one in eight millennials "boomeranged" back to their parents' home due to the recession, after having lived on their own. More than a third of millennials in their late twenties have "boomeranged."

Parents were concerned too. More than one-third (38 percent) of parents reported that financial problems were their primary concern about their emerging adult child, and half reported that they were worried about how long their child was taking to become financially independent.

And, in a troubling role reversal, many millennials are now concerned not only about their own future, but their parents' as well. Jackie voiced her worry this way: "I'm very overwhelmed and scared. I didn't have any support system. Undergrad and grad, I put myself through school. I had to do everything, between loans to pay for this crazy-expensive education, and then just the cost of living. Then also my mom, she has no type of retirement, no type of savings. She gets paid really bad now. She's always struggled. So looking back maybe five years ago, I was always like, oh, I'll be able to take care of her. Now I'm looking at where I am. I can't see a clear path, moving ahead."

Some millennials feel infantilized by their lack of autonomy; the combination of too much debt and too little income makes it virtually impossible to move forward as adults. The faltering economy and limited potential for economic gain have caused one in four young people to delay marriage, one in three to put off starting a family, and close to half to delay buying a home. One woman, who has a graduate degree and a good public-sector job with the New York City government, described her frustration: "It makes me feel really young. My parents were married and had two babies and owned a house when they were my age."

When people in their twenties and thirties compare themselves to their parents, they inevitably come up short. Seventy percent said they believed it was easier for their parents to achieve the American Dream, and 60 percent believed their parents had much better opportunities for building their careers. Half of all millennials believe they are worse off than their parents were at the same age. They're probably right. In 2014, the *Wall Street Journal* reported that Americans who were under the age of thirty-five in 1995 earned wages that were 9 percent higher than those of millennials in the same age bracket today. And yet perceptions of this generation as lazy or unambitious persist. Young people bristle when confronted with these characterizations. Jeannie put it this way: "We're being squeezed from every possible angle. It's really scary. Then at the same time, you'll hear that we're not working as hard as past generations — but that's not true at all."

The legacy of the financial crisis is likely to affect this generation for a long time: a US Chamber of Commerce Foundation study found that even after economic recovery, college graduates who enter the workforce during a weak economy continue to experience relative wage loss for at least fifteen more years. That wage loss translates into less ability to save and prepare for retirement, to feel confident that they can start a family and provide for it. For the past several generations, children have been raised to believe they would do better than their parents. Not anymore.

Like so many of my check-casher and payday-lender customers, a significant number of millennials have a deep distrust of the financial-services system. Nearly one in four trusts "no one" when it comes to advice about money. And banks fare worst among financial-services providers. A recent *Time* magazine article related that 71 percent of millennials would rather go to the dentist than listen to a banker. All four of the largest banks made it to the top-ten list of millennials' least-loved brands. A third of this group believe they will soon be leading a bank-free lifestyle, and more than half think that banks are all the same.

At least part of this dissatisfaction stems from the perception that banks are nickel-and-diming millennials as customers. Those I interviewed complained about the high cost of using out-of-network ATMs and about other fees they found frustrating and often inexplicable. Millennials don't think banks should be charging them when the banks are holding on to their money. Eighty-three percent of millennials say that fees are the most important factor in choosing a financial-services provider. They question the rationale behind so-called maintenance fees: "What the hell are maintenance fees?" They wonder why they're charged so much for international transactions: "No fees for international transactions! It's an increasingly globalized world."

But millennials aren't stuck with these banks. They're coming of age at a time when they have very different options than their parents did. Not only are banks a worse deal than they used to be, but millennials have other places where they can get their financial needs met. For many, banks simply aren't a good fit. Not surprisingly, millennials are the predominant adopters of online banking. A whopping 94 percent who do have bank accounts actively use online banking, and 74 percent say that mobile banking is very important to them, compared to 42 percent of baby boomers. But they're not necessarily thrilled with these services. Over half of the overall population surveyed for a recent study said they would switch banks in order to get access to a better app, and the largest group of potential switchers was made up of millennials. Nearly two-thirds of this group also said they would spend three dollars per month for a banking app, compared to about one-fourth of total respondents. And nearly three-quarters report that they would be more excited about new financial services offered by Google, Apple, PayPal, or Square than by their nationwide bank.

Unlike previous generations, millennials think of their relationship to banks as transactional rather than relationship-driven, probably because they came of age during a time when banks invested less and less in relationships. That's one reason they are more likely than older generations to consider a branchless bank.

Financial innovators know millennials aren't happy with banks, and they're tripping over one another in a rush to come up with solutions that work for the largest generation ever. The Millennial Disruption Index, which identifies which industries are most likely to be transformed by millennials, found banking to be at the highest risk for disruption. The market opportunity is huge. Four out of five millennials carry a supercomputer — also known as a smartphone — everywhere they go. A fast-growing field called fintech, or #fintech for the social-media-savvy, is working around the clock to figure out how to connect to potential customers by way of their phones.

Venmo is a free "digital wallet" linked to users' checking accounts. Once a user signs up, she can use the app to transfer money to other Venmo users immediately and (almost) for free. A recent study that looked at the concentration of millennials using apps found that Venmo ranked second. As of 2014 over half of millennials were already using Venmo or another payment company, compared with 27 percent of Americans age fifty and over. In the quarter ending in June 2015, users transferred $1.6 billion through the app, up 247 percent (from $486 million) during the same quarter one year earlier. Many use Venmo to settle up after a shared meal or cab ride, as well as for bigger items like plane tickets or rent. No one has to worry about paying someone back, having the right change, or carrying and cashing checks.

Millennials are ten times more likely than their older counterparts to use online peer-to-peer lenders like Lending Club and Prosper. Peer-to-peer lending, or P2P, requires far less paperwork than other loans and is perceived to be more transparent than payday loans. P2P platforms act as exchanges that enable borrowers to connect with investors who have money to loan. These loans rely on a wider range of information — such as SAT scores — to assess borrowers' creditworthiness and therefore reach consumers who might not qualify otherwise. Their average interest rates have been lower than those of credit cards since 2010. P2P emerged in 2006 and has grown quickly, particularly among millennials, who appreciate "the convenience of transacting online and are less loyal to banks." While consumer bank loans and credit card business have been declining every quarter since 2007, P2P lending has grown at an average rate of 84 percent per quarter.

Mobile banks like Simple, Moven, and GoBank have no brick-and-mortar locations but offer partnerships with countless ATM locations, robust mobile apps that allow for personalized budgeting categories, and promises of "no surprise fees." GoBank, for example, allows customers to choose a monthly fee of zero to nine dollars. The amount they pay is completely up to them. GoBank also features a Fortune Teller, which users can consult when they are, say, contemplating a large purchase. Perhaps, while shopping for a winter coat, you see a pair of boots that you don't absolutely need but you really love. You consult GoBank's Fortune Teller, which does a quick analysis of your finances and may tell you "Buy Prada" or "Buy nada," depending on how flush you are.

These mobile banks market themselves to fee-averse millennials and are designed for smartphone rather than computer use, enabling customers to make payments and track spending while on the move. These entities are technically banking services, not banks; they work with banks behind the scenes to insure deposits and handle the actual banking transactions behind the mobile apps. Mobile banks focus on creating a low-cost, easy-to-use, transparent experience, providing for the consumer the sense of satisfaction and ease that previous generations enjoyed in their banking relationships — and that many check-cashing and payday-loan customers value.

(Meanwhile, when I downloaded the banking app for my megabank over the summer so that I could deposit a large check while on vacation, I discovered that it wouldn't accept checks of more than a thousand dollars.)

Many banks are actively minimizing their footprints by closing branches and opening micro branches and souped-up ATMs. In late 2014, PNC Bank announced plans to convert three hundred locations to tellerless branches featuring "super-charged ATMs." And in February 2015, Chase reported that it would be closing three hundred branches by the end of the year in order to cut $1.4 billion. The bank cited lagging demand for teller services as the reason. Yet while the shuttering of branches in all neighborhoods seems like a certainty, it's unclear how banks intend to engage millennials in the online arena where so many bank.

The millennials I interviewed impressed me with their money-saving and budgeting tactics. Some use digital apps like Mint.com and Level Money to help them budget and track spending. Mint users connect all of their financial accounts — banking, investing, credit cards — to the site, which pulls together all of their information so that users can see everything in one place. Users can create savings goals and set a budget for personalized categories like groceries, clothing, entertainment, and transportation. The app keeps track of all charged expenses by category and notifies the user when they've overspent in any category. Mint.com launched in 2007 and currently boasts over thirteen million users in the United States. Level Money bills itself as the "Mint for millennials." Its founders believe millennials don't think in traditional budgeting categories, so the app simply takes the user's monthly income, sets aside what's necessary to pay bills and to save (the app recommends 7 percent), and then shows the user what's available to spend every day. Its founder, Jake Fuentes, was quoted as saying, "What we wanted wasn't a budget, but the digital equivalent of opening your wallet and seeing how much money you have left."

Some of the millennial payday-loan borrowers I interviewed used Credit Karma to help rebuild their credit after their scores plummeted when they couldn't repay their debts. Melanie saw advertisements for Credit Karma and got the app "because my credit was so crappy, and I actually really like it. If I have a credit card with a $500 limit and I spend $250 on it, the red arrow on the app, which indicates my credit score, goes down. I see it drop. It's devastating, because I worked pretty hard to get it up. It's like a slap in the face. It's motivating. The next paycheck, $500 straight to that credit card. It's paid off."

Others use more old-fashioned methods to budget. Anna organizes her cash into a series of envelopes, each of which represents one week of the month. Seeing the cash helps her remain aware of what she has left and for how many days it has to stretch. Tess, another woman who has switched from using her debit card to cash, described how she analyzes every purchase, no matter how small. "It takes up a lot of mental space when you have to do those calculations all the time. It'll be Wednesday. I'm looking in my wallet and I'm like, I have no food at home. I can either go to the grocery store and buy some things, do this whole process, cook. I'm super-late. I have a ton of homework. Or I can stop and get this ten-dollar thing to eat, but what is that going to mean for me tomorrow? How am I going to negotiate that on Friday?"

The millennials I spoke with have become particularly strategic about food. Once this topic came up, focus-group participants began swapping stories and tricks. Emily told the others, "I've developed some strategies with food. For instance, if I go to the cafeteria, I will just get side items. If you get them in a to-go box, they give you a lot more. They just fill up the box. That's the whole meal: side items. And they're two dollars per side, by the way, so you can get two sides. That's a meal." Claire subscribes to a ten-dollar "winter box" of fruit and vegetables that the New York City nonprofit Grow NYC targets to low-income New Yorkers. When we spoke, she had just purchased a box that came with a surfeit of apples. "It's very reasonable, although you have to work to eat it. I incorporate apples into almost every meal. I'm not a major fan of apples, but I apple everything up." The others in the group laughed, but it was nervous laughter — Claire's story had hit close to home.

Some recognize that the tradeoffs may have long-term consequences. Ruth remarked that her choices about diet aren't good for her. "I've noticed the way in which I consume food — the type of food, the frequency. I definitely am bargain shopping, but I'm also seeing myself eat a lot more junk food. It's cheaper, it was on sale. I know healthwise I can't afford to." Others spoke of putting off doctor and dentist visits because they couldn't afford them.

One woman went on Medicaid but wasn't happy about the care she got from eligible providers. Another relayed the consequences of skimping on dental care: "I had a couple of cavities early in the year in January, and it was really expensive. I used up whatever my allotment was for the year, so I was going to have to pay for any future dental work out of pocket. So I skipped my six-month checkup, and then the next time I went to the dentist, I needed a root canal—which was fourteen hundred dollars. Who knows if that's a direct correlation, because I skipped it, but it ended up costing me a lot more money."

I was surprised to learn how many millennials had used alternative financial services like payday lenders, check cashers, prepaid debit cards, and pawnshops. Like the "new nonprime" folks who have relatively high incomes and own their homes, my millennial interviewees don't fit the stereotype of the alternative financial-services user.

Greta once earned a six-figure income through her business, but she had to file for bankruptcy after leaving an abusive marriage. She relies on $400 per month in food stamps and the $194.50 that she receives every two weeks in public assistance to support herself and her two small children. The fact that she doesn't pay rent right now helps. But, she says, "The per diem is in the single digits. So the last few days before the next money is due, I'm so tight that often I'm not able to buy my kids sweets or whatever. Having been on public assistance and going through shelters and banks and seeing everything I have, I was forced to use a lot of alternative measures because I didn't have a bank account for quite a while."

Greta is now working to make a fresh start by pursuing a master's degree at a well-respected program. Because her public assistance money doesn't stretch very far, she still uses a check casher. "I need to go to a check-cashing place even if I pay through the nose because I need the money this weekend to feed my kids. If I had a check and I put it in the bank, it would clear in two to three business days. But if it's Friday, that means Wednesday of next week. Between now and Wednesday, I don't have anything. So even though check cashing is expensive, at that moment it's not really an option whether it's a good deal or not, because it's just not a choice." Most people probably wouldn't think of Greta as being in the same boat as Michelle, my RiteCheck customer who took out eight dollars on her EBT card, paying a two-dollar service fee. We assume that educated, neatly dressed, accomplished students don't share the struggles of the black and brown "underbanked" living in the poorest neighborhoods. But many do. It's time we understood that a much larger group of people is feeling the effects of economic insecurity.

A 2013 online survey found that almost half (45 percent) of all millennials had used some alternative financial product or service in the past year. A similar survey conducted in 2012 reported that more than half had used a prepaid debit card, one in four had used a check casher, and more than one in five had used a pawnshop. Analyzing the widespread use of alternative financial services among millennials, a *Forbes* magazine article said that millennials have a "mistrust of traditional financial instruments and a pragmatism about not digging themselves a deeper hole than they already find themselves in due to student loan debt and a weak job market."

Sixty-three percent of respondents to the 2013 survey who used emergency cash products reported positive or neutral relationships with their bank. Jared pawned video games when he was short on cash in college. He found the owner of the pawnshop to be trustworthy and helpful. "The guy knew who I was. He did this for tons of us students. They didn't have money at the end of the month, so they brought something that they had." Comparing this experience to how he felt going to the bank, Jared said, "When I walked into a bank, even if I knew the people, I knew I wasn't going to walk out and be like, 'I really got something I needed from going to the bank today.'"

For Amanda, payday loans were just one of a battery of strategies she used to get by. She also participated in research studies that would pay her fifty dollars or more and met "people in these groups that, literally, that's how they got money." Like the customers I met at RiteCheck, Jackie and Sam both went to check cashers or to Walmart to cash their paychecks when they needed the money right away and couldn't wait for their checks to clear. Others went to check cashers to buy money orders in order to pay bills or took cash advances against their credit cards — another form of high-interest debt.

We continue to perpetuate the myth that children whose families are economically stable can build on and grow the assets of their parents and grandparents and that children whose families have little can work hard and create a stable foothold. That narrative has never been true for many who are disadvantaged. And a secure future now seems unlikely for many more young people.

During these discussions I learned that many of my students borrowed and lent money informally. Some shared bank accounts with siblings, parents, and friends. And several participated in informal but highly structured saving and lending groups, a strategy many RiteCheck customers also used. Months after I had left my post as a teller, I decided to return to the South Bronx to find out more about how and why so many people manage their money informally.

7

BORROWING AND SAVING
UNDER THE RADAR

VICKY, DRESSED IN A PARKA, BOOTS, AND JEANS, HER HEAD
wrapped in a hat and scarf, gives Blanca a hug and greeting, and
sits down to unwrap.

"*Hace tanto frío hoy!*" Vicky exclaims, shaking out her shoul-
der-length brown hair. It's February, and New York has had a cold,
snowy, and apparently endless winter.

"*Si, pero hay sol,*" says Blanca. At least the sun is out.

Blanca is a petite woman with short hair dyed a soft reddish
brown, rectangular plastic glasses, and intelligent eyes that twinkle when she's joking around, which is often. She's wearing slacks
and a bright sweater, her feet clad in the kind of pink mesh slip-
pers you can buy for a couple of dollars in Chinatown.

Vicky has come to Blanca's neat one-bedroom apartment in
Mott Haven, in the South Bronx, to make her two-hundred-dol-
lar payment to the informal savings and loan fund, or *tanda,* that
Blanca has operated for eight years. The payments are due every
Wednesday. Some members, like Vicky, stop by the apartment to
pay. They may sit awhile, have a cup of coffee or a glass of tama-
rind water, and chat. Others drop off their money with Esme, Blanca's *comadre,* who works in a bodega on 138th Street; she'll give
the money to Blanca later. Blanca and Esme aren't blood relatives,
but the term *comadre* signifies a deep relationship — more like kin-
ship than friendship. Still others, like Blanca's daughter, Sylvia,

who lives in North Carolina, deposit their payments directly into Blanca's Wells Fargo account. Blanca herself travels to a few members' homes to collect the money. In these cases, they give her a *propina,* a tip, ranging from ten to fifty dollars.

Today, as Vicky and Blanca chat, Javier, Blanca's twenty-something grandson, walks to the kitchen through the living room and fixes himself a plate of food, greeting the women as he passes by. Dalia, one of Blanca's friends, has brought her four-year-old son, Pablo, with her today, making the apartment more lively than usual. Pablo has long, black hair pulled into a ponytail; his little body is in constant motion. The TV plays cartoons and the sound is on. Blanca scolds Pablo when he gets too close to the screen — he's a rambunctious child — but she winks and smiles at us behind his back; she's stern only to his face.

At sixty-four years of age, Blanca has a story that is a variation on those of so many immigrants who have come to the United States in search of something better. Blanca moved here from Honduras in 1983 after a divorce left her to care for her three children — a twelve-year-old daughter and nine-month-old twin sons. Right after the divorce, Blanca had moved to San Pedro Sula for work and left her children in El Rosario with her mother, knowing the arrangement wouldn't work over the long term. She applied for a tourist visa but was rejected when the US consulate called her boss for a reference. Blanca had just gotten a loan from him, and he feared that she would run off without paying him back. Soon after, a man she knew got her a Mexican visa, and they crossed the border into Mexico and eventually into the United States by land.

Blanca left everything behind, including her children. A year later, once she had gotten settled in the Bronx, she married, and a year after that she returned to Honduras for her then fourteen-year-old daughter. Blanca's low income allowed her to bring only one guest into the United States; she was making nine thousand dollars per year then. It wasn't until 1999, more than fifteen years after she had left, that Blanca managed to bring her sons, who hardly knew her, and her mother.

Blanca's children are grown now. Sylvia, her daughter, moved to North Carolina with her husband in 2007. Sylvia had started the *tanda* and a business selling gold jewelry; Blanca took over both of them when her daughter moved. Sylvia and her husband own a bodega and use the money they save through the *tanda* to invest in and grow their business. One of Blanca's sons is married and lives in Houston. The other now lives in New Orleans, where he has a five-year-old son. Blanca doesn't see or talk to her sons very often these days, but she remains very close to her daughter.

In addition to the living room's large television, two oversized couches face each other, and shelves along one wall display knick-knacks and family photos. But all of the action happens at the table that abuts the wall; it's Blanca's command-and-control center. Prescription bottles, tubes of hand lotion, a tray of gold earrings for sale, and neat stacks of mail occupy the strip of space where the table meets the wall. Blanca's ledger, a worn book in which she records payments, is also here. A painting of the Last Supper hangs above the table; Jesus gazes down benevolently at the talk about the frigid winter and neighborhood gossip. Blanca sits in the seat closest to the kitchen. From here she takes phone calls and pivots to microwave a waffle for Pablo or get a drink for a visitor. Today she gets a call from a *tanda* member telling her when he'll be by to drop off his payment. Someone else calls to ask Blanca about the location of another meeting she'll attend later.

Esme, Blanca's *comadre,* works at a local bodega/bakery often scented with the sugar and vanilla of freshly baked *pan dulce.* Esme has what the urban-studies author Jane Jacobs calls "eyes on the street" — she knows everyone and sees everything. Esme is young, energetic, and sharp. She passed up invitations to join other *tandas* because she didn't know the people running them well enough to trust them with her money. She emphasizes how important it is to know the person who runs the *tanda* very well before you join.

Worldwide, many people commonly use *tandas* like the ones Blanca operates to save and borrow, yet these associations are virtually invisible to policymakers and to those of us who manage our money in other ways. The US term for this kind of group is ROSCA — rotating savings and credit association — and it is known around the world by more than two hundred names. Koreans call this type of organization a *kay*, Brazilians have named it *consorcio*, and Caribbeans assign the word *susu*. Members employ the funds for a wide range of purposes: putting a down payment on a car, funding a trip home, or investing in a business. Sometimes members have bank accounts and also belong to ROSCAs. A member might use the ROSCA to save for a very large purchase like a home, participating in the ROSCA for several rounds and moving those savings to a bank until she has enough for the purchase.

ROSCAs differ from place to place and from community to community, but the core structure is fairly consistent. Every week, each member pays in a set amount of money — this is called the "hand." In Blanca's *tanda*, the hand is two hundred dollars per week, and there are fifteen numbers. Each round of the *tanda* lasts for a set number of weeks (the "round"), in this case, fifteen. Each member of the ROSCA gets a number that corresponds to the number of a week. The member with number one gets the first bundle of money, called the "drawer," and the member with the number fifteen gets the last. For those with the lowest numbers, the ROSCA operates as an informal loan fund — these members get a large sum of money quickly and then effectively pay back the loan over the ensuing weeks. For those at the end of the list, the ROSCA operates as a savings mechanism. It's impossible for a ROSCA member to withdraw money before it's his turn to receive the drawer—a setup quite different from a bank account. Some members want to save more than two hundred dollars each week and take more than one number. Blanca's daughter and son-in-law have seven numbers between them; they put in fourteen hundred dollars each week and get seven infusions of six thousand dollars over the course of the round.

Places in the queue are often determined by longevity—those who have been in the *tanda* the longest get the first places in line. One of Blanca's *tandas* works this way. The organizer typically gets the first place to compensate for doing the work and taking on the risk of running the ROSCA. When people who have higher numbers need their money more quickly, they pay Blanca for a lower number. When Blanca talks about this transaction, she says, *"El-los me dan una propina"*—they give me a tip. She doesn't say that they pay her. Clearly, she views these transactions differently from straight-up payments.

Other ROSCAs use a lottery or bidding system. In the bidding system, whoever bids the most gets to choose his place in the ROSCA. That bid then translates into a discounted contribution for the rest of the members. For some, the lottery is simply a random drawing.

ROSCAs rely on social capital—the trust, norms, and networks that operate within a community. The role and status of the banker are key. Everyone in Blanca's *tandas* has some connection to her, and those at a further remove must cultivate the relationship before being accepted into the group. For example, it took Toni nearly three months of weekly visits, and growing connections to others in Blanca's circle, like Esme, before Blanca trusted her enough to let her join. Blanca minimized the risk of accepting Toni, a relative stranger, by giving her the last number.

Group pressure within a ROSCA makes it more likely that members will make payments on time. But Blanca's *tanda* is different — most members know only one or two other people in the group, plus Blanca; some know only Blanca. There are no meetings, no attempts to create community. This ROSCA is not about building trust among members. As the newest member, Toni, put it, "You know, it's a little strange that I'm lending my money to all of these people I've never even met. I've put in nine hundred dollars already and I honestly don't have any idea where my money is."

This isn't true for all ROSCAs. In some, the connections between members are a fundamental part of the group, and participation in the ROSCA actively builds those relationships. The researcher Shirley Ardener wrote recently about her experience attending a meeting of a ROSCA at the University of Buea in Cameroon; most participants were lecturers from the school. Ardener described how, over drinks, people watched the money being collected and counted "to much banter, teasing accusation and counter accusation, and hilarity."

At times Blanca has had to put in the money owed by a member who misses a payment, but she views that as part of what it takes to maintain her reputation as a trustworthy coordinator; it's the cost of doing business.

Some ROSCAs serve more specific purposes. Some exist to purchase certain consumer goods in a quantity great enough for each member to get the item at a discount. If everyone needs a dishwasher, for instance, the leader of the group will negotiate a price with a vendor for ten dishwashers, resulting in a discount for all members. Boston-based Ethiopian cab drivers participate in *iddirs,* their version of ROSCAs, to save for their funerals. Participants think of this "death money" as a separate category from other funds. Historically, observers have often judged this type of funeral saving as irrational.

These value judgments carry over into the present with respect to ROSCAs. When I described Blanca's *tandas* to a banker, he shook his head and sighed in exasperation. "If we could only talk to those people and explain to them how much better off they'd be if they put their money in a bank!" he said. He couldn't understand why the *tanda* worked better than a bank for Blanca's participants.

People have used informal saving and lending strategies for centuries. Some don't trust banks, and others can't get what they need from banks. The "under the mattress" savings method is alive and well, and it turns out that highly organized practices for saving and lending exist worldwide, and immigrants have brought a number of them to the United States and continue to use them here.

Six percent of the US population over the age of fifteen saved in informal lending groups in 2011. This count is likely low; determining the size and scope of this sector is difficult because it is completely unregulated. The sociologist Viviana Zelizer hypothesizes that we dismiss or fail to notice practices like these, which she calls "circuits of commerce," because "they don't fit neatly into established frameworks." They've been marginalized as a result. Our focus on firms and production systems limits our understanding of the complexity of economic structures.

Though the designation "informal" suggests a casual system, many of these financial practices are highly codified. Some, like a small loan to a family member or friend, might be more informal in the typical sense of the word. Others, like loan sharking — lending at illegal interest rates — have clear rules, and there are consequences for failing to abide by them. Some practices, like *tandas,* are perfectly legal, while others, like lending at prices above the usury rate, are not.

The sociologist Sudhir Venkatesh, who studied the informal economy of a black neighborhood in Chicago, defines the "underground economy" as "a widespread set of activities, usually scattered and not well integrated, through which people earn money that is not reported to the government and that, in some cases, may entail criminal behavior." Informal economic activities of all kinds tend to be more prolific in low-income communities. Venkatesh argues that this is partly because of "the neglect of outside actors . . . who refuse to allocate enough resources to black inner cities to create true economic security there."

I witnessed the same kinds of activity during the time I spent in the largely Latino communities of the South Bronx. During my shifts at RiteCheck, a neighborhood man often came in hawking bootleg DVDs — *Sonido bueno garantizado!* One day someone would come in selling perfume; the next day it would be chocolate. Gregorio came into RiteCheck several times a day, walking briskly through the store, picking up small bits of trash and talking to himself, often about relationships. He has some sort of mental disability but appears to function well enough. Like many people in the neighborhood, he sells things on the street in the warmer months — used or discarded items he picks up in his ramblings. Gregorio has worked out an arrangement with RiteCheck by which he can keep the things he sells in a broom closet off the store lobby. In return, he picks up the lobby and sweeps the sidewalk out front.

Blanca's jewelry business is completely informal. She sells her wares from her home or takes them to the homes of prospective buyers. These countless financial transactions and exchanges, Venkatesh found, "wove together the social fabric" of a neighborhood.

Informal finance is particularly hard to measure. Many actors within this sector, especially those engaged in illegal activities, try to hide transactions, making it difficult to identify and count, and analyze them. We do know that these informal practices form an important aspect of the consumer financial-services system and that they're closely connected to mainstream and alternative components. We also know that engaging in informal transactions can be risky and expensive, subjecting the participant to potential fraud or even financial collapse. So why do so many people manage their money this way? Why not instead benefit from the interest and the deposit insurance that come with a savings account?

Many informal practices are responses to market failure — the products and services people want and need aren't available from mainstream or alternative financial-services providers. Sure, I could save my money in a bank, but there's nothing stopping me from taking out that money whenever I want. I don't trust myself to leave the money in the bank, and the structure and rules of a ROSCA force me to save over time. Many participate in ROSCAs because of the discipline they impose. I might promise myself that I'll put two hundred dollars into my savings account every week, but it's easier for me to break that promise to myself than it is to break the agreement I've made with the ROSCA, wherein shirking my duty can result in embarrassment, humiliation, or being shut out of other community groups. Or I might trust myself to save, but I want to avoid the pressure from friends and family who know I have money saved and want to borrow it. Some researchers have found that networks of family and friends can make it hard for an individual to save and accumulate assets, particularly in low-income communities. If I don't have access to my money because it's tied up in a ROSCA, I'm less likely to be besieged by people asking me for loans.

Sometimes members don't want to get their money when it's their turn to receive the pot. They appreciate how the *tanda* forces them to save, and they ask Blanca to hold the money for them longer. In such cases, Blanca functions as a "money guard." She provides this service only for people in her *tandas,* but it's a relatively common practice. Let's say I work cleaning houses and get paid in cash. Perhaps I don't trust myself not to spend the money. Or my husband gambles, so I don't want to bring the money home for fear that he'll find it and use it to place bets. In order to keep my money safe, I give it to a trusted friend or associate — a money guard — to hold until I need it.

Perhaps I need a small amount of credit and I have no credit file and no payday lender in my state. The loan shark meets that need for me. Maybe I've defaulted on a loan through no fault of my own — my spouse left me and ran up the joint credit card. I may be locked out of formal credit markets, but a friend or family member, or the person who runs my ROSCA, is still willing to extend credit to me. These informal services fill critical needs in many communities. This isn't to say that the arrangements are always ideal, but sometimes they are the best option.

Blanca keeps a waiting list for people who want to join her *tandas*. She could probably expand but doesn't want to take on the extra risk and the burden of collecting even more payments. Blanca's apparent rigidity sometimes creates tension in the community. One woman who sold mangoes nearby wanted to join the *tanda*. Blanca refused to let her participate because she didn't know the woman well enough. The woman became angry and tried to tarnish Blanca's name in the neighborhood, saying that Blanca had not been good to her. These incidents don't seem to ruffle Blanca very much; it's all part of the package. The incident does illustrate that the *tanda* banker has to have a certain status in the community and the kind of personality that can absorb criticism.

As the operator of the group, Blanca used to get the first number, meaning that every fifteen weeks she was able to "borrow" three thousand dollars to invest in the jewelry business. Now that her business is established, Blanca no longer needs the first number, but she continues to benefit by running the *tandas*. This isn't the only way the *tanda* and the jewelry business are connected. *Tanda* participants often use some of their savings to buy jewelry from Blanca. It seems possible that participants feel somewhat obligated to patronize Blanca's jewelry business, that it's a way of thanking her for her good management of the *tanda*.

When members can't make it to the South Bronx, they deposit their "hands" directly into Blanca's bank account. Policymakers and consumer advocates tend to see the mainstream and informal financial-services systems as separate, but in these cases the banks, part of the mainstream system, are actually enabling the informal system to function more efficiently.

A critical element of any credit system is the borrower's demonstrated capacity to repay a loan, and the lender's ability to evaluate the riskiness of the borrower. Banks and credit card companies rely on credit scores calculated by credit bureaus. In the informal component, where this kind of information is not available, lenders need other kinds of information. The connections Blanca has with members of her *tandas* play the role of credit scores in mainstream credit markets.

Informal economic activity isn't confined to low-income people. It is the rare contractor in New York City who reports all of her income. The thousands of recent college graduates working as babysitters and nannies in New York City alone tend to be paid in cash or by personal check, and it is the norm not to report this income on tax returns. Estimates put the size of the US informal economy at between 5 and 10 percent of the GDP, and up to 40 percent of the labor force is thought to be informal. But the proportion of informal activity is higher in some communities than others. Saving and lending practices are no exception.

Blanca herself offers a window into the complexity of informal financial services. The *tandas* she operates function completely on trust, as we've seen, and new members are people she knows well or who come to her from members of her existing network. Aside from payments that are a day or two late, she has never had trouble with members failing to make their payments. Blanca also exercises quite a lot of flexibility in how she operates a *tanda*. One member told Blanca she was going home to Mexico for the holidays a couple of weeks before her number came up. Blanca gave her her lump payment early, minus what she still owed, knowing it would be useful to her to have it for the holidays.

Blanca also makes loans of a couple hundred or a thousand dollars to her *tanda* members. They know she has a lot of money coming into and going out of her household and that she's willing to help them cover an unexpected expense or bills until the next paycheck. When I ask what she charges for this service, she shrugs. "*Nada. Pero cuando me pagan, me regalan algo. Si yo presto mil dólares, me regalan como cien.*" She doesn't charge interest, but her "borrowers" typically give her some money when they repay her. Blanca's use of the verb *regalar* is interesting here. The word *regalo* in Spanish means "gift," so what she's really saying here is that her borrowers "gift" her, say, a hundred dollars in return for the thousand-dollar loan. Blanca doesn't view that hundred dollars as a payment the way I might view the interest on my mortgage as a payment.

Blanca and her patrons use language that shows how they think about these types of funds or payments in different ways. This practice has a long history. Zelizer shows that, historically, "different monies were used differently and even kept separately." The words for different kinds of money — *tip, gift, bonus, ransom, salary, allowance* — distinguish one kind from another and also represent different webs of social relationships.

Before he died, my father-in-law would give my husband and me a check at holiday time. Rather than depositing it into our joint account and using it to pay bills, we would think about how we could use it for something special — a weekend getaway or some small luxury we wanted for our home. When I studied small-scale self-employment endeavors of women in the 1990s, I learned that many did something similar; they earmarked the "extra" income they made from their business ventures for a specific purpose — tuition at a parochial school, gifts, or a designated savings fund for retirement. The majority of the *tanda* participants I interviewed earmark those savings and treat the *tanda* money differently from the other money that flows into and out of their household. "The earmarking of money," Zelizer writes, "is a social process: money is attached to a variety of social relations rather than to individuals." Nowhere is this more true than in a ROSCA.

When you step back and look at the big picture of what Blanca does, it becomes clear that she facilitates saving, borrowing, and protecting money for a group of about twenty-five people. In essence, she operates as a very small savings and loan for the people within her circle. The network is geographically concentrated in Mott Haven but extends far beyond. Vicky's number is toward the end of the *tanda* queue. The *tanda* forces her to save; when it's her turn to receive the pot, she sends most of the money to her family in Oaxaca, Mexico, where she has two children. Blanca's "savings and loan" has an international reach.

The transactions Blanca and others who run ROSCAs facilitate take place informally, but their networks are not limited to the informal component of the consumer financial-services sector. Most of the people in Blanca's network rely on all three components of the consumer financial-services system: mainstream, alternative, and informal. Blanca has bank accounts at Wells Fargo and at Citibank, and, as we've seen, some of her members transmit their payments directly into her bank account. Vicky has held an account at Chase ever since her employer started using direct deposit. She cashed her checks at the check casher before but now uses only mainstream and informal financial services.

ROSCAs don't always work well. Lidia, who is from Guerrero, Mexico, had never put savings in one until she met Dolores at her church a couple of blocks from RiteCheck. Dolores, a newcomer to the church, told Lidia about the *tanda* she was running and Lidia decided to join. It was 2013, and a major hurricane followed by another storm had recently devastated her Mexican hometown. Lidia wanted to save in order to send money back home. Unfortunately, after six weeks, Dolores left with all the money. Lidia, who has three children with her and two in Mexico, lost fifteen hundred dollars, an enormous sum for her. When Lidia and the other members tried to reach Dolores, they discovered that she had moved and that her phone number had been disconnected. Now, apparently, Dolores is at it again, running another *tanda* in another neighborhood. Lidia says she won't ever participate in a *tanda* again because she can't afford the risk.

One cold February day in 2015, more than a year after I had completed my stint as a teller, I stopped in at RiteCheck between meetings to say hello to Cristina and Ana Paula, have a cup of tea, and warm up in the store. I told them I was trying to learn more about how people used informal networks to manage their money. I had already met Blanca and was particularly interested in meeting loan sharks — *usureros* or *prestamistas*, in Spanish. Nearly everyone we spoke with knew someone who would lend money informally. Oftentimes these lenders are embedded in the community, and their knowledge of residents helps them with their business.

"You can get a couple of hundred dollars — two hundred, five hundred — from these guys in the street," Cristina tells me. "Everyone who lives here knows who they are." We were brainstorming about how I could meet one of them when a tall middle-aged man came to Cristina's window and told her he wanted to leave some money for someone else to pick up, and could she give him an envelope? The man put $130 in the envelope and wrote on the outside *To: Aguero, From: J.*

After he left, Cristina waved the envelope at me. "Here you go. This is definitely a loan payment. Aguero lives right on the block. He's in here every day. He'll definitely be here soon to pick up this envelope."

"Can you introduce me to this Aguero? Do you think I could interview him?" I asked.

We decided it would be better for Jackie to tell Aguero about me and to see if he would be willing to talk to me rather than for me to wait for him that day at the store. Sure enough, Aguero came in the next week, and, as arranged, Jackie introduced us. I recognized him from the months I worked as a teller, but I had never realized he was a moneylender. He's an older Puerto Rican man, maybe in his late sixties, with silver hair and kind eyes. He didn't strike me as the kind of person who would break your kneecaps if you couldn't pay back your loan. I told him about my research and asked if we could talk. He answered a few questions — telling me he charges twenty to twenty-five dollars for a hundred-dollar loan and that he has been lending money in the neighborhood for many years. But then he got restless and said he needed to leave.

When I realized that Aguero had come to the store every day that I had worked there, and that everyone but me knew he was a moneylender, I was reminded yet again of how my "outsider" status limited my view of what went on in the neighborhood and at RiteCheck.

Lety, who sells tamales in the neighborhood, knows Daniella, a neighborhood informal lender. Over tea at Ray's Pizza, Daniella said she worked part-time as a home health aide and supplemented that income with work "on the streets." Questioned about what that meant, Daniella replied, "I sell money."

Daniella makes monthly loans of about a thousand dollars to people in the neighborhood, charging a hundred dollars for that amount. She knows the going rate in the neighborhood and says her loans are the cheapest. Recently, she also started making much smaller loans. She had an aneurism a few months back and lost some of her hours at her regular job. A lot of women in the neighborhood need these small loans to pay utility bills when they are at risk of being disconnected, she says. A religious woman, Daniella sees herself as helping others in need.

"*Hay tanta necesidad en la calle,*" she says. "So I don't charge a lot of interest." She quotes a passage from the Bible about usurers who won't go to heaven if they take advantage of others' needs. Daniella doesn't make short-term weekly loans for the same reason — she believes these loans are abusive.

Daniella's informal lending business evolved organically. Friends saw that she was financially savvy and liked to save. In addition to her business, Daniella owns two two-bedroom apartments in the neighborhood. She rents them to single men, usually undocumented, who come to the United States to work. Daniella's monthly cost for each apartment is eleven hundred dollars and she charges fourteen hundred dollars in rent. Daniella's friends began to ask her for quick loans, and she soon realized she could turn a profit on her own thriftiness. She expanded the network of people she lends to by asking others, like the shopkeeper at her local bodega, to refer potential borrowers to her.

Like Blanca, Daniella works only with people she knows or who are referred by a trusted source. When she has to turn down other people, she softens the blow by using a little fiction, saying she has to defer the decision because she needs to talk to *"la mujer arriba"* — the woman above. There is no "woman above," but this nonexistent superior comes in handy as the person who rejects the loan applicant. When Daniella reports the decision this way, it depersonalizes the transaction and deflects blame from Daniella. When she does make loans, Daniella asks her customers to sign a form that states how much money they have received and when the loan is due. In fine print, the form states that the loan carries no interest — Daniella includes this so that she can't be accused of doing anything illegal. In Blanca's *tandas,* no papers change hands.

When policymakers and consumer advocates talk about financial health, they generally distinguish between income and assets. Income, assuming there's enough of it, helps people with their day-to-day needs, while assets provide a cushion for hard times. People generally need to save in order to accumulate assets, and Americans typically lag when it comes to savings. According to the Organization for Economic Cooperation and Development, the United States has a savings rate of 4.87 percent, somewhat below the EU's at 6.54 percent and far below countries like Sweden and Switzerland, which have savings rates of 15.8 percent and 17.8 percent, respectively. Over the past forty years, savings in our country have dropped significantly, from a peak of 13 percent, and this drop has occurred during a period characterized by a decline in wages and a rise in financial instability.

The reasons for this plunge in savings include a shift to a consumption mentality — we have a whole lot more stuff than we ever did. The average size of a home in the United States has gone from 1,725 square feet in 1983 to 2,598 in 2013. But we're also paying for a lot more things out of pocket that used to be covered by the government and our jobs. And it's tough to save when incomes have dropped or remained flat, and in general have become so much less predictable.

But somehow, a lot of people who are living very close to the edge are managing to put away money, and, as we've seen, ROS-CAs are a key ingredient in their ability to save successfully. Annie is using the money she saves in Blanca's *tanda* to build a home for her mother in Honduras; it will be completed this year. Carolina uses the *tanda* to pay her tuition at a local community college. Even though she has had to provide for her two younger siblings since their mother was deported to Mexico in 2011, Carolina has been able to avoid student loans. She studies early childhood education and plans to get her BA next and then her master's degree at Columbia. She works part-time at a daycare center on New York's Upper East Side and goes to school in the evening. She beams when she tells us that her younger brother is in college and that her sister will be starting as a freshman in the fall.

The networks created and reinforced through ROSCAs spread information about members, enabling those involved to reduce the risks and transaction costs of lending to one another without having a typical credit-scoring system. This pooling of information offers "stronger economies of scale when small amounts are involved" and helps "predict individual repayment probabilities."

These informal practices are not confined to lower-income communities or to people who are credit-constrained. When Linda Silva Thompson, a dean at an urban commuter college in the Bronx, discovered that a ROSCA for college faculty and staff had been operating for over twenty years, she decided to join and learn more about it. The ROSCA participants range from maintenance staff to high-level administrators. None are unbanked. All employees of the college are required to have their checks deposited directly into a bank or credit union.

Participating in this ROSCA has enabled Linda to see a complex web of financial activity, much of it informal, that she was completely unaware of during her first five years on the job. Because Linda has a private office with a desk that locks, one of the participants — a maintenance worker — has asked her to act as his "money guard" — keeping his cash safe in her office until he can turn it in to the ROSCA's banker.

I also discovered that many of my students use informal strategies to manage their finances. Some described arrangements with family and friends that allow for give-and-take when a family member is going through a particularly difficult — or a particularly good — time. Claire says, "My sister and I lend money between each other quite frequently. It's never been a huge amount of money, so it's never gotten into an awkward place. Honestly, for me, I don't even think about it. I almost think we're one, in a weird way." For the past ten years, Nancy has shared a checking account that she opened with close friends from high school. Once roommates, the friends no longer live near one another; they deposit money into the account whenever they have something extra, and use the "pot" to travel to see one another. No one keeps track of how much each friend contributes, and, Nancy says, "We have no issue with that. There's moments that I get a good job and have more than someone else, so I make sure that I put as much in as I can. We've never had an issue in terms of 'you put more; I put more.'"

Different immigrant groups have brought ROSCAs, under various names, to this country. Ife, who is Nigerian, worked in city government, joining with other city employees from Nigeria to create a ROSCA. "Every paycheck, we'd put in two to three hundred dollars and maybe we'd save for, like, six months. There'd be one person in charge of it. It'd be maybe a checking account that they opened up, or they'd stash it somewhere under their bed. At the end of the six months, everything was tallied and everybody got what they saved."

Amira, who is Egyptian and married with two children, participates in ROSCAs called *gamayas* in her community. These *gama-*

yas are used not only for money but also for household items and food. The Muslim American community in which Amira lives has sophisticated systems that spread the job of caring for families in need. "One of the *gamayas* we do," Amira explained, "is for new people that are coming into the community. They'll do it with food. One family will buy fifteen chickens and other groceries and donate it to a family for that month. Then it happens the next month. When we first got married, that was really helpful."

Amira also has a joint checking account with her parents, who live in Minnesota, and her brother-in-law, who lives in Ohio. "The beginning of marriage is very difficult, when you're both students and trying to get set up," Amira said. "When we got married, we were super-broke, and my husband's brother was financially more stable at the time than we were. So having the Chase account with him and with my parents meant that they could get us money here."

Amira credits the tightly knit Arab American community in her Brooklyn neighborhood to her family's ability to survive in New York City. "Being surrounded by Arab Americans, Muslim Americans, Egyptian Americans has been really, really helpful. Our own community has taken us in. Like if my husband and I have a meeting, we can leave the kids at the mosque. There's a sense of belonging of sorts, where you can actually trust a person, having never met them. You can leave a four- and a five-year-old there. I guess my point is, what's helped us with becoming mentally stable in this city, and financially stable, is the community that surrounds us."

Jack works at the US Department of Housing and Urban Development; he also participates in a ROSCA through his job. "We're not supposed to do them, but we do. There's a group checking account we set up with the Federal Credit Union. They pull a hundred dollars from my paycheck, and I get paid bimonthly, so that's two hundred per month."

Indeed, research shows that the "sharing economy" is on the rise. This economy values shared resources and collaboration over accumulation and ownership, and it operates as a system of providers and users, although people often act in both roles. Providers offer goods and services to be shared, and users rent, pay for, or barter for what's being offered. Best known for services like Zipcar, Lyft, and Airbnb, it extends to crowdfunding as well as the sharing of equipment and media. Advances in technology — mobile apps and web platforms — allow individuals to connect and then facilitate services and transactions. While almost less than one in ten adults has participated in the sharing economy as providers, consumers under age thirty-five make up 38 percent of the total. Half of millennials belong to or expect to join a sharing service within the next year.

Policymakers and most mainstream and alternative financial-services providers have failed to look closely at the informal component of the consumer financial-services system. If they did, they would understand that it is vibrant and widespread, and that it fills needs that the market has left unmet. Although many of the people who use ROSCAs are technically unbanked, they are saving and borrowing, using the pooled contributions they receive to build assets and take on "good debt" like paying for college or building a home to which they can retire in their home countries. If their participation in these ROSCAs was recorded, many would have good credit scores. Those without credit histories qualify only for expensive credit or no credit at all.

Some entrepreneurs do understand the potential of ROSCAs and their customers, and they are working hard to bring this potential to new products and services. Mike Mondelli has created a new credit-scoring model that would enable the participants in Blanca's *tanda* to get credit scores. And José Quiñones created a nonprofit organization, the Mission Asset Fund, that keeps ROSCA members' money safe and helps them build credit scores. We'll learn more about Mondelli, Quiñones, and four other innovators in the next chapter.

8

INSIDE THE INNOVATORS

A CONFLUENCE OF FORCES HAS CREATED A MOMENT RIPE for innovation and wholesale change in the consumer financial-services industry, with a slew of innovators poised to seize the opportunities. Enormous advances in technology, significant changes in consumer behavior, and a radically revised regulatory environment are coming together in ways that offer hope for more efficient, effective, and equitable provision of consumer financial services. This moment is notable for its rarity — this business sector "hasn't changed materially in hundreds of years," according to Brett King, an expert in retail banking.

Creative destruction, a term coined by the Austrian economist Joseph Schumpeter, denotes the process by which capitalism destroys old economic orders and reinvents them through innovation. Here's an example of this process at work: innovations in refrigeration and transportation technologies enabled the creation of supermarkets, which ultimately put many smaller food shops out of business. More recently, Amazon, in its use of the Internet, its innovative approaches to shipping, and the creation of the Kindle reader, profoundly changed book selling.

Technology always plays a big role in times of creative destruction, and the present moment is no different. Never before has so much information about each and every one of us been more available to more people. Although this situation raises important questions about privacy — we're seeing how debt collectors and identity thieves abuse these resources — many innovators in consumer financial services are focused on how to harness this information for profit and for good. Information about consumers can lead to the creation of products and services better suited to their needs.

Advances in technology enable us to do new things with the smartphones that most of us carry every day. We can move money between accounts, pay the babysitter, and avoid overdrafting with simple, readily available apps. Dave Birch, a director at Consult Hyperion, a firm that specializes in electronic transactions, predicts that "in fifty or one hundred years . . . people will see the mobile phone as the critical inflection point in the history of payments." Mobile phones have already revolutionized financial services in Kenya, where nineteen million (90 percent of adults) of the country's forty-four million inhabitants manage their money through a system called M-PESA (M for "mobile"; *pesa* means "money" in Swahili).

Others are rethinking the "plumbing" of the financial-services system. There is no reason why it should take several days for the check you deposit to appear as cash in your bank account. It shouldn't cost so much to send money to relatives overseas. Those in the financial technology, or "fintech," industry use the term "friction" to describe these inefficiencies, and some entrepreneurs are hell-bent on removing it. This change would lower costs to banks and other financial-services providers, and hopefully they'll pass these savings on to consumers. The costs of these inefficiencies hit lower-income and disadvantaged groups the hardest, so if savings are passed on to consumers, it would represent a significant gain.

For the most part, banks and alternative financial-services businesses are not known as nimble innovators or entrepreneurs. Historically, banks have valued safety and have been slow to embrace change. The big-bank innovations we've witnessed over the past several years — the credit default swaps and complex global-finance deals — have nothing to do with normal retail customers like you and me. Banks' staid culture, combined with the huge aversion to risk they've adopted in the wake of the financial crisis, makes them poorly poised to take advantage of new customer-focused opportunities.

Meanwhile, alternative financial-services providers have a great deal of experience serving consumers with less than ideal financial profiles, but most lack the scale and capacity to harness new technology and use behavioral research to tweak their offerings. Like banks, alternative financial-services providers are not known as innovators. As direct deposit becomes the norm, check cashers are concerned about the viability of their business. Payday lenders worry about forthcoming federal regulations that are bound to cut into their profits. But neither check cashers nor payday lenders have come up with new products or services that would help them diversify.

Enter the innovators. Over the past few years, a new crop of entrepreneurs with background in engineering, finance, and policy has arrived on the scene. They see the knotty problems that characterize consumer financial services and they are driven to solve them. Like all successful entrepreneurs, they get energized by figuring out how to deal with tough challenges. They think they can build a better mousetrap. And some of them believe they can make the world a better place while providing safe, affordable financial products and services to the growing number of people who need them.

Two of the six innovative firms profiled here, Oportún and Fenway Summer, offer new loan products targeted at people who use payday loans. Two work on more systemic problems: L2C has come up with a more accurate credit-scoring model, and Ripple is working on a system that will move money quickly and immediately, so that no one has to wait for a check to clear. The Mission Asset Fund is a nonprofit organization that formalizes the ROSCAs described in Chapter 7. And the final innovator, KeyBank, is a midsize regional bank that has returned to the idea that building relationships with all of its customers, not just those who are better off, is an essential part of creating a strong business.

CHANGES IN CONSUMER BEHAVIOR

Two key changes in consumer behavior are creating new markets for these and other innovators. The first change goes right back to the importance of trust. Trust in banks is at an all-time low. According to popular opinion, banks are responsible for the financial meltdown, the subprime crisis, the loss of jobs, and the decline in assets that so many consumers are experiencing. Consumers don't think banks operate in their best interest — an enormous opportunity for entrepreneurs. The other change concerns the way people manage their money. Five years ago, no one would have predicted just how much consumers are willing — and able — to do with their smartphones. Smartphone use grew by 50 percent in 2013 alone, from 1 billion to 1.5 billion users globally.

CHANGES IN THE REGULATORY ENVIRONMENT

On the regulatory side, the financial crisis has made it easier for some entrepreneurs to compete with big banks. The Consumer Finance Protection Bureau (CFPB) is working on rules that will make it harder for banks to profit from overdrafts and for payday lenders to make loans to people who clearly won't be able to repay them. These people will need new sources of credit, and some innovators are trying to meet this need. Raj Date, the founder of the startup Fenway Summer, says that "regulation makes already-too-conservative big institutions even more conservative and slow. And that helps if you're small."

Meanwhile, banks are getting mixed messages from the federal government regarding how to think about the "underserved." On the one hand, recent focus on the "unbanked" and "underbanked" has put pressure on banks to reach out to these potential customers. On the other hand, the creation of the CFPB has banks and alternative financial-services providers worried about a new layer of regulation and how it will affect them. Some believe the new attention being paid to consumer protection has had an unintended consequence: less advantaged customers find themselves even more underserved. New oversight of overdrafts could convince banks to pull back on their checking account offerings. These accounts are seen as the gateway to broader participation in mainstream financial services, so once the checking accounts go away, the entry point disappears.

These changing regulations have also caused banks to put more resources into compliance, to make sure the rules set by all five federal and the myriad state regulators are being followed. This increased spending on compliance may shift resources away from innovation.

And so, while the intent behind the regulation is a good one — keeping banks from making bad loans to people who can't pay them — one could argue that the same regulation is pushing people to use more expensive forms of credit, like payday loans.

The big banks are complaining about the increased scrutiny they've experienced since the crisis. But others, like Marla Blow, who heads Fenway Summer's credit card division, doesn't have much sympathy for these banks: "They will say that they get regulatory scrutiny because now they're deemed to be too big to fail," she said, "meaning that they go through extra exams and people are looking at them even more closely. And I pretty openly said to people, 'So cry me a river. Because you're a gigantic financial institution and somebody's looking at you? Hard, huh? Hard to live on the billions and billions of dollars you're making every quarter, and the price you pay is you've got a little bit of extra scrutiny?'"

CULTURAL DIFFERENCES

Entrepreneurs tend to be frisky and stubborn, willing to take risks and fail. They're made of different stuff than the people who step into well-established firms and take the reins from a long line of predecessors. Entrepreneurial culture bears little resemblance to banking industry culture. Banks prefer to watch the little guys experiment. If their projects appear promising, banks would rather purchase them than try to create a culture of innovation in-house. Marla Blow contrasted her prior experience at Capital One with the environment she's working in now: "There's just not that culture in large banks to really do a project and see if there's a sign of life and then if there is, slowly add to it and grow it," she says. "They weirdly have this idea that if something is not worth five billion dollars right out of the gate, then they're not going to do it."

The products and services that innovators are bringing to market not only rely on new technology — they often leverage new research from fields like behavioral economics and psychology. Some innovations are designed explicitly to achieve a "double bottom line" — to make a profit for investors while also delivering bet-ter products at better prices to those who are not currently well served by the financial-services industry. Unlike the mega-banks that put profit above all else, many innovators are explicitly work-ing to do well by doing good.

These firms have real potential to impact the three factors my payday-lender and check-cashing customers cited as the reasons they chose to use alternative financial services: cost, transparency, and service.

The innovators featured in this chapter are by no means the only ones doing important and interesting work, but they are rep-resentative of the range of talent and creativity that's out there right now. And they are attacking the problems from a variety of angles, demonstrating that in financial services, as in most things, there's more than one way to skin a cat.

L2C

Like many entrepreneurs populating the fintech field, Mike Mon-delli is a refugee from mainstream financial services. He worked as a stockbroker at Morgan Keegan while getting his MBA at Geor-gia State. But Mondelli didn't like the work and soon set out on his own to fill some of the gaps he saw in the marketplace. One of these concerned cell phones. Mondelli read somewhere that ap-proximately half of the people acquiring cell phones had to put down a deposit ranging from one hundred to one thousand dol-lars, based on providers' perceptions of their risk. That's a lot of money — more than many could afford.

Mondelli believed he could come up with a more accurate as-sessment of customers' risk factors, which would enable a larger number of people to get phones by putting down a small deposit, or even no deposit. He created a model to test his hypotheses and then tried to sell it to cell-phone providers. They weren't convinced. In order to show that he stood behind his model, he guaranteed his assessments. If a customer defaulted within the first two years, Mondelli's firm, L2C, would pay the cell-phone company up to $350 of what the customer owed at the time of default. If Mondelli's assessment was correct, his firm would get 20 percent of the customer's monthly payment; if the monthly payment was fifty dollars, L2C got ten.

Mondelli and his team proved that the lenders' assessment model was less than accurate, particularly for people, such as immigrants and young people, who have no credit history or a very "thin" one. When cell-phone business disappeared as big cell-phone companies bought up the smaller local and regional ones, Mondelli continued to develop his risk-assessment model.

Mondelli's firm, L2C, uses data different from what the big three credit bureaus — Experian, TransUnion, and Equifax — use to generate our individual FICO scores. (FICO stands for the name of the company that originated this scoring mechanism: Fair Isaac Corporation.) The big three look at whether you pay your mortgage, auto loan, installment loans, and credit card bills, and whether you pay them on time. The traditional FICO score is also based on how much available debt you have, and how much of it you're currently using. If your credit card limit is $10,000 and you're using $1,000, you'll have a better credit score than if you're using $9,000.

FICO scores reflect what Mondelli calls a balance-sheet view of consumers, taking into account only the liability side of the balance sheet. This way of computing a credit score tends to disqualify a whole swath of would-be borrowers who get shut out of the credit market entirely or pushed to more expensive forms of credit, like payday loans. "If you're going to make a loan, you also want to see the assets side and the income statement," Mondelli says, "not just the liabilities. So we get a sense of a person's checking account performance, their discretionary spending, and other loans." The L2C model also assesses whether the consumer owns a home, what it's worth, and the balance of the mortgage. Finally, the L2C credit score assesses the consumer's stability — "Can you send them a bill? Can you find them? How long have they lived where they live? How frequently do they move?"

TransUnion purchased L2C in 2014. When I visited Mondelli at L2C in Atlanta, the firm was in transition. On the large floor it had occupied in a generic office building, most of the workspaces had been vacated. Some of L2C's staff had been let go, and others were moving.

TransUnion recently began using a product called Credit Vision Link, the first one to incorporate both the data that credit bureaus have historically used and the alternative data that L2C includes. In addition to using this much broader range of information, Credit Vision Link also looks at a consumer's performance over a thirty-month period, whereas traditional credit scores look at a single moment in time. Say it's January and you want to apply for a credit card. If you're like many people, the balance on your other cards is pretty high because you've spent a lot of money over the holidays. If your credit score was determined by the traditional snapshot approach, your new card would probably come with a higher interest rate and worse terms than it would have if Credit Vision Link had rated you based on its thirty-month perspective.

The possible ramifications of this new credit-scoring model are huge. More than sixty million Americans have no FICO score at all because credit bureaus use data they cannot provide. And if you don't have a credit score, it can be very hard to get a loan, rent an apartment, or convince an employer to hire you. Credit Vision Link can score all sixty-two million of these people. After scoring, about 20 percent end up with a prime credit score of 660 or higher, gaining them access to much cheaper credit than they could get without a credit score.

Then there's the subprime group, the people whose low scores make them ineligible for well-priced credit. When Mondelli and his team rescored people with subprime credit scores, they found that they could increase the scores of about 23.5 million of them, from subprime to prime or super-prime. Mondelli's conviction and drive have moved the needle on financial inclusion.

RIPPLE

It's natural to focus on products, services, and the institutions that offer them when we think about how to improve the consumer financial-services system. But a critical part of the system — the infrastructure that undergirds the institutions, the rails on which the system runs — is invisible to consumers. This infrastructure is critical to the way money moves from person to person, place to place, and institution to institution. And it's responsible for a whole lot of the "friction" that slows the system down. As we saw in Chapter 1, one of the main reasons people use check cashers is because banks make them wait to access their money, whereas check cashers offer instant liquidity — albeit at a price.

Chris Larsen, a serial fintech entrepreneur, is betting that his firm, Ripple, can eliminate much of that friction. Like many fintech startups, Ripple is headquartered in San Francisco. Its modern, minimalist-style offices occupy a high floor in a building in the financial district. Larsen, fit and in his midfifties, displays a youthful energy as he describes his firm.

Larsen's vision for Ripple is to create what he calls an "Internet of value" comparable to the Internet of information we're all familiar with. Before the Internet, it took time for information to move from one place to another. And it cost money. Now the process is free and instantaneous. Ripple aims to create an analogous system for value, whereby money and property can be transferred globally, in real time, for free.

Larsen considers where the Internet of value is now, compared to where the Internet of information was in 1993, when few people had email accounts and research and data were stored at universities and in libraries, prohibiting easy access. Looking at the potential for the Internet of value, Larsen says, "We're laying the pipes now for a pretty major transformation."

Engineers make up two-thirds of Ripple's hundred-member staff. The remaining third are mostly people who work in compliance — making sure the company conforms to regulatory policy — and experts in the capital markets. The company employs a chief cryptograper and a scrum master, job titles that seem better suited to a sci-fi novel than a finance startup. Staff members have come to Ripple from NASA, Apple, Google, and the Federal Reserve. They've worked in the life sciences, including neuroscience, and as hackers. Every single one of them loves solving tough problems — like eliminating friction.

How will the Internet of value do this? It will connect all of the networks, both public and private, that now move money but are disconnected. "Banks pay a lot to send money from one place to another," Larsen tells me. "And a lot of payments fail — they get stuck somewhere between the starting point and the endpoint."

"If you're underbanked, your money probably moves from a non-bank provider to a small bank to a regional bank to global," Larsen explains. "Your money might go several hops. Every hop is taking a cut. Every hop is slowing you down. That's a problem." When the transfer is immediate, it's costless and riskless. "That's a huge, huge changeup," Larsen said.

One application of Ripple technology handles "cross-border payments" — value being moved from one country to another. My RiteCheck and Check Center customers frequently sent money to friends and relatives in their home countries, and in other parts of the United States, and they paid a lot for those transactions. The way we do this now, Larsen says, "is built on old 1970s infrastructure, where you have all the problems of uncertainty, failure rates, time delay, and enormous cost." Larsen estimates that it costs about $1.6 trillion dollars to move the $22 trillion in cross-border payments that are transferred annually.

Banks will benefit from Ripple's technology because it will lower their costs significantly. Consumers will benefit because they'll be able to send and receive their money faster and more cheaply, and to access their money as soon as they deposit a check. Once this technology becomes ubiquitous, a big barrier to using banks will be removed.

FENWAY SUMMER

Raj Date thinks kinetically and speaks quickly, as though there is simply too much information in his brain vying to come out at the same time. After studying engineering at Berkeley, Date got his law degree at Harvard, and then spent time at McKinsey, the elite consulting company, and at Capital One and Deutsche Bank, before working side by side with Senator Elizabeth Warren to set up the Consumer Finance Protection Bureau (CFPB).

Date spent three years at the agency and then set out on his own, creating a for-profit firm to create a set of products — a mortgage product, a credit card, and a student loan — designed for people who couldn't access safe, high-quality financial products. Date called his new firm Fenway Summer and brought in a highly talented staff consisting mostly of people he had worked with at Capital One and the CFPB. He bought a two-hundred-year-old townhouse in the heart of Georgetown and hung out a shingle.

The choice of an old townhouse for the headquarters of a financial firm speaks to the kind of culture Date has built. He prioritized creating a small team with talent and experience in the capital markets, in credit, and in regulatory environments. These categories of professionals don't often sit next to each other at big banks; they're siloed off in separate departments. At Fenway Summer, everyone knows what everyone else is up to.

Although it seemed counterintuitive in an industry like banking, Date believed Fenway Summer's small size and high level of expertise would give it an advantage over larger banks: "If you're very big, it's very hard to care about little tiny things that will probably fail anyway. If you're Bank of America, are you really going to put your A team on some subscale new idea that will probably fail? Or are you going to have them work on this thing over here that is on fire? You should probably focus on those big problems."

Date's working hypothesis is that, with the right people in place, his firm can tackle market failures and make a profit in a way that's fair for consumers. Fenway Summer hopes to impact the market most directly through its products. Build, the credit card, is one of them. Launched in late 2015, Build is meant to provide a viable credit option for people who now take out payday loans.

Marla Blow, a seasoned credit-card-industry executive with degrees from the Wharton School and Stanford's Graduate School of Business, joined Fenway Summer in early 2014 as CEO of FS Card, the startup credit card venture. (FS Card is the name of the business, and Build is the name of its credit card.) The first thing you notice about her is that she is a black woman, a rarity in a sector overwhelmingly dominated by white men. You get the sense that she is a pro at shifting her affect, depending on the room she's in.

Ahead of the official launch of Build, she received the first physical card in the mail, complete with magnetic stripe, and could hardly contain her excitement at having a tangible object that represented the culmination of years of work. She beamed as she handed it across the table. "That's really a magnetic stripe!" she said. "You could actually take that up the street and buy something with it."

Blow, who worked closely with Date at Capital One and at the CFPB, wanted to make a difference. She had read Barbara Ehrenreich's book *Nickel and Dimed,* which exposed the plight of low-wage workers. The book made Blow think hard about how so many people live with financial instability. "Another part of the problem that really spoke to me," she said, "is people of color, my family members, people I know, who are going through this in a very visceral way."

Blow loves figuring out what makes people tick. She went through a phase when she read mountain-climbing books like Jon Krakauer's *Into Thin Air,* a harrowing account of the author's disastrous climb up Mount Everest in 1996. After she finished the book, she read everything else about that climb because she is "fascinated by the psychology of people who push themselves that far." Blow sees her interest in human psychology as an attribute well suited to her work. She finds it fascinating and troubling when people choose a payday loan rather than a credit card. Creating the Build card, for Blow, is about helping people make better choices.

Fenway Summer incubated its credit card business with the

view that a credit card is the right product to meet the borrowing needs of subprime consumers in a changing small-dollar lending market. During the 1980s and 90s, when access to credit expanded, it was relatively easy to get a credit card, and banks developed cards specifically for the subprime market. But as we saw in Chapter 4, card issuers often duped consumers with low introductory rates, then quickly switched them to higher ones once the consumer signed up for the card. Blow says this was "the easy way to do credit in the subprime space. You offer credit to people at a low price that does not reflect the risk, and then when they pay one day late, you just ratchet up their interest rate dramatically. It might go from 9.9 percent to 19.9 percent, retroactively applied to balances that they've already built out."

When the CARD Act prohibited credit card companies from doing many of the things that lay at the core of their business models, many pulled out of the market altogether. They've retreated to the safer prime and super-prime markets. Their departure created the space for Fenway Summer to come in and try to do things differently.

Blow's perspective on card providers changed when she left Capital One and went to the CFPB. She'd heard Capital One executives blame the CARD Act for forcing them out. But she knew the problem was not the regulation. It was the providers' unwillingness to consider a different approach to the problem.

Blow and her team at Fenway Summer believe it's possible to provide credit to subprime consumers without tricking them — and make a profit too. They believe that upfront pricing without hidden fees more effectively builds positive customer relationships, and their hypothesis appears to be on target. Response to the Build card has been robust, particularly among payday-loan users.

KEYBANK

Not long after I finished my teller work, I gave a talk about my early findings to a diverse audience of financial-services professionals. I spoke about the high cost, poor service, and lack of transparency my customers had received at banks, and how they trusted the tellers at the check casher more than the bank tellers. Bruce Murphy, executive vice president and head of corporate responsibility at KeyBank, participated in the panel following my talk. He acknowledged banks' general failure to serve the "financially excluded" and talked about the ways KeyBank was trying to address the problem. After the close of the session, Bruce slipped me his card and said, "Why don't you come visit us at KeyBank, Lisa. I'd love to show you what we're up to."

Nine months later I flew to Cleveland, where KeyBank is headquartered. Murphy had scheduled a full day of meetings for me — I met with everyone from Murphy's boss, CEO Beth Mooney, to a woman who teaches financial education classes for KeyBank in one of the city's poorest neighborhoods. Spirits were running high in the offices of the upper-level managers at KeyBank because first-quarter earnings had just been announced, and they were very good. Murphy took this as confirmation of something he has been working to prove throughout his career — that in banking, it is still possible to do well while doing good.

Throughout the day, every person I met repeated the bank's mantra: "mission and margin." In other banks I've visited, the community development work, as it's often labeled, tends to be separated from "real work." It was relatively easy for me to get interviews with the people who work in a bank's community development department, but very difficult to get access to the people who made the big decisions about direction and strategy. Murphy, on the other hand, has direct access to KeyBank's CEO, Beth Mooney, as he did with her predecessor.

Murphy says "a light bulb went on" when KeyBank recognized that the less-well-off wanted the same things that the rest of their clients wanted. He explains, "Any new client thinking about joining the institution cares about reasonable fees, quick problem resolution, whether it's easy to do business. The most likely reason that a client would leave a financial institution? 'They hit me with a fee. They were unreasonable in handling it. I don't trust them anymore.'"

KeyBank created its Access Account, a "hassle-free" bank account, and marketed it broadly, not just to people with lower incomes. Since introducing the Access Account in the summer of 2014, KeyBank has experienced client growth at a faster rate than that of the prior five years. This result came from focusing on what the bank's clients have in common rather than what separates them. "We recognize that our clients come to us with different assets, different liabilities, different credit issues," Murphy said. "We work with everyone on an individual basis, but when it comes to how we build their trust, there's a very common set of issues."

When I asked whether KeyBank had sacrificed profits by cutting fees, Murphy acknowledged that decisions made over the past two years, such as cutting fees and eliminating debit resequencing, have decreased the bank's fee income. "But what's the upside?" Murphy asked. "Clients trust us. Clients build relationships with us. And the word of mouth that happens draws others in."

KeyBank also began offering check-cashing services in many of its branches for people who tended not to use banks, or who used both a bank and a check casher. Whereas most banks fear the "reputational risk" of providing alternative financial services, KeyBank sees check cashing as one more way to meet the needs of people in the communities it serves.

Recognizing the demand for small-dollar credit, Key also created a small-dollar revolving loan product for the bank's existing customers who would otherwise not qualify for one of the bank's loans. KeyBank relies on the proprietary information the bank has about its customers and uses it to inform these lending decisions. As Murphy describes it, KeyBank builds "a personal relationship score that allows us to go much deeper into the credit-score bands than a traditional bank would."

Many of the payday borrowers I interviewed complained that they couldn't get this kind of loan from their bank, despite the fact that they had been loyal to the bank for years and their records showed that they got regular paychecks and did not overdraw their account. Why couldn't these banks repay them for their loyalty? Andy, a computer technician, was extremely frustrated that his bank didn't have confidence in him. "Banks used to care about you," he said. "But traditional banks are very resistant now and they're not helping their customers. If I walk in there with a pound of money, they're more than happy to spend it and make money off it, but they're not willing to look at people like me and say, 'Hey, this person has been with us for thirteen years, you know? The check comes every week. He's been employed with this company for thirteen years.' They don't do any of that."

As a midsize bank, with $93 billion in assets, KeyBank is much smaller than the mega-banks that now occupy such a huge part of the market. But it is still the twenty-seventh-largest bank in the country, much bigger than the community development banks and credit unions that also have strong missions. KeyBank's advantage is that it's large enough, and diversified enough, to experiment with new products and business lines without taking on too much risk. KeyBank shows that innovation doesn't always depend on cutting-edge technology. It can be as simple as a mindset: wanting, as Murphy says, "to serve all of the clients in our community, from the low-income and underbanked to the wealthiest."

MISSION ASSET FUND

The office of Mission Asset Fund (MAF) sits in the middle of a busy commercial block in San Francisco's Mission District. The brightly painted space buzzes with activity. José Quiñones started MAF in 2008, convinced that he had a better way to combat financial exclusion compared to the strategies he saw being promoted. Where policymakers saw an unbanked community, Quiñones saw people, all over San Francisco's Mission District, saving money. They just weren't saving it in banks. They were using ROSCAs like the ones described in Chapter 7. Rather than try to change their behavior, Quiñones thought, why not try to make what they were already doing work better?

Quiñones recognized how well ROSCAs worked for people like Blanca and the members of her circles. He understood the importance of meeting people where they were, something that happens far too infrequently, especially in lower-income communities and communities of color. Instead of dismissing the ROSCA out of hand, he embraced it — that is his innovation.

But Quiñones also recognized its drawbacks — the risk of theft and the lack of connection to mainstream financial services. MAF initiated its Lending Circles Program to expand and formalize the use of ROSCAs — to keep members' money safe so that people like Dolores, the *tanda* leader we met in Chapter 7, can't run off with it. The program also reports on-time payments to credit bureaus so that participants can build their credit scores. And when clients are ready, MAF helps them open bank accounts. In 2011, MAF expanded the program to the entire Bay Area and in other cities, partnering with nonprofit organizations to introduce their constituents to the idea of lending circles. Since its founding, MAF has worked with fifty-two hundred participants to start eleven hundred lending circles. It's not the kind of scale that will move the needle, but it does highlight the importance of beginning with consumers and what they are already doing.

Quiñones believes the communities he serves are severely misunderstood. "The assumptions about consumers are wrong," he says. "And if the assumptions are wrong, the policy will be wrong. A lot of policy derives from the notion of deficits. The assumption is that if you're Latino, you're fucked up. If you're white, you're okay. If we shift away from deficits, we can get to a different vision of what could be possible."

OPORTÚN

Oportún, an alternative lender in Redwood City, California, makes small installment loans at an average interest rate of 33 percent — well below what the typical payday lender charges but above what many think is acceptable. Raul Vazquez, Oportún's CEO, often meets people who raise their eyebrows when he tells them Oportún's interest rate. "They're thinking about their own credit card or mortgage," he said. "They don't understand that people with little or no credit history have very limited options when it comes to borrowing money, and those options can be very expensive."

Vazquez, an industrial engineer by training, came to Oportún in 2012 after a career in retail and e-commerce. It was a big leap, "bigger than I thought," says Vazquez. As he sits in a busy diner south of San Francisco, his passion for what he does is clear. His dark eyes shining, he explains that he was drawn by the opportunity to learn the financial-services business and by Oportún's mission to help the Latino community. His parents both come from small mining towns in Mexico. "Having grown up along the border, basically in El Paso, I felt like I really understood the customers and spoke the language. Perhaps most important, I could really see the value of helping people get through an emergency or move forward with their lives by giving them access to responsible, affordable, credit-building loans," Vazquez says. "The business is fascinating because it's at the intersection of purpose and profit. Because as you know, there are some very distinct differences in how the Hispanic community thinks about dealing with companies, the distrust that exists, the distrust they have of larger financial institutions, given the experience many of them may have had in their own countries or that their family members might've had."

Oportún's founders chose a target interest rate of 36 percent; the average rate is currently a bit lower. They believed that this rate would allow them to do responsible lending and also build a viable business. "As a mission-driven company committed to helping our customers, we started with the goal of lending at a reasonable rate, even if that meant losing money while we figured out the right cost structure," Vazquez said. "We've always had a high standard for what responsible lending should look like and our challenge has been to develop the right business model to make it sustainable." It took eight years for Oportún to begin to make a profit.

The other factor that drives the business model is scale: the more loans you can make, the more efficient you can be, and the lower your costs. Oportún currently has 170 locations in five states and makes larger loans than payday lenders do — up to six thousand dollars for returning customers. Like the Build card and Key-

Bank's new revolving line of credit, Oportún's loans compete with payday loans on price, and they prioritize transparency, service, and the kind of relationships that most banks and credit card providers no longer invest in.

Two important threads connect these innovation stories. One is that nearly everyone I spoke with approached their business in the same way: as a knotty problem they wanted to solve. That focus led the way. Their first priority was not to make a boatload of money, create a particular product, avoid penalties, or skirt regulations. The innovators wanted to find a solution for a particularly difficult problem.

Second, an unusually high number of the people I interviewed had been touched by financial insecurity in a deep and personal way. Garry Reeder, head of the advisory practice of Fenway Summer, grew up poor, in a trailer park. Marla Blow has seen her relatives suffer at the hands of unscrupulous financial-services providers. Beth Mooney, CEO of KeyBank, had a brother who lost his way and found himself drowning in debt. Raul Vazquez grew up in an immigrant family that struggled financially. When you witness firsthand what financial insecurity can do to people, it changes the way you think. It's no longer "those people" who are struggling. It's "my people."

It's impossible to predict the cumulative effect of innovative startups (only a few are described here) on the consumer financial-services industry. There is no shortage of promising ideas. Right now, smart, creative people are tackling every aspect of the problems discussed in this book. The potential for transformation is right here in our backyard.

9

REJECTING THE NEW NORMAL

THE CONSUMER FINANCIAL-SERVICES SYSTEM IS BROKEN. This system, which consists of not only banks, check cashers, and lending circles, but also policymakers, regulators, and credit bureaus, fails to provide Americans with the products, services, and information they need to achieve financial stability. As a result, too many Americans are unable to participate fully in the economy and in civil society.

The first step toward improving the system is to change how we talk about it. Framing the problem as "banked versus unbanked" has helped spotlight problems of financial exclusion, but it has also placed a value judgment on some people's financial decisions without understanding their situations, implying that the un- and underbanked are somehow deficient. This understanding of the problem also tacitly affirms that banks are the good guys. They're not. This paradigm has outlived its useful life. It's time to move on.

What if, instead of focusing narrowly on people's "poor choices" — failing to save, patronizing predatory lenders, running up fees — we worked harder to understand the options available to people and the context in which they make those choices? Looking at the problem systemically will lead to a much different conversation and ultimately to transformational solutions.

The problem is not that people are unbanked, but that they lack high-quality, affordable financial services and the resources to attain the stability that once defined what it meant to be middle class.

A conversation about financial health has begun in certain corners of the consumer financial-services field, providing the reframing that's needed right now. The Center for Financial Services Innovation (CFSI) has pioneered the idea of making financial health — also called financial wellness or well-being — a central goal. According to CFSI, "financial health is achieved when an individual's day-to-day financial system functions well and increases the likelihood of financial resilience and opportunity." The Consumer Financial Protection Bureau recently created a financial well-being scale, which measures four attributes of financial health: control over one's finances, capacity to absorb a financial shock, having financial goals and being on track to meet them, and being able to make choices that allow one to enjoy life. For a growing number of Americans, these attributes are unattainable.

According to this scale, virtually none of the consumers I interviewed for this book would qualify as financially healthy. Not Dina from Chapter 6, the woman who recently finished graduate school and landed her dream job but is so saddled with student debt that even shopping for shoes feels like a distant fantasy. Not Karen from Chapter 5, who has a good job but takes out payday loans to cover the bills for her father's assisted living facility. And certainly not Michelle from Chapter 1, who was willing to pay two dollars to access the last ten dollars remaining on her Electronic Benefits Card.

In a study of US financial health, CFSI found that 57 percent of Americans — 138 million people — are struggling financially, more than double the number of adults the FDIC categorized as unbanked or underbanked in its most recent survey. The problem is much, much larger than we thought. It's big enough, in fact, to fuel

a movement. Universal financial health is a goal that has the potential to unite us.

Improving the financial-services industry will go a long way toward securing Americans' financial health. In our modern capi-
talist system, no one can be financially healthy without reliable financial services that enable a person to save, spend, borrow, and
plan. Financial services are necessary to universal financial health
but not sufficient to achieve it. As we've seen, a large part of the
problem is that wages, benefits, and government programs provide much less of a buffer against hard times than they have in
the past. People cannot be financially healthy if they work full-
time and cannot pay for basic necessities, if one medical issue can
force them to deplete all their assets, or if the prospect of crushing
debt means forgoing advanced education. Even if every single one
of the recommendations I'm about to lay out is adopted, financial
health will still be out of reach for a large and increasing number
of Americans. Why? They simply do not have enough money.

In order to make financial health a reality for all Americans,
we need to ensure that anyone who works hard for forty hours
each week can earn enough to support a family. We need to provide everyone with the opportunity to work and a strong safety net
that will help people manage when work doesn't work. We need
to provide stable housing and affordable health care, so that one
illness or accident can no longer send a family into debt so deep,
they cannot get out. Planning for the future shouldn't involve the
kind of tradeoffs today's young people are facing — whether to invest in themselves by pursuing an advanced degree or forgo it and
take care of their parents, whether to go to college when that decision might mean decades of indebtedness and the inability to own
a home or have a child. When people invest in their own education

— their human capital — it's good for all of us because human capital increases productivity, which helps fuel the economy. We have good reason to care about one another's financial health.

There is more than one way to tackle this much larger set of problems, and many ideas exist: creating a universal basic income, implementing a federal jobs-creation program, providing greater subsidies for childcare, housing, education, and health care. We have the resources and the ideas. What we need now is political will.

In addition, we need to rethink our assumptions about the way people make decisions. Most people have very good reasons for doing what they do with their money. The job of policymakers and financial-services providers is, first, to understand these choices and the needs that drive them *without prejudgment*, and second, to make financial systems work better and enable people to make sound choices.

Behavioral economists have joined the conversation about financial inclusion in recent years, adding insight into how people make decisions about money: people are not the "rational actors" that classical economists imagine them to be. Michael Barr, a professor and former assistant secretary of the US Department of the Treasury, argues that the context in which people make decisions is powerful. "We have a persistent tendency to underestimate the power of the situation relative to the presumed influence of the consumer's intention, education, and personality traits." Remember Ariane, the teller I worked with at Check Center, who took out five payday loans to fix her car so she could get to work? The situation she found herself in — choosing between taking out payday loans or losing her job — overrode her knowledge; as she told me, "I know it's bad." The upside of this finding is that the effect of context on decision making is predictable. We can find ways to protect people at vulnerable moments.

The way choices are presented — what the economists Richard Thaler and Cass Sunstein call "choice architecture" — is also critical to making a good decision. Employee enrollment in retirement plans provides a good illustration. When a worker is lucky enough to get a job that includes a retirement plan, she must usually make several decisions — whether to participate, how much to contribute, how to allocate contributions across different investments. Most plans require workers to "opt in" — in other words, you have to choose to participate. Researchers have found that simply changing the default option from "opt out" to "opt in," or raising the default amount of the contribution, can make a big difference in whether and how much people save for retirement.

Interventions like these make it more likely that people will behave in financially healthy ways, and we should certainly think more about how to "nudge" people to make the best choices they can in whatever financial situation they find themselves.

As currently structured, our financial-services system — and the larger economic context in which it sits — makes it hard for people to attain financial health unless they already have a cushion, a stake, a network that can come to their rescue when the chips are down.

It doesn't have to be this way.

Until the will arises to make sweeping transformational changes, there are ways to improve the consumer financial-services system that will support greater financial health. The previous chapter discussed promising private-sector ideas. The policy ideas presented next range from broad changes to smaller tweaks that address the issues that vex consumers most. These ideas had to meet one essential criterion to be included here: have a fighting chance of improving the financial health of individuals and families.

CHANGE THE RELATIONSHIP BETWEEN
BANKING AND GOVERNMENT

My enthusiasm for the innovations described in the previous chapter might imply that the free market can take care of all the problems plaguing the consumer financial-services system. It won't. While innovation is important, this isn't simply a problem of unleashing that innovation and letting it transform the system. Innovation can lead to both healthy and unhealthy outcomes. Remember trans fats and artificial coloring?

I argue for renewed government involvement in the consumer financial-services sector, the kind of involvement our nation's founders fought for. They believed banks were a necessary part of our national economic infrastructure and that bank policy should focus on serving the public. But the focus of policy has shifted from promoting equality of access to "favoring bank profitability and efficiency over public needs." In the consumer financial-services system we now have, the government supports our banks — remember the bailout? — but does not hold banks accountable to serve all Americans equally well. We should be demanding more in return.

If we think of the relationship between the government and the banking industry on a spectrum — with complete public-sector provision of financial services on one end and a completely unregulated market at the other end — it's clear that we've moved too far to the "unregulated" end. The government has allowed banks to focus too narrowly on profits, creating no incentive for them to provide safe, affordable services for everyone. The market is now rigged in favor of the wealthy and in favor of large financial institutions.

Banks benefit from government in all kinds of ways. The FDIC insures consumer deposits. Loan guarantees and direct injection of public funds into banks, especially those deemed "too big to fail," enable them to borrow at lower rates and take bigger risks. A recent study found that the biggest banks have been among the top recipients of government subsidies, grants, loans, and tax credits over the past fifteen years. And banks continue to operate with the knowledge that the government will rescue them should anything go wrong.

We've seen that alternative and informal financial services have emerged and grown to fill needs unmet by the market, but check cashers and payday lenders aren't the best options for improving financial health. A popular policy response these days is to focus regulation on the check cashers and payday lenders, or to punish or simply shut down these so-called predators. But the alternative sector exists and has expanded because healthier options don't exist for many, many people.

The big banks have demonstrated a lack of interest in providing the financial products and services we need at a price we can afford. They will not address the problem on their own. The only way to guarantee that all of us will have the ability to achieve financial health is for the government to intervene and play a much larger role in the provision of financial services.

The three following options entail this greater government involvement. First, the government could subsidize banks to serve those customers who are not profitable. Although it may seem counterintuitive to pay banks for what many argue they should be ethically bound to do, there are precedents for this kind of policy. The Lifeline program, which provides discounted landline and wireless telephone service to thirteen million Americans, is an example. The Reagan administration initiated the Lifeline program, which enjoys bipartisan support and is funded in part by contributions from telecommunications companies. A similar model could be adapted for financial services through provision of free or subsidized savings and checking accounts.

Alternatively, the federal government could enable mission-oriented banks and credit unions to extend their reach. I hear about them when I talk with people who are happy with their financial institutions. It's hard to imagine the will to "make banking boring again." But a set of banks and credit unions — Amalgamated, Carver, the Lower East Side People's Credit Union, to name a few — remain locally rooted and guided by a strong sense of mission, though their numbers have declined. Rather than wax nostalgic about the good old days, we should support the banks that already serve people best. The Community Development Financial Institutions Fund, a federal pot of money created in 1994 to support these businesses, is a step in the right direction, but the amount of funding is a pittance compared to what's needed.

In *Phishing for Phools,* Akerloff and Shiller label as heroes the rare business people "who restrain themselves from taking advantage of customers' psychological or informational weaknesses." I had the good fortune to speak with many of these financial-sector heroes. They run mission-oriented banks and credit unions that endeavor to make a profit without manipulating and deceiving their customers. But the world isn't so easy for those who work on the side of the angels. Our economic system, which prizes competition and profit above all else, simply doesn't reward them for prioritizing safety, affordability, and transparency.

A third option would be for the federal government itself to provide banking services. One way to do this is through the postal service. Many countries provide safe, affordable financial services through their postal systems, and this was once done in the United States as well. For about fifty years, until 1967, the postal service enabled people to make savings deposits. Mehrsa Baradaran, a legal scholar and advocate of postal banking, calls this "the most

successful experiment in financial inclusion in the United States."
The Office of the Inspector General of the United States Postal
Service (USPS) issued a white paper in 2014 arguing for such a solution, and the case has its merits. The postal service has a strong
brand and a large footprint, but it's unclear whether the USPS has
the capacity to distribute financial services efficiently, particularly in urban areas. This white paper argued that the USPS could
both serve the underserved and make money, an attractive prop-
osition, given the agency's financial situation. Postal banking is a
compelling idea, but we shouldn't assume that it will be profitable.
It should be considered and, if it makes sense, backed by government, simply because it's the right thing to do.

ENABLE BETTER DECISION MAKING

It's impossible to make healthy financial choices without the right
information. Consumers need access to clear, easy-to-understand
information that will help them make the best financial decisions
for their individual situations.

Government can hold financial-services providers accountable by requiring them to make it easier for consumers to compare
products and make informed choices. The solution is not more
disclosure — which tends to result in long fine-print documents
that no one reads or understands — but simple, clear ways to compare products and make choices. Financial-information boxes
that resemble the nutrition-information boxes on packaged food
would provide consumers with clear, standardized information
about fees, interest rates, penalties, and the like. The information
on packaged food allows consumers to easily compare two kinds
of breakfast cereal, yogurt, or frozen pizza right in the supermar-

ket aisle, so they can make healthier choices. There's no reason why a standardized "fact box" can't replace the opaque technical language, asterisks, and fine print that typically accompany financial products.

Some progress has already been made in this area, but no single standard has been adopted by all companies, making comparisons difficult; also, these efforts at transparency are voluntary, not required. The Consumer Financial Protection Bureau should continue its initiatives to make this information consistent across the full range of consumer financial products.

But it's not just the products that consumers need to understand — it's also the providers. It's impossible for consumers to keep up with which financial institutions are providing the best products at the lowest prices. Here too, precedents for creating such a system exist. In 2010, the New York City Department of Health implemented a system for communicating to consumers the results of its restaurant inspections. Every establishment that serves food must now post a sign in its window with a large blue grade — A, B, or C — to state how it fared in its most recent inspection. It used to be that you had to go online and search for that information. Michael Barr recommends using just such an easy-to-understand symbol, a gold seal or the like, to identify financial institutions judged to offer safe and affordable bank accounts.

We know that some banks treat their customers better than others and some payday lenders engage in illegal collections practices, while others don't. Using a rating system modeled on the one used by the US Department of Health would inform customers as to how well financial-services providers do their job.

In order to make the best of these rating systems, it has to be easy for people to move from one financial institution to another. Right now it's anything but. Moving would be simpler if we each had a universal, portable financial identity that we control. When we move from one bank or credit union to another, that identity would go with us. Information about how we use financial products and services, and what we pay for them, could be included as part of this identity.

Even if consumers were able to access clear and complete information about financial services easily, they would still need well-developed skills and knowledge in order to make sound decisions. A recent study conducted by the Urban Institute found that financial coaching positively affected participants' financial health on a range of outcomes, including nonretirement savings balances, credit scores, budgets, and ability to deal with financial stress. This kind of coaching will require a significant investment, but the returns are potentially great.

CREATE A SANDBOX FOR INNOVATORS

Even with so much fertile ground for innovators, it's unclear whether the best ideas will reach the consumers they could benefit most. Government regulation is one of the most difficult pieces of the puzzle. There's a risk that some potentially significant innovation will be, as JoAnn Barefoot puts it, "strangled in the cradle." Ripple's Chris Larsen believes we need a government framework for managing innovation. He cited the global framework for electronic commerce set up during the Clinton administration as an example of what's needed. "It was on the list of the administration's top fifteen things they had to worry about in the world. You don't have that right now. It's not on the administration's radar," he said.

In the UK, the Financial Conduct Authority (FCA) created Project Innovate to foster competition and growth among financial-services companies that are developing products with the potential to improve consumers' experience and outcomes. As part of the initiative, FCA created a "regulatory sandbox" as a safe space where businesses can test new products without being subject to regulatory considerations.

This sandbox environment cuts down on risk by allowing innovators to test products before jumping through every regulatory hoop. Less risk can help innovators get much-needed investment funding. The sandbox can also reduce the time it takes to develop and introduce a new product.

Without a government framework for managing innovation, some projects that have potential to improve consumers' experiences are abandoned at an early stage in development, before their true value can be assessed, because of hurdles in funding or regulation. The ability to manage regulatory risk can allow more of these products to reach the consumers they are designed to help.

Getting these ideas adopted will be no easy task, particularly the ones that require government to be more aggressive in regulating banks and ensuring that all Americans have access to safe, affordable financial services. In the wake of the financial crisis, Paul Krugman argued that "policymakers are still thinking mainly about rearranging the boxes on the bank supervisory organization chart. They're not at all ready to do what needs to be done." That's what movements are for. They pressure government to change because change is necessary. The healthy food movement and the minimum-wage movement, both grassroots efforts, have made extraordinary gains in recent years. We can learn from their successes.

We can start the financial rights movement with a manifesto that clearly lays out Americans' right to financial products and services that are safe, affordable, fair, transparent, and universally available. Financial insecurity connects so many of us who have no idea we're linked — from Andy, the computer programmer in Dallas who should be looking forward to retirement but cannot, to Michelle in the South Bronx who pays a high proportion of her welfare benefits in order to get her cash right away, to Kendra, the army vet who has given up on the American dream. Whether or not we suffer from financial insecurity ourselves, it's a certainty that a neighbor, a coworker, a sibling, your child, or the person who cuts your hair or cleans your teeth stays up at night worrying about money. Our culture places so much pressure on us to be able to make it on our own. But the odds are stacked against all of us now, in ways they've never been before. It's time to demand a change.

It's been two years since Ariane, my fellow Check Center teller, left for a better job at a veterinarian's office. The regular hours and better pay meant that life was more predictable, but Ariane aimed higher. She wanted to leave the working poor and join the middle class — the "old" middle class, in which a college degree and a regular paycheck purchased financial security. So she paid off her payday loans, what Suze Orman would call "bad debt," and took out student loans, considered "good debt" because she was investing in herself, in order to go to college full-time. Ariane is almost finished with her associate's degree and will enroll in a four-year college as soon as she graduates. "I couldn't decide between anthropology and environmental science because I love them both," she said. Ariane's professors beg her to take more courses with them because she brings so much to the classroom. She ultimately decided on environmental science because "I think it'll be easier to find a good job with that degree."

Ariane isn't sure she made the right decision about taking out student loans, but going back to school seemed the only way to improve her situation. She knows the economy isn't great and that there's no guarantee she'll get the kind of job she aspires to when she's done with school. She's trying desperately to climb a ladder that may not exist anymore for someone like her.

Between food stamps, subsidized childcare, financial aid from her community college, and student loans, Ariane gets by somehow and has not taken out more payday loans. But it would be a stretch to say she's financially healthy. After paying off her old payday loans and the overdraft fees that she had accrued at her bank, Ariane opened a new bank account. "I'm twenty-five years old and I'm moving forward in my life," she declared. "It seemed like the right thing to do." But with finances extremely tight, she recently overdrew her account by ten dollars. Her bank began hitting her with charges that quickly mounted to three hundred dollars. "It doesn't seem fair," she said. "I don't even want a bank account now." She now uses a prepaid debit card to manage her money. "There's nothing left over to save anyway," she said. "When I'm out of money, that's it."

Making the system work better for Ariane and every other American who suffers from financial insecurity won't be easy. It will require the recognition that all of us deserve access to safe, affordable financial services, and then the will and the resources to make this happen. This is a fixable problem with no shortage of promising ideas to solve it. But in order to repair the system, we need a shared understanding that access to good financial services is a right, not a privilege of the fortunate few. We need to demand financial justice.

AUTHOR'S NOTE

People often ask me whether I went undercover when I worked as a teller and a loan collector. I did not. In each case, the higher-ups at the business knew I was a professor and researcher. I told them what I was hoping to learn. When I began each job, I also briefed the tellers with whom I worked. For me, this was the most ethical approach to my research, and because I was more interested in the consumers than the businesses, I felt confident that I could learn the kinds of things I set out to learn without concealing my identity.

Not being undercover has its tradeoffs, one of them being that my presence almost certainly changed the behavior of the people around me. There's no way for me to know exactly how it changed. But the real question is whether my findings changed in significant ways because of it. I will never know the answer to that for sure, but I did everything I could to confirm my preliminary findings. I used multiple methods, including participant observation, interviews, focus groups, and survey data. I discussed my findings with other researchers in this field. This range of methods and data allowed me to keep re-examining my data as the research progressed. I spent enough time at each site to observe patterns of behavior over time, and I assume, though I cannot definitively conclude, that people became comfortable enough with my presence to go about their normal work and interactions.

I began with a set of questions about why so many people were using alternative financial services if these services were harmful. That question led me to my fieldwork in the South Bronx. There, my initial questions generated additional questions, which expanded my area of inquiry. What began as an ethnographic study of a single neighborhood seen through the perspective of a check-cashing store evolved into a much larger study of the consumer financial-services industry. The evolution of my questions led me back to other data and studies, which drew me back to fieldwork, to interviews with financial-services providers and policymakers, and back to the fieldwork again, both in the South Bronx and elsewhere. The entire project was iterative, and I went where it took me until I began to see larger patterns. I wrote some of the book in the first person in order to give readers a sense of my journey and how the project unfolded over time.

Issues always arise when a researcher who is different from the people she is researching enters "their space." The academic term for this is "positionality." It refers to where the researcher stands in comparison to the people she is observing, often focusing on relationships of power and privilege. I would be remiss if I didn't address how I negotiated my difference relative to the people and communities I studied. I strove to remain aware of my own position and to think through how it might shape my research and my interpretation of interviews, interactions, and other events. Whenever possible, I tested my interpretations with those who had greater "insider" status, such as the tellers with whom I worked.

My "difference" was most obvious at RiteCheck, located in a mostly Spanish-speaking neighborhood. I was taller, blonder, whiter, more educated, more financially secure, and older than most of the other tellers, and Spanish is not my first language, although my ability to speak it enabled me to serve customers who preferred to speak Spanish; approximately 80 percent of our customers were Spanish-speaking. For those reasons, I was an "outsider" at RiteCheck. I blended in more, visually at least, at Check Center, although I was older, more educated, and more financially stable than the other tellers and loan collectors there.

The fact that the other tellers and loan collectors at both jobs were the "experts," teaching me how to do their jobs, helped normalize the dynamic. I needed them and their expertise to make it through the workday. And after many days of working together, managing long lines of customers, spelling each other with breaks, talking about our children, we developed trust. But my relative privilege meant that I was not dependent on the jobs I held and therefore had a different relationship with management. I could switch the day I worked easily if I had a conflict, and I did not work on Thanksgiving, Christmas, or New Year's Day, whereas my colleagues did. Although I did truly worry about being fired when my drawer was short, the consequences would not have been nearly as dire for me as they might have been for others.

But the fact that I had never used a check casher or payday lender also meant that I didn't see and understand everything going on in front of me — the reasons behind the transactions I was facilitating. Having colleagues who were much more experienced with customers' needs and their rationale for managing their money the way they did proved invaluable. Cristina, Joana, Ariane, and the other tellers became key informants, helping me make sense of practices that my own position and background prevented me from understanding. The stories I relay about Carlos the contractor, Michelle, the woman who used her EBT card, and Aguero, the informal lender, illustrate this dynamic.

I conducted interviews at both RiteCheck and Check Center after I finished my teller work, in part to get at the situations I may have missed working at the window. My research assistant and I interviewed approximately fifty customers one-on-one at each site, and another forty-five with payday borrowers for a related project. When we conducted these interviews, and all of the other interviews and focus groups referenced in this book, we told the interviewees who we were and why we were doing the research. Each interviewee signed an informed consent form that described the research, and was paid to participate. The names of all consumers who were interviewed and who participated in focus groups for this book have been changed. The names of the tellers have also been changed. No composite characters are used. All interviews were completely voluntary.

My prior experience of conducting research in lower-income communities, along with the work of other ethnographers, caused me to question the conclusions being drawn solely from quantitative data. There was scant qualitative work that focused on consumer financial services, particularly the alternative and informal components of the industry. But even putting myself behind the teller window for months didn't enable me to understand everything that was happening. Once Cristina knew I was also interested in informal financial services, she introduced me to Aguero, the loan shark, and the Mexican women who purchased money orders at RiteCheck every Wednesday morning. But even with an open mind and the help of my fellow tellers, it's likely that I didn't see everything.

The customers I waited on and the hotline callers with whom I spoke did not know I was a researcher. There was no practical way to convey that information, and at that point in my research, I was more interested in patterns than in individual stories. When I tell the story of any individual in this book, he or she represents a larger group with similar experiences.

Toni Castro, one of my research assistants, participated in two rounds of Blanca's *tanda*. She also conducted many of the interviews with RiteCheck customers in the South Bronx. Toni is Mexican, and Spanish is her first language. We hypothesized that it would be easier for her to gain the trust of locals than it would have been for me. I accompanied her many times to Blanca's apartment to make payments or just to chat, and Toni also introduced me to the other people who anchor Chapter 7. Toni introduced herself as a student and when I was with her, she introduced me as her professor. Toni's social class and education also positioned her as more privileged than most of the people she got to know in Mott Haven. But her physical appearance and accent enabled her to approach and engage people more easily than I could. She was more likely to get invited into people's homes, which allowed her to gain a more complete understanding of the people she met and interviewed.

Another question I get asked is whether RiteCheck and Check Center are representative of the larger groups of check cashers and payday lenders, respectively. The answer is "yes and no." Yes, in the sense that I believe working at any check casher or any payday lender would provide me with similar lenses on the consumers who patronize such businesses. My primary reason for working in these businesses was to understand what consumers did and why. I think those motivating factors would have been very similar regardless of where I worked.

The "no" part of my response has to do with the businesses themselves. I am fairly certain I would not have gotten the kind of access I had from just any check casher or payday lender. Joe Coleman is not your typical check casher. I don't think many people in his position would have embraced my research idea so completely. Coleman was genuinely curious about how his business looked through my eyes. He saw my research as a kind of test of his belief that RiteCheck brings value to his customers and the neighborhoods in which his stores operate.

Coleman is widely known and well-respected in the alternative financial-services industry and among people who are concerned about financial inclusion, and he was essential to helping me find a payday lender who would give me the kind of access I enjoyed at RiteCheck. Rob Zweig and John Weinstein were similarly accommodating at Check Center.

From my experience on the hotline, I know that there are payday lenders who obey the law and treat their customers well, and those that don't. Indeed, one of the reasons I wanted to volunteer on the hotline was to talk with people who had had a range of experiences with different lenders. The study I did with MDRC, using Clarity data that involved interviewing another set of payday borrowers, provided yet another dimension to this work. But I worked at only one check casher and one payday lender and I cannot say how typical those businesses are.

I was paid the going wage for entry-level tellers at both businesses; they were required by law to pay me. I donated those wages, some to the Virginia Poverty Law Center, which hosts the Predatory Loan Help Hotline, and some to the scholarship fund of the Financial Services Centers of America, one of the primary trade associations of the alternative financial-services industry.

I wrote this book because I believed my findings could supply current policy debates with new information. I also realize that my project raises new questions, some of which I am already beginning to address with additional research that will test, improve on, and expand our understanding of how consumer financial services work and how they can be improved.

ACKNOWLEDGMENTS

This book began with a question that turned into a quest. And, like all good quests, this one involved a journey, a series of vexing obstacles, a few riddles, and a terrific group of trusty sidekicks and wise elders.

Joy Cousminer, the founder of Bethex Federal Credit Union, unknowingly planted the seed for this book when she brought Joe Coleman to one of my classes. I am indebted to Joe for his intellectual curiosity and for trusting me enough to hire me and give me complete access to his business and his staff. I learned so much in my four months at RiteCheck. I never would have landed my second job, at Check Center, if Joe hadn't vouched for me to Rob Zweig and John Weinstein, who also opened their business to me. Thanks to Joe, Rob, John, and all of the other check cashers and payday lenders I met who shared their perspectives and experience with me. I am grateful for their openness and willingness to engage with me.

My coworkers at RiteCheck and Check Center, especially Cristina, Joana, Ariane, and Delia, proved to be not only terrific coworkers but also wise informants. Their kindness, generosity, and humor made our time together enjoyable. In critical ways, their knowledge and insight shaped my understanding of alternative financial services and the people who use them.

Dana Wiggins, who runs the Predatory Loan Help Hotline, is a tireless advocate for people who are struggling with debt and feeling hopeless. Dana generously introduced me to members of the Virginia Partnership to Encourage Responsible Lending, trained me on the hotline, and answered countless questions about legal issues, history, and policy.

One of the biggest obstacles I faced on my quest was making sense of 150 years of bank policy and figuring out how that history affected our situation today. I owe huge debts to JoAnn Barefoot, Chuck Muckenfuss, Bob Kuttner, Lyn Farrell, and Ellen Seidman for guiding me through a morass of legislation and telling me about the many parts of the process that nobody writes down. Ellen in particular was kind, patient, supportive, and willing to read draft after draft of key chapters. I only hope my condensed version of their stories does justice to the richness and depth of their knowledge and experience.

The innovators featured in Chapter 8 — Chris Larsen, Bruce Murphy, José Quiñones, Raul Vazquez, Raj Date, Marla Blow, and Mike Mondelli — spent precious time away from business to talk with me. Members of their staff who do not appear in these pages provided additional insight. Arjun Schütte, founder and managing partner of Core Innovation Capital, helped me understand what innovation means in the fintech space and introduced me to Mike and Chris.

Every writer who has a day job struggles to amass the big chunks of time that are critical for thinking through ideas, rearranging the pieces of the puzzle, and getting them all down on paper. For the gift of time I thank The New School's provost, Tim Marshall, and executive dean Mary Watson, who both provided me with course releases and allowed me to take an early sabbatical in order to complete this book. I spent the 2015–16 academic year as a scholar at the Russell Sage Foundation, which provided me with a quiet office, research support, a daily hot lunch, and a community of supportive scholars — in short, the best environment one could hope for when writing a book. Thank you to Sheldon Danziger and Ivan Ramos for a wonderful year, to Claire Gabriel and Katie Winograd for research support, to Galo Falchettore for his assistance with graphics, and to Jackie Cholmondelev and Maria Cesarczyk for their nourishing lunchtime sustenance. Fellow scholars Prudence Carter, David Gamson, and Steven Greenhouse offered friendship, lively conversation, and a sympathetic ear.

Financial support from the New York Community Trust, the MetLife Foundation, The New School, and the Consumer Credit Research Foundation enabled the fieldwork, travel, research assistance, and writing time necessary to complete this project. Thank you to Evelyn Stark and Rick Love at the MetLife Foundation and Pat Swann at the New York Community Trust. Evelyn not only supported my work financially but also engaged with me intellectually throughout the process and connected me to her wide network.

MetLife also supported a project in which I partnered with MDRC for an analysis of payday borrowers. Tim Ranney of Clarity Services gave us access to his rich data, without which we could not have done that work. I thank my collaborator Rick Hendra and Steve Nuñez and the rest of the team at MDRC. I'm very happy our work together is continuing.

Mina Addo, Toni Castro, and Andrea Marpillero-Colomina, my three top-notch research assistants at The New School, contributed to every aspect of this book, from standing on street corners collecting Money Stories, to traveling around the country with me to conduct interviews, to chasing down obscure statistics and policies. Thank you all for your energy and enthusiasm, your attention to detail, and your being game for whatever this project needed. I am so grateful to have worked with you, and I look forward to cheering from the sidelines as you all go on to become first-rate scholars.

So many people read and commented on pieces of this work at various stages. My first thanks go to the writing group I've been a part of since 2013, which grew out of the 2013 Summer Writers Colony at The New School. Madge McKeithen provided important insight and encouragement when I was just beginning to try my hand at writing for a wider audience. Mary Little, Rae Francoeur, Candy Schulman, and Nancy Woodruff have been a steadfast source of encouragement and honest criticism over the entire period during which I researched and wrote this book.

Many others read my work and helped me wrestle through ideas, including Jennifer Tescher, Anne Stuhldreher, Rachel Schneider, Arjan Schütte, Alec Gershberg, Lana Swartz, Rick Hackett, Tim Ranney, Darrick Hamilton, Greg Fairchild, Kris Rengert, Cliff Rosenthal, Mae Watson Grote, Cathie Mahon, Amy Brown, Mark Willis, Ron Grzyzwinski, Mary Houghton, Manuel Castells, Sarah Pink, Giorgos Kallis, Sarah Banet-Weiser, Jim Ziliak, Tali Mendelberg, Kate Zaloom, Rick Hackett, Giorgos Kallis, Prudence Carter, Jeff Smith, and Rachel Sherman.

My agent, Adam Eaglin at Cheney Literary, was the best guide an academic author tiptoeing into the foreign waters of trade publishing could hope for. Adam's wise and steady counsel skillfully guided me through the process from beginning to end. My editor, Deanne Urmy, brought her deep insight and valuable experience to the project. Deanne read many drafts of this book and shaped it in subtle and not-so-subtle ways. Readers have Deanne to thank for her gentle suggestion that I cut the ten-page summary of usury going back to ancient Babylonia.

My children, C.C. and Milo, are never happy when work takes me away from home, which it often did for the fieldwork pieces of this project, but I know they understood my passion for it, and I hope they see what a marvelous gift it is to be able to do meaningful work that you love. I thank them both for their curiosity, their patience, and their understanding. My husband, Alec, kept the home fires burning when I was on the road or needed to sequester myself to write. When I asked him several years ago, "What if I got a job as a teller?" he got it immediately and supported the project 100 percent. Throughout the research and the writing, Alec was my constant sounding board, helping me refine and articulate many key ideas in this book.

I couldn't do without the moral support and cheerleading of my sisters, Leslie and Jody, and my mother, Lois. They always have my back, make me laugh, and keep me connected to my roots.

Finally, I am enormously grateful to the people who were willing to share their stories with me. It's not easy to talk about money in our culture, and for some, it meant revisiting painful moments in the past and decisions that they wished they hadn't made, while thinking about a future that seems bleak. I hope we can all benefit from their courage, sharing, and perseverance.

NOTES

INTRODUCTION:
WE'RE ALL UNDERBANKED

PAGE

xiv *the percentage of Americans:* Susan Burhouse et al., "2013 National Survey of Unbanked and Underbanked Households" (Washington, DC: FDIC, October 2014). https://www.fdic.gov/householdsurvey/2013report.pdf

xv *Payday lending grew:* Eva Wolkowitz, "2013 Financially Underserved Market Study" (Chicago: Center for Financial Services Inclusion, December 10, 2014). http://www.cfsinnovation.com/content/2012-financially -underserved-market-sizing-study#sthash.1QQKl1ou.dpuf

xvi *A ChexSystems report that:* Jessica Silver-Greenberg, "Over a Million Denied Bank Accounts for Past Errors," *New York Times,* July 30, 2013. http://dealbook.nytimes.com/2013/07/30/over-a-million-are-denied -bank-accounts-for-past-errors/?_r=0

approximately 6 percent: Involuntary bank closure statistic comes from Consumer Financial Protection Bureau, "CFPB Study of Overdraft Programs: A White Paper of Initial Findings" (Washington, DC: CFPB, June 2013). http://files.consumerfinance.gov/f/201306_cfpb_whitepaper_ overdraft-practices.pdf

More than one million: This figure is from Silver-Greenberg, "Over a Million Are Denied Bank Accounts."

xvii *"banked" (they use only banks):* Burhouse et al., "2013 National Survey of Unbanked and Underbanked Households."

One in five African American households: Ibid.

"mainstream banking services": Julie Menin, "Bad Alternative to Banks," letter to the editor, *New York Times,* November 14, 2014.

xviii *Jacob Hacker writes that:* Jacob Hacker, *The Great Risk Shift: The New Economic Insecurity and the Decline of the American Dream* (Oxford, UK: Oxford University Press, 2008).

A recent study conducted by: Burhouse et al., "2013 National Survey of Unbanked and Underbanked Households."

xix *put their trust in banks:* GlobeScan, "Seven Years on from the Financial Crisis, Trust in Banks Remains at All-Time Low" (Toronto, Ontario: GlobeScan, July 2, 2015). http://www.globescan.com/news-and-analysis/blog/entry/seven-years-on-from-the-financial-crisis-trust-in-banks-remains-at-all-time-low.html

1. WHERE EVERYBODY KNOWS YOUR NAME

3 *More than half of:* Joel Schectman, "The South Bronx Is a Banking Wasteland," *New York Daily News,* March 10, 2009. http://www.nydailynews.com/new-york/bronx/south-bronx-banking-wasteland-article-1.367439

less than one in ten: Ibid.

encompassed within New York's 15th: Formerly the 16th, before redistricting, effective January 3, 2013.

"It is going through": C. J. Hughes, "Mott Haven, the Bronx, in Transition," *New York Times,* March 25, 2015. http://www.nytimes.com/2015/03/29/realestate/mott-haven-the-bronx-in-transition.html?_r=0

nearly half used food stamps: New York City Department of City Planning, Population Division, "DP03 Selected Economic Characteristics" (New York: NYC Dept. of City Planning, January 2014), p. 3. http://www.nyc.gov/html/dcp/pdf/census/puma_econ_10to12_acs.pdf#bx01and02; US Census Bureau, American Fact Finder, "2007–2011 American Community Survey Five-Year Estimates: Food Stamp/SNAP" (Washington, DC: US Census Bureau, 2011), p. 1. http://factfinder.census.gov/faces/tableservices/jsf/pages/productview.xhtml?pid=ACS_14_5YR_S2201&prodType=table

vast sections of the area: Mindy Thompson Fullilove and Roderick Wallace, "Serial Forced Displacement in American Cities, 1916–2010," *Journal of Urban Health: Bulletin of the New York Academy of Medicine,* vol. 88, no. 3 (May 24, 2011): 381–89. http://link.springer.com/article

/10.1007/s11524-011-9585-2; Urban Oasis, "Digital HOLC Maps." https://dl.dropboxusercontent.com/u/3961868/HOLC%20Maps/HOLC /BronxHOLC-MED.jpg

Home to waves of Polish: Jill Jonnes, *South Bronx Rising: The Rise, Fall, and Resurrection of an American City* (New York: Fordham University Press, 2002).

In 1969 the New York City: Ibid., p. 181.

4   *25 percent of the Bronx's:* Ibid., p. 199.

8   *Frey also found that:* Alexander Von Hoffman, *House by House, Block by Block: The Rebirth of America's Urban Neighborhoods* (New York and Oxford, UK: Oxford University Press, 2004), p. 41.

16   *A twenty-five-year-old:* Susan Weinstock et al., "Overdrawn: Persistent Confusion and Concern About Bank Overdraft Practices" (Washington, DC: Pew Charitable Trusts, June 2014), p. 3. http://www.pewtrusts. org/~/media/Assets/2014/06/26/Safe_Checking_Overdraft_Survey_ Report.pdf

more than ten overdrafts: Trevor Bakker et al., "Data Point: Checking Account Overdraft" (Washington, DC: Consumer Financial Protection Bureau, July 2014), p. 5. http://files.consumerfinance.gov/f/201407_cfpb_ report_data-point_overdrafts.pdf

17   *"opt out" and have transactions:* Board of Governors of the Federal Reserve System, "What You Need to Know: New Overdraft Rules for Debit and ATM Cards" (Washington, DC: Federal Reserve, June 22, 2010). http://www.fnbfs.com/personal/what-you-need-to-know.pdf; Carter Dougherty, "Banks Face Hit from CFPB on $30 Billion in Overdraft Fees," *Bloomberg Businessweek,* August 1, 2014. http://www.businessweek .com/news/2014-07-31/banks-face-hit-on-30-billion-in-overdraft-fees -from-cfpb-rules#p1

maximum amount that can: Bakker et al., "Data Point," p. 4.

renewed its commitment: Heather Landy, *"American Banker's* 2013 Survey of Bank Reputations," *American Banker,* June 25, 2013. http://www .americanbanker.com/magazine/123_7/american-bankers-2013-survey -of-bank-reputations-1060105-1.html

don't recall opting in to: Weinstock et al., "Overdrawn," p. 15.

consumers would rather have: Ibid.; Bakker et al., "Data Point," p. 4; Consumer Financial Protection Bureau, "CFPB Study of Overdraft Programs: A White Paper of Initial Findings" (Washington, DC: CFPB, June 2013), pp. 28–31.

The Pew report relies on a nationally representative sample of 8,042 respondents, age 18 and older, who within the past year had paid overdraft penalty fees, paid overdraft transfer fees, had transactions declined at no cost, or never attempted to spend more than what was in their accounts. The sample was identified using random-digit dialing of households and randomly generated cell phones. Within each household, one single respondent was randomly chosen. Many of the questions asked respondents to remember back in time: "Thinking about the most recent time during which your checking account balance was negative, about how much was the cost of the initial transaction that caused the overdraft?" This method raises some questions about the reliability of survey participants' recall and the potential of providing less-than-accurate answers because of shame or perceived judgment. The CFPB study used a representative sample of account-level and transaction-level checking histories from several large banks. The study reviewed transaction histories for the eighteen-month period spanning January 2011 through June 2012 to determine which account transactions resulted in overdraft or were returned for nonsufficient funds. The study reviewed monthly summaries at the account level in order to limit the analysis to active accounts.

19 *median length of these disclosure:* Pew Charitable Trusts, "Checks and Balances, 2014 Update" (Washington, DC: Pew, April 2014), p. 5. http://www.pewtrusts.org/~/media/assets/2014/04/09/checksandbalancesreport2014.pdf

it's clear that a money order: FIS Global, "FIS Consumer Banking PACE Index: Understanding Performance Against Customer Expectations (PACE)" (Jacksonville, FL: FIS, 2015), p. 6. http://learn.fisglobal.com/closethegaps

A recent FIS Global report showed that 77 percent of banked consumers didn't think banks met their expectations in basic areas such as fair and transparent pricing.

20 *"What a banker might call":* Brett King, *Breaking Banks: The Innovators, Rogues, and Strategists Rebooting Banking* (Singapore: John Wiley & Sons, 2014), p. 137.

2. BANKONOMICS,
OR HOW BANKING CHANGED
AND MOST OF US LOST OUT

25 *Debates about the perils:* Woodrow Wilson, "The Democratic Party's Appeal," *The Independent,* October 24, 1912.

 This special issue includes the feature "The Political Parties: Their Appeal to the Nation by the Presidential Candidates William H. Taft, Woodrow Wilson, Theodore Roosevelt, Eugene V. Debs, Eugene W. Chafin, Arthur E. Reimer."

Thomas Jefferson, Woodrow Wilson: Louis D. Brandeis, *Other People's Money and How the Bankers Use It* (Washington, DC: National Home Library Foundation, 1933).

bankers' self-interested business: Mehrsa Baradaran, *How the Other Half Banks: Exclusion, Exploitation, and the Threat to Democracy* (Cambridge, MA: Harvard University Press, 2015).

the pendulum has swung: Ibid., p. 154.

27 *have dwindled in number:* Victoria Finkle, "Is Dodd-Frank *Really* Killing Small Banks?" *American Banker,* August 18, 2015. http://www.american banker.com/news/law-regulation/is-dodd-frank-really-killing-commu nity-banks-1076157-1.html

30 *"gold mine of checking":* Haberfeld quotation comes from Neil Christy, "To Fee or Not to Fee?" *BankDirector.com Magazine,* June 3, 2011. http:// www.bankdirector.com/magazine/archives/2nd-quarter-2002/to-fee -or-not-to-fee

 The vast majority of overdraft fees — 90 percent — comes from just 5 percent of banks' customers. "Cash-strapped" customers pay an average of $499.02 annually to maintain their checking accounts, compared to the $17.85 spent by high-balance customers. This differential paints a stark picture of how those living on the edge pay stiff penalties for interacting with banks, which have figured out how to make a considerable profit off them. An FDIC study found that account holders in low-income areas were more likely than others to incur multiple overdrafts, raising concerns that consumers from potentially vulnerable groups may shoulder a disproportionate share of overdraft fees and other checking account costs. These customers likely overlap significantly with the consumers who use alternative financial services. So why do policymakers and consumer advocates continue to push banks?

The average charge per: Claes Bell, "Checking Fees Rise to Record Highs in 2012," Bankrate.com, September 24, 2012. http://www.bankrate.com /finance/checking/checking-fees-record-highs-in-2012.aspx#slide=5; "Average Nonsufficient Funds Fee," infographic, Bankrate.com, December 8, 2004. http://www.bankrate.com/brm/news/checkingstudy2004 /interest/nsf-fee.asp

average ATM fees: Allison Ross, "Checking Account Fees Surge to New Highs,"Bankrate.com,2014.http://www.bankrate.com/finance/checking /checking-account-fees-surge-to-new-highs-1.aspx

up to twenty-five dollars: Blake Ellis, "Nine Most Annoying Bank Fees," infographic, *CNN Money,* June 16, 2011. http://money.cnn.com/galleries /2011/pf/1106/gallery.annoying_fees/index.html

31   *the bank will charge:* Pew Charitable Trusts, "Checks and Balances, 2014 Update" (Washington, DC: Pew, April 2014), p. 9.

As of 2010, banks had to allow consumers to opt in to overdraft protection, but research shows that many consumers don't know whether they've opted in or out. As of 2012, 54 percent of consumers who had overdrawn their checking account in the past year with their debit card did not think they had chosen this service.

In 2014, Americans paid: Consumer Financial Protection Bureau, "CFPB Study of Overdraft Programs: A White Paper of Initial Findings" (Washington, DC: CFPB, June 2013), pp. 28–31.

Overdraft fees peaked at just over $37 billion in 2009 and have declined slightly since, partly due to regulation and consumers' choice of more affordable banking options.

32   *Dodd-Frank required banks:* Michael Muckian, "Five Ways to Increase Non-Interest Income," *Credit Union Times,* May 16, 2014. http://www .cutimes.com/2014/05/16/5-ways-to-increase-non-interest-income

nearly half of all consumers: Weinstock et al., "Overdrawn: Persistent Confusion and Concern About Bank Overdraft Practices" (Washington, DC: Pew Charitable Trusts, June 2014).

Pew Charitable Trusts conducted this nationally representative survey of 1,804 adults, to explore their experiences with debit card and ATM overdrafts and to learn about account-holder knowledge, understanding, and attitudes about overdraft fees.

Having a checking account is: First Data and Marketing Strategies International, "How Financial Institutions Can Build Customer Relationships and Long-Term Success," white paper, 2011, p. 6. https://www.firstdata.com/downloads/thought-leadership/fi-segmentation-wp4.pdf

all of which generate: Alan Friesen, "Core Deposits: More Customers Equals More Profits: The Bank with the Most Customers Wins!" *Bank Director,* 2nd quarter, 2009. http://www.haberfeld.com/pdf/AlanView pointArticle.pdf

33 *banks are doing everything:* Martha C. White, "Why Banks Love Debit Cards Again," *Time,* March 28, 2013. http://business.time .com/2013/03/28/why-banks-love-debit-cards-again/

Despite these two huge suits: Pew Charitable Trusts, "Checks and Balances," p. 3.

34 *"have lost an essential tool":* Jessica Silver-Greenberg and Robert Gebeloff, "Arbitration Everywhere: Stacking the Deck of Justice," *New York Times,* DealBook blog, October 31, 2015. http://www.nytimes .com/2015/11/01/business/dealbook/arbitration-everywhere-stacking -the-deck-of-justice.html

"they tend to do them": Ibid.

George Akerlof and Robert Shiller: George A. Akerlof and Robert Shiller, *Phishing for Phools: The Economics of Manipulation and Deception* (Princeton, NJ: Princeton University Press), p. xi.

36 *made it a common catchphrase:* Renee Haltom, "Failure of Continental Illinois," *Federal Reserve History,* November 22, 2013. http://www.federal reservehistory.org/Events/DetailView/47

37 *"other people's money": Other People's Money* is the title of Louis Brandeis's 1914 treatise.

"virtue-less cycle": Edmund Conway, "Bank of England Says Financiers Are Fuelling an Economic Doom Loop," *The Telegraph,* November 6, 2009. http://www.telegraph.co.uk/finance/financialcrisis/6516579 /Bank-of-England-says-financiers-are-fuelling-an-economic-doom -loop.html

the remaining 6,395 banks: Ryan Tracy, "Tally of US Banks Sinks to Record Low," *Wall Street Journal,* December 3, 2013. http://online.wsj.com/articles/SB10001424052702304579404579232343313671258; Steve Schafer, "Five Biggest US Banks Control Nearly Half of Industry's $15 Trillion in Assets," Forbes.com blog, December 3, 2014. http://www.forbes.com/sites/steveschaefer/2014/12/03/five-biggest-banks-trillion-jpmorgan-citi-bankamerica/#1dfa5ee51d43

declined by 85 percent: Finkle, "Is Dodd-Frank *Really* Killing Small Banks?"

38   *opening checking accounts:* Federal Reserve Bank of Chicago, "Chicago Fed History: 1940–1964" (Chicago Fed, 2015). https://www.chicagofed.org/utilities/about-us/history/chicago-fed-history-1940-1964

"the banking industry that": Paul Krugman, "Making Banking Boring," *New York Times,* April 9, 2009. http://www.nytimes.com/2009/04/10/opinion/10krugman.html?_r=0

"3-6-3 era" of banking: Federal Reserve Bank of Chicago, "Chicago Fed History: 1940–1964."

economic equivalent of 9/11: Robert G. Kaiser, *Act of Congress: How America's Essential Institution Works, and How It Doesn't* (New York: Vintage Books, 2014), p. 13.

39   *"a save-your-country moment":* Ibid., p. 9.

"make markets for consumer": Consumer Financial Protection Bureau, "About Us" (Washington, DC: CFPD, updated March 9, 2015). http://www.consumerfinance.gov/the-bureau/

wrote an article titled: Elizabeth Warren, "Unsafe at Any Rate," *Democracy: A Journal of Ideas,* no. 5 (Summer 2007). http://www.democracyjournal.org/5/6528.php?page=all

It is impossible to buy: Ibid.

40   *show their constituents that:* Kaiser, *Act of Congress,* p. 134.

voters wanted policymakers: Ibid.

Before the CFPB, four federal: The Office of the Controller of the Currency (OCC), the Office of Thrift Supervision (OTS), the Federal Deposit Insurance Corporation (FDIC), and the Federal Reserve Board (the Fed).

"a new and powerful agency": The White House, Office of the Press Secretary, "Remarks by the President on 21st-Century Financial Regulatory

Reform," press release, June 17, 2009. https://www.whitehouse.gov/the
-press-office/remarks-president-regulatory-reform

Until we got the CFPB: Ellen Seidman, interview by Lisa Servon, September 30, 2014.

    The CFPB also has extremely wide jurisdiction. Unlike the other regu-
latory agencies, the CFPB deals both with banks and with alternative financial-services providers. The CFPB writes the rules for everyone, even
if it doesn't examine everyone.

41   *"competed with each other"*: Kaiser, *Act of Congress*, p. 192.

    they just kept adding: Ellen Seidman, interview by Lisa Servon, Septem-
ber 30, 2014.

    people who work to ensure: Laura Noonan, "Banks Face Pushback over
Surging Compliance and Regulatory Costs," *Financial Times*, May 28,
2015.   https://next.ft.com/content/e1323e18-0478-11e5-95ad-00144feab
dc0

    In 2015, the *Financial Times* estimated that some banks spend as much
as $4 billion annually for compliance activities ranging from internal con-
trols to prevent money laundering to producing data for financial stress
tests.

42   *an acceptable credit risk*: Kenneth T. Jackson, *Crabgrass Frontier: The
Suburbanization of the United States* (New York: Oxford University Press,
1985).

    unsuitable for investing: Ibid.

    residents of these redlined: Jim Greer, "Race and Mortgage Redlining
in the United States," paper presented at the Western Political Science
Association Meetings, Portland, OR, March 22–24, 2012. http://wpsa
.research.pdx.edu/meet/2012/greer.pdf

    so-called "changing neighborhoods": Michael Westgate, *Gale Force — Gale
Cincotta: The Battles for Disclosure and Community Reinvestment* (Cha-
tham, MA: Education and Resources Group, Inc., 2011), p. 147.

    savings and loan banks: Ibid., p. 41.

    Research on discrimination in: Sandra Phillips, "The Subprime Mortgage
Calamity and the African American Woman," *Review of Black Political Economy*, vol. 39, no. 2 (November 15, 2011). http://link.springer.com
/article/10.1007/s12114-011-9107-1

African American and Latino borrowers: US Department of Justice, "Justice Department Reaches $335 Million Settlement to Resolve Allegations of Lending Discrimination by Countrywide Financial Corporation," press release, updated June 22, 2015. http://www.justice.gov/usao-cdca /dojcountrywide-settlement-information

eight major banks caught: Taylor Gordon, "Eight Major American Banks That Got Caught Discriminating Against Black People," *Atlanta Black Star,* March 3, 2015. http://atlantablackstar.com/2015/03/03/8-major -american-banks-that-got-caught-discriminating-against-black-people/

43   *protest credit discrimination:* The Truth in Lending Act (TILA) of 1968, the Fair Credit Reporting Act of 1970, and the Equal Credit Opportunity Act (ECOA) of 1974 all aimed to level the playing field for people seeking all kinds of loans.

reforms aimed at declaring: Baradaran, *How the Other Half Banks,* p. 49.

it wasn't because they were: Jonathan Macey and Geoffrey Miller, "The Community Reinvestment Act: An Economic Analysis," *Virginia Law Review,* vol. 79, no. 102 (March 1993): 302. http://digitalcommons.law .yale.edu/cgi/viewcontent.cgi?article=2662&context=fss_papers

44   *higher broker fees than those:* US Federal Trade Commission, "FTC, DOJ, and HUD Announce Action to Combat Abusive Lending Practices," press release, March 30, 2000. https://www.ftc.gov/news-events/press -releases/2000/03/ftc-doj-and-hud-announce-action-combat-abusive -lending-practices

after controlling for borrower: Robert B. Avery, Kenneth P. Brevoort, and Glenn B. Canner, "Higher-Priced Home Lending and the 2005 HDMA Data," *Federal Reserve Board Bulletin,* September 18, 2006, revised. http://www.federalreserve.gov/pubs/Bulletin/2006/hmda/default .htm

offered subprime mortgages: Phillips, "The Subprime Mortgage Calamity and the African American Woman."

comparable white male applicants: Ibid.

more likely to be unbanked: Michael Corkery and Jessica Silver-Greenberg, "Banks Reject New York City IDs, Leaving 'Unbanked' on Sidelines," *New York Times,* December 23, 2015. http://www.nytimes .com/2015/12/24/business/dealbook/banks-reject-new-york-city-ids -leaving-unbanked-on-sidelines.html?ref=topics&_r=0

3. THE NEW MIDDLE CLASS

47 *"Middle-Class Betrayal?"*: Seth Freed Wessler, "Middle-Class Betrayal? Why Working Hard Is No Longer Enough in America," *NBC News,* March 16, 2015. http://www.nbcnews.com/feature/in-plain-sight /middle-class-betrayal-why-working-hard-no-longer-enough-america -n291741

"Dear Middle Class": Lynn Stuart Paramore, "Dear Middle Class: Welcome to Poverty," *Salon,* January 8, 2014. http://www.salon .com/2014/01/08/dear_middle_class_welcome_to_poverty_partner/

middle class is "shrinking": T. J. Raphael, "The American Middle Class Is Shrinking," *Public Radio International,* December 13, 2015. http://www .pri.org/stories/2015-12-13/american-middle-class-shrinking

"screwed": Kevin Drum, "Chart of the Day: Even the Rich Think the Middle Class Is Getting Screwed," *Mother Jones,* March 15, 2015. http:// www.motherjones.com/kevin-drum/2015/03/chart-day-even-rich -think-middle-class-getting-screwed

"doing worse than you": Haley Sweetland Edwards, "The Middle Class Is Doing Worse Than You Think," *Time,* April 8, 2015. http://time .com/3814048/income-inequality-middle-class/

"turning proletarian": Joel Kotkin, "The US Middle Class Is Turning Proletarian," *Forbes,* February 16, 2014. http://www.forbes.com/sites /joelkotkin/2014/02/16/the-u-s-middle-class-is-turning-proletarian /#2715e4857a0b284313c82f29

"the precariat, an emerging class": Guy Standing, *A Precariat Charter: From Denizens to Citizens* (London: Bloomsbury, 2014), p. 1.

"unnecessary and amoral": Ibid., p. x.

48 *Nearly half of Americans now:* Christopher Matthews, "Nearly Half of America Lives Paycheck-to-Paycheck," *Time,* January 30, 2014. http:// time.com/2742/nearly-half-of-america-lives-paycheck-to-paycheck/

Nearly half could not come: Kasey Wiedrich et al., "Treading Water in the Deep End: Findings from the 2014 Assets and Opportunity Scorecard" (Washington, DC: Corporation for Enterprise Development, January 2016). http://assetsandopportunity.org/scorecard/about/main_findings/

"enjoys less opportunity": Ronald Brownstein, "Meet the New Mid-

dle Class: Who They Are, What They Want, and What They Fear," *The Atlantic,* April 25, 2013. http://www.theatlantic.com/business /archive/2013/04/meet-the-new-middle-class-who-they-are-what-they -want-and-what-they-fear/275307/

"redefined to mean not": FTI Consulting, "Allstate/National Journal Heartland Monitor XVI Key Findings," memorandum (Washington, DC: FTI Consulting, April 15, 2013). http://heartlandmonitor.com/wp -content/uploads/2013/04/Tab-5-ASNJ-Heartland-Monitor-16-Key -Findings-Memo-04-15-13-1230-PM-ET.pdf

50   *"in the eighteen-month period"*: Tim Ranney and Mike Cook, "Chang- ing Patterns and Behaviors of Unsecured Short-Term Loan Consumers" (Clearwater, FL: Clarity Services, 2011). https://www.nonprime101.com /wp-content/uploads/2015/02/1376498431_Clarity-Services -Consumers-Behavior-White-Paper.pdf

2015 study using updated: MDRC (Manpower Demonstration Research Corporation), "The Subprime Lending Database Exploration Study: Ini- tial Findings," unpublished paper (New York: MDRC, December 23, 2015).

lost their prime score: Ibid.

"More and more economic risk": Jacob Hacker, *The Great Risk Shift: The New Economic Insecurity and the Decline of the American Dream* (Oxford, UK: Oxford University Press, 2008).

51   *"mainstream American opinion"*: Timothy Noah, *The Great Divergence: America's Growing Inequality Crisis and What We Can Do About It* (New York: Bloomsbury Press, 2012), p. 18.

"wanted to raise the marginal tax": Ibid.

52   *has been larger in the "lost"*: Lawrence Mishel, "The Wedges Between Pro- ductivity and Median Compensation Growth" (Washington, DC: Eco- nomic Policy Institute, April 26, 2012). http://www.epi.org/publication /ib330-productivity-vs-compensation/

worker compensation has increased: Alyssa Davis and Lawrence Mishel, "CEO Pay Continues to Rise as Typical Workers Are Paid Less" (Wash- ington, DC: Economic Policy Institute, June 12, 2014). http://www.epi .org/publication/ceo-pay-continues-to-rise/

worked more than one job: Jonathan Morduch and Rachel Schneider,

"Spikes and Dips: How Income Uncertainty Affects Households," *US Financial Diaries,* October 2013. http://www.usfinancialdiaries.org/issue1-spikes

The *US Financial Diaries* project collected detailed financial data from two hundred low- and moderate-income families in the United States over the course of a year. More on the methodology here: http://www.usfinancialdiaries.org/issue2-method917

53 *individuals are working part-time:* Rob Valletta and Leila Bengali, "What's Behind the Increase in Part-Time Work?" *Federal Reserve Bank of San Francisco Economic Letter,* August 26, 2013. http://www.frbsf.org/economic-research/publications/economic-letter/2013/august/part-time-work-employment-increase-recession/13/

less bargaining power to negotiate: Kathleen Madigan, "The High Share of Part-Time Workers Helps Explain Weak Wage Growth," *Wall Street Journal,* May 8, 2015. http://blogs.wsj.com/economics/2015/05/08/the-high-share-of-part-time-workers-helps-explain-weak-wage-growth/

number has not changed: Ibid.

54 *"we become less effective":* Sendhi Mullainathan and Eldar Shafir, *Scarcity: The New Science of Having Less and How It Defines Our Lives* (New York: Times Books, 2013), p. 15.

Pay attention next time: Dunkin' Donuts "crew members" typically start at minimum wage. See Dunkin' Donuts Crew Member application at http://www.job-applications.com/dunkin-donuts-crew-member/

Several B & N positions start at or near minimum wage. See Barnes & Noble job application at http://www.job-applications.com/barnes-and-noble-application/

compared to 27 percent: Janelle Jones and John Schmitt, "Update on Low-Wage Workers," CEPR blog, June 7, 2014. http://cepr.net/blogs/cepr-blog/update-low-wage-worker-1979-2013

more than half are women: David Cooper and Doug Hall, "Raising the Federal Minimum Wage to $10.10 Would Give Working Families, and the Overall Economy, a Much-Needed Boost" (Washington, DC: Economic Policy Institute, March 13, 2013). http://www.epi.org/publication/bp357-federal-minimum-wage-increase/

55 *even after you account:* Ibid.; Lawrence Mishel, "Low-Wage Workers Have Far More Education Than They Did in 1968, Yet They Make Far

Less," *Economic Snapshot* (Washington, DC: Economic Policy Institute, January 23, 2014). http://www.epi.org/publication/wage-workers-education-1968/

entirely failed to factor in: Laura Shin, "Why McDonald's Employee Budget Has Everyone up in Arms," *Forbes,* July 18, 2013. http://www.forbes.com/sites/laurashin/2013/07/18/why-mcdonalds-employee-budget-has-everyone-up-in-arms/

"employers shifted away": Amy Traub and Catherine Ruetschlin, "The Plastic Safety Net: 2012" (New York: Demos, May 22, 2012). http://www.demos.org/publication/plastic-safety-net

56 *More than three-quarters:* Ray Boshara, William Emmons, and Bryan J. Noeth, "The Demographics of Wealth: How Age, Education, and Race Separate Thrivers from Strugglers in Today's Economy" (St. Louis: Federal Reserve Bank of St. Louis, February 2015). https://www.stlouisfed.org/~/media/Files/PDFs/HFS/essays/HFS-Essay-1-2015-Race-Ethnicity-and-Wealth.pdf

combined to make these: Ray Boshara, "Policy Perspectives on Fostering Consumer Financial Health," paper presented at Emerge Conference, Los Angeles, June 4, 2014. http://cdn.americanbanker.com/media/pdfs/CFSI14-Boshara.pdf

violating the federal Age: Jonathan Stempel, "US Agency Claims Darden Won't Hire 'Old White Guys' for Dining Chain," Reuters, February 12, 2015. http://www.reuters.com/article/darden-lawsuit-idusl1n0vm25r20150212#vykrxzo7jyszt9vy.97

57 *many older Americans:* Helaine Olen, "The Semi-Retirement Myth," *Slate,* March 2, 2015. http://www.slate.com/articles/business/moneybox/2015/03/baby_boomers_delaying_retirement_it_s_a_myth_because_retirement_is_inevitable.html

59 *cost of living increases:* Pew Research Center, "Views of Job Market Tick Up, No Rise in Economic Optimism" (Washington, DC: Pew, September 4, 2014). http://www.people-press.org/2014/09/04/views-of-job-market-tick-up-no-rise-in-economic-optimism/

medical debt makes up: Mike Patton, "US Health Care Costs Rise Faster Than Inflation," *Forbes,* June 29, 2015. http://www.forbes.com/sites/mikepatton/2015/06/29/u-s-health-care-costs-rise-faster-than-inflation/

That may sound manageable: Hashem Said, "High Price Paid by Americans with Onerous Medical Debt," *Al Jazeera America,* June 5, 2015. http://america.aljazeera.com/watch/shows/ajam-presents-hard -earned/articles/2015/6/5/high-price-crippling-medical-debt.html; Board of Governors of the Federal Reserve System, "Report on the Economic Well-Being of US Households in 2014" (Washington, DC: Board of Governors of the Federal Reserve System, May 2015). http://www.federal reserve.gov/econresdata/2014-report-economic-well-being-us-house holds-201505.pdf; Bourree Lam, "US Housing Costs: Up, Up, Up, Up," *The Atlantic,* August 22, 2014. http://www.theatlantic.com/business /archive/2015/08/shelter-cpi-housing-rent-inflation/401849/

struggle to pay off a $400: Consumer Financial Protection Bureau, "Consumer Credit Reports: A Study of Medical and Non-medical Collections" (Washington, DC: CFPB, December 2014). http://files.consumerfinance. gov/f/201412_cfpb_reports_consumer-credit-medical-and-non-med ical-collections.pdf; Consumer Financial Protection Bureau, "CFPB Spotlights Concerns with Medical Debt Collection and Reporting," press release, December 11, 2014. http://www.consumerfinance.gov /newsroom/cfpb-spotlights-concerns-with-medical-debt-collection -and-reporting/

housing prices went up: Lam, "US Housing Costs: Up, Up, Up, Up."

60 *prices have grown by:* The Data Team, "Daily Chart: American House Prices Reality Check," *The Economist,* November 3, 2015. http://www .economist.com/blogs/graphicdetail/2015/11/daily-chart-0

increased from 37 percent: Allison Charette et al., "Projecting Trends in Severely Cost-Burdened Renters, 2015–25" (Cambridge, MA: Enterprise Community Partners and Harvard Joint Center for Housing Studies, September 2015). https://s3.amazonaws.com/KSPProd/ERC_ Upload/0100886.pdf

families that devote more: US Department of Housing and Urban Development, "Affordable Housing" (Washington, DC: HUD, no date). http:// portal.hud.gov/hudportal/HUD?src=/program_offices/comm_planning /affordablehousing/; Harvard Joint Center for Housing Studies, "Record Number of American Renters Feel the Strain of Housing Cost Burdens," interactive map (Cambridge, MA: Harvard Joint Center for Housing Studies, June 2015). http://harvard-cga.maps.arcgis.com/apps/Map Series/index.html?appid=0ffea521479a4585b383169bf00e2aa9

"in thirty-three states": Elise Gould and Tanyell Cooke, "High-Quality

Child Care Is Out of Reach for Working Families" (Washington, DC: Economic Policy Institute, October 6, 2015). http://www.epi.org/publication /child-care-affordability/#introduction-and-key-findings)

Childcare costs exceeded rent: EPI basic family-budget thresholds measure the income families need in order to attain a modest yet adequate standard of living in 618 communities. EPI's basic family-budget threshold for a two-parent, two-child family ranges from $49,114 (Morristown, Tennessee) to $106,493 (Washington, DC). The median family budget area for this family type is $63,741.

"have done little or nothing": Pew Research Center, "Most Say Government Policies Since Recession Have Done Little to Help Middle Class, Poor" (Washington, DC: Pew, March 4, 2015). http://www.people-press .org/2015/03/04/most-say-government-policies-since-recession-have -done-little-to-help-middle-class-poor/

4. THE CREDIT TRAP: "BAD DEBT" AND REAL LIFE

63   *"finance a 'want'":* Suze Orman, "IOU 101," *O, The Oprah Magazine,* July 2008. http://www.oprah.com/money/Good-Debt-or-Bad-Debt-Financial -Freedom-by-Suze-Orman

64   *86 percent had to take on:* Amy Traub and Catherine Ruetschlin, "The Plastic Safety Net: 2012" (New York: Demos, May 22, 2012), p. 10. http:// www.demos.org/publication/plastic-safety-net

The average household: Erin El Issa, "2015 American Household Credit Card Debt Study," *Nerd Wallet.* http://www.nerdwallet.com/blog/credit -card-data/average-credit-card-debt-household/#Vp5zv1L9zfc

social norms associated with: Carl Packman, *Loan Sharks: The Rise and Rise of Payday Lending* (Cambridge, UK: Searching Finance Books, 2012).

against "moral and natural law": Thomas Aquinas, *Summa Theologica,* translated by the Fathers of the English Dominican Province (London: R. T. Washburne, Ltd., 1918), pp. 330–40; reprinted in Roy C. Cave & Herbert H. Coulson, *A Source Book for Medieval Economic History* (New York: Biblo & Tannen, 1965), p. 182. http://legacy.fordham.edu/halsall /source/aquinas-usury.asp

65   *Interest rates embody:* Lauren K. Saunders, "Why 36 Percent: The History, Use, and Purpose of the 36 Percent Interest Rate Cap" (Boston: National Consumer Law Center, April 2013). https://www.nclc.org/images/pdf/pr-reports/why36pct.pdf

Until the 1920s, employers: Ibid.

hide from borrowers the true cost: Ibid.

all states capped interest: Ibid.

In the late nineteenth and early twentieth centuries, loan sharks dominated the small-dollar market. The usury rate for larger business loans was 6 percent, which resulted in higher returns than the amounts earned on small loans. The 36 percent rate cap was an effort to entice legitimate lenders to participate in the small-dollar market; the higher interest rate would make small loans profitable and therefore attractive to larger lenders.

based on lenders' personal: Federal Reserve Bank of Boston, "Credit History: The Evolution of Consumer Credit in America," *The Ledger,* Spring/Summer 2004. https://www.bostonfed.org/education/ledger/ledger04/sprsum/credhistory.pdf

dealt with only the well-to-do: Ibid.

if, in his opinion: Louis Hyman, *Debtor Nation: The History of America in Red Ink* (Princeton, NJ: Princeton University Press, 2011).

66   *required that a man cosign:* Rose Eveleth, "Forty Years Ago, Women Had a Hard Time Getting Credit Cards," *Smithsonian Magazine,* January 8, 2014. http://www.smithsonianmag.com/smart-news/forty-years-ago-women-had-a-hard-time-getting-credit-cards-180949289/?no-ist

a corporate employer: Hyman, *Debtor Nation.*

discounted a woman's income: Eveleth, "Forty Years Ago."

women continue to pay more: Gary R. Mottola, "In Our Best Interest: Women, Financial Literacy, and Credit Card Behavior" (Washington, DC: FINRA Investor Education Foundation, April 2012). http://www.finrafoundation.org/web/groups/foundation/@foundation/documents/foundation/p125971.pdf

faced discrimination when: Hyman, *Debtor Nation.*

credit became an indispensable: Federal Reserve Bank of Boston, "Credit History."

finance these purchases: Eli M. Remolona and Kurt C. Wulfekuhler, "Finance Companies, Bank Competition, and Niche Markets," *Quarterly Review, Federal Reserve Bank of New York,* Summer 1992, p. 25. https://www.newyorkfed.org/medialibrary/media/research/quarterly_review/1992v17/v17n2article3.pdf

67 *gave American consumers:* Andrea Ryan, Gunnar Trumbull, and Peter Tufano, "A Brief Postwar History of US Consumer Finance," Harvard Business School Working Paper 11-058 (Cambridge, MA: HBS, 2010). http://www.hbs.edu/faculty/Publication%20Files/11-058.pdf

cash, checks, and money orders: By 2008, 57 percent of consumer payment activity was conducted electronically — representing $4.5 trillion spread across seventy-five billion transactions. See Ryan et al., "A Brief Postwar History of US Consumer Finance."

the first card issuer that: Federal Reserve Bank of Boston, "Credit History."

Diners Club was a "charge card" rather than a credit card, as it didn't actually offer credit to its members; it was effectively a deferred payment scheme whereby customers would pay the amount they charged at the end of the payment period. But its development was an important piece of the growth and evolution of the credit card industry as a whole. See Lana Swartz, "Gendered Transactions: Identity and Payment at Midcentury," *WSQ: Women's Studies Quarterly,* vol. 42, nos. 1 and 2 (Spring/Summer 2014). https://muse.jhu.edu/journals/wsq/v042/42.1-2.swartz.pdf

heralded the expansion: Federal Reserve Bank of Boston, "Credit History."

Many states eviscerated: Saunders, "Why 36 Percent."

The Supreme Court case *Marquette v. First Omaha* permitted states to charge the interest rate of their home state rather than the rate in the state where the loan was being made. As a result, many states repealed their interest rates in order to attract banks to locate there. In addition, severe inflation reduced the supply of credit; getting rid of rate caps allowed more "product" to flow into the market. See *Marquette Nat. Bank v. First of Omaha Service Corp.,* 439 US 299 (1978).

loopholes that enable: Colin Morgan-Cross and Marieka Klawitter, "Effects of State Payday Loan Price Caps and Regulation" (Seattle: Evans School of Public Affairs, University of Washington, December 2, 2011). https://

evans.uw.edu/sites/default/files/public/STATE%20PAYDAY%20LOAN
%20PRICE%20CAPS%20%26%20REGULATION.pdf

Until credit scores began: Dean Foust and Aaron Pressman, "Credit
Scores: Not So Magic Numbers," *Bloomberg Business,* February 6, 2008.
http://www.bloomberg.com/bw/stories/2008-02-06/credit-scores-not-
so-magic-numbers; Philadelphia Media Network, "History of Credit
Scores," philly.com, February 26, 2008. http://www.philly.com/philly
/business/cars/research/general_cars/General_History_of_Credit_
Scores.html

68   *connection between card issuers:* Following enactment of the Truth in
Lending Act, midsize and regional retail chains ended their own credit
card programs and began accepting bank credit cards. Banks were increasingly supplementing interest income with user and retailer fees;
therefore they were less sensitive to limits on interest rates. Midsize retailers and regional chains couldn't compete. In a countermove, by the
late 1970s large retail lenders opened banks and moved into the general credit card business. See Ryan et al., "A Brief Postwar History of US
Consumer Finance."

policy has abetted this trend: Ibid.

virtually eliminated caps: Jose Garcia, "Borrowing to Make Ends Meet: The
Rapid Growth of Credit Card Debt in America" (Washington, DC: Demos,
November 7, 2007). http://www.demos.org/publication/borrowing
-make-ends-meet-rapid-growth-credit-card-debt-america

allowing them to be determined: Ibid.

average late-payment fee: Ibid.

By 2009, it had climbed: Index Credit Cards, "Credit Card Late Fees Average $34.09, Over-the-Limit Fees Average $36.53," indexcreditcards.com,
October 6, 2009. http://www.indexcreditcards.com/creditcardlatefees/

69   *"bring money out of the shadows":* Bari Tessler Linden, "The Antidote
to Money Shame," Bari Tessler Linden blog, November 7, 2013. http://
baritessler.com/2013/11/money-shame/

"flip your rich switch": Nan Akasha, "Money Archetypes and Guilt and
Shame," Nan Akasha blog, May 29, 2012. http://www.nanakasha.com
/money-archetypes-guilt-shame

rise in bankruptcy filings: Jill Lepore, "The Warren Brief," *The New Yorker,*

April 21, 2014. http://www.newyorker.com/magazine/2014/04/21/the-warren-brief

left one partner economically: David Himmelstein et al., "Medical Bankruptcy in the United States, 2007: Results of a National Study," *American Journal of Medicine,* vol. 22, no. 9 (August 2009). http://www.amjmed.com/article/S0002-9343(09)00404-5/pdf

cut down on abusive: Kathleen Day, "Bankruptcy Bill Passes; Bush Expected to Sign," *Washington Post,* April 15, 2005. http://www.washingtonpost.com/wp-dyn/articles/A53688-2005Apr14.html

70   *claims about bankruptcy fraud:* Ibid.; Lepore, "The Warren Brief."

to entice new categories: The "democratization" of credit began in the 1970s, following regulatory changes requiring banks to avoid discriminatory lending practices and to meet the needs of local communities. The 1978 Supreme Court decision in *Marquette v. First Omaha* allowed credit card companies to charge whatever rate was legal in the state where they were based and permitted banks to charge higher interest rates to riskier borrowers. This increase in credit availability was also facilitated by growth of markets where lenders could sell their loans. See S. Mitra Kalita, "The 'Democratization of Credit' Is Over: Now It's Payback Time," *Wall Street Journal,* October 9, 2009. http://www.wsj.com/articles/SB125511860883676713S

only 43 percent: Sandra E. Black and Donald P. Morgan, "Meet the New Borrowers," *Current Issues in Economics and Finance: Federal Reserve Bank of New York,* vol. 5, no. 3 (February 1999). http://www.nyfedeconomists.org/research/current_issues/ci5-3.pdf

that number had risen to: Ibid.

twenty solicitations for every: Garcia, "Borrowing to Make Ends Meet."

defined as having credit: Nick Clements, "Bad Credit? Banks Want to Give You Credit Cards," *Forbes,* May 20, 2015. http://www.forbes.com/sites/nickclements/2015/05/20/bad-credit-banks-want-to-give-you-credit-cards/2/#43f366d966d4

work with less seniority: Black and Morgan, "Meet the New Borrowers."

riskier than traditional ones: Ibid.

71   *to hold unskilled jobs:* Ibid.

median outstanding credit card: Board of Governors of the Federal Reserve System, "Report to the Congress on the Profitability of Credit Card Operations of Depository Institutions" (Washington, DC: Board of Governors of the Federal Reserve, June 2014). https://www.federalreserve .gov/publications/other-reports/files/ccprofit2014.pdf

The average credit-card interest rate declined slightly during this same period, from 18.02 percent in 1989 to 15.79 percent in 1995.

quickly racked up debt: Black and Morgan, "Meet the New Borrowers."

72   *paying $15 billion:* The CARD Act put an end to this practice in 2009.

Citibank had sold its: Michael Barr, ed., *No Slack: The Financial Lives of Low-Income Americans* (Washington, DC: Brookings Institution Press, 2012), p. 284.

73   *to cut way back on:* Associated Press, "Citigroup Ordered to Refund $700 Million in Credit-Card Case," *New York Times,* DealBook blog, July 21, 2015. http://www.nytimes.com/2015/07/22/business/dealbook /citigroup-must-refund-700-million-in-credit-case.html?_r=0

their credit limits fell: Larry Santucci, "A Tale of Two Vintages: Credit Limit Management Before and After the CARD Act and Great Recession," Federal Reserve Bank of Philadelphia, Payment Cards Center, Discussion Paper 15-01, February 2015. http://papers.ssrn.com/sol3/papers .cfm?abstract_id=2646080

Between 2008 and 2010, average credit limits fell by 14 percent on open accounts and 32 percent on new accounts.

people had already begun: Ibid.

pay for the kinds of things: Traub and Ruetschlin, "The Plastic Safety Net."

half of households: Ibid.

experiencing the highest: Catherine Ruetschlin and Dedrick Asante-Muhammad, "The Challenge of Credit Card Debt for the African American Middle Class" (Washington, DC: Demos and NAACP, December 2013), p. 3. http://www.demos.org/sites/default/files/publications/CreditCard Debt-Demos_NAACP_0.pdf

Over half of African American: Ibid.

74   *compared with 85 percent:* Ibid., p. 2.

own one dollar for every: Rakesh Kochhar, Richard Fry, and Paul Taylor, "Wealth Gaps Rise to Record Highs Between Blacks, Whites, and His-

panics" (Washington, DC: Pew Research Center, July 2011). http://www
.pewsocialtrends.org/2011/07/26/wealth-gaps-rise-to-record-highs
-between-whites-blacks-hispanics/

four times more likely: Traub and Ruetschlin, "The Plastic Safety Net,"
p. 11.

the result of cards being canceled: Ibid.

1 percent used funds from: Ibid.

75   *his database of subprime borrowers:* While I could not find evidence to
support Ranney's belief, I did talk with Larry Santucci, a researcher at
the Federal Reserve of Philadelphia. Santucci researches credit cards
and thought Ranney's hypothesis is plausible as one fact that has contributed to the overall decline in credit scores.

two-thirds of the resources: Scott L. Fulford, "How Important Is Variability in Consumer Credit Limits?" Federal Reserve Bank of Boston
Working Paper No. 14-8, May 2014, p. 4. https://www.bostonfed.org
/economic/wp/wp2014/wp1408.htm

cut off many consumers: Ibid.

overall credit limits fell: Ibid., p. 1.

paying more than 20 percent: Greater numbers of African Americans and
Latinos paid these high rates; 33 percent and 34 percent, respectively.
See Traub and Ruetschlin, "The Plastic Safety Net," p. 8.

much higher interest rates: Kelly Dilworth, "Average Credit Card Interest Rates Rise to 15.07 Percent," CreditCards.com, October 2014.
http://www.creditcards.com/credit-card-news/interest-rate-report
-100114-up-2121.php

5. PAYDAY LOANS:
MAKING THE BEST OF POOR OPTIONS

77   *Payday loans are illegal:* For the number of states where payday loans
are illegal, see Pew Charitable Trusts, "State Payday Loan Regulation and Usage Rates" (Washington, DC: Pew, July 11, 2012). http://
www.pewtrusts.org/en/multimedia/data-visualizations/2014/~/media
/data%20visualizations/interactives/2014/state%20payday%20loan%20
regulation%20and%20usage%20rates/report/state_payday_loan_
regulation_and_usage_rates.pdf

usage has increased dramatically: For a summary of the emergence of the payday loan industry, see Bruce Miller (Managing Director, Stephens), "Credit: Where We Are and Where We're Going," paper presented at FiSCA at 25 Conference, Chicago, October 2012.

growing from a $10 billion: For data on the growth of the payday loan industry, see Bruce Miller (Managing Director, Stephens), "Mergers and Acquisitions Activity in the Alternative Financial-Services Industry: The Current Environment and Thoughts on the Future," paper presented at FiSCA Conference, Chicago, October 2012.

82   *Center for Responsible Lending:* Center for Responsible Lending website.

86   *more payday lending stores:* Christopher Lewis Peterson and Steve Graves, "Usury Law and the Christian Right: Faith-Based Political Power and the Geography of American Payday Loan Regulation," *Catholic University Law Review,* vol. 57, no. 3 (2008).

87   *Banks have retreated from:* Federal Deposit Insurance Corporation, "The FDIC's Small-Dollar-Loan Pilot Program: A Case Study After One Year," *FDIC Quarterly,* vol. 3, no. 2 (2009). https://www.fdic.gov/bank/analytical/quarterly/2009_vol3_2/SmallDollar.pdf

88   *two possible answers:* I cannot summarize all of the academic literature here, so I have done my best to provide a reasonable summary. For more studies that find that payday lending exacerbates financial distress, see Brian Melzer, "The Real Costs of Credit Access: Evidence from the Payday Lending Market," *Quarterly Journal of Economics,* vol. 126, no. 1 (2011); Dennis Campbell, Asis Martinez-Jerez, and Peter Tufano, "Bouncing out of the Banking System: An Empirical Analysis of Involuntary Bank Account Closures," *Journal of Banking and Finance,* vol. 36, no. 4 (April 2012); Scott E. Carrell and Jonathan Zinman, "In Harm's Way? Payday Loan Access and Military Personnel Performance," *Review of Financial Studies,* vol. 24, no. 9 (2014); Paige Skiba and Jeremy Tobacman, "Do Payday Loans Cause Bankruptcy?" Vanderbilt Law and Economics Research Paper No. 11-13, November 9, 2009.

Studies finding that payday lending can be beneficial include Adair Morse, "Payday Lenders: Heroes or Villains?" *Journal of Financial Economics,* vol. 102, no. 1 (October 2011); Bart Wilson et al., "An Experimental Analysis of the Demand for Payday Loans," *Social Science Research Network,* April 28, 2010; Dean Karlan and Jonathan Zinman, "Expanding Credit Access: Using Randomized Supply Decisions to Estimate the Impacts," *Review of Financial Studies,* vol. 23, no. 1 (2010); Donald Morgan and Michael R. Strain, "Payday Holiday: How Households Fare After Payday Credit Bans," Federal Reserve Bank of New York Staff Report No. 309, February 2008; Jonathan Zinman, "Restricting Consumer Credit Access: Household Survey Evidence on Effects Around the Oregon Rate Cap," *Social Science Research Network Electronic Journal*, vol. 34, no. 3 (November 2008).

failed to provide the small-dollar: Morse, "Payday Lenders: Heroes or Villains?"

the event of a financial setback: Wilson et al., "An Experimental Analysis of the Demand for Payday Loans."

benefits of the loans: Morgan and Strain, "Payday Holiday"; Gregory Elliehausen, "An Analysis of Consumers' Use of Payday Loans," Financial Services Research Program Monograph No. 41, January 2009; Marc Anthony Fusaro and Patricia J. Cirillo, "Do Payday Loans Trap Consumers in a Cycle of Debt?" working paper, November 16, 2011; Morse, "Payday Lenders: Heroes or Villains?"

borrowers who use payday: Alex Kaufman, "Payday Lending Regulation," Finance and Economics Discussion Series (Washington, DC: Federal Reserve Board, Divisions of Research and Statistics and Monetary Affairs, August 15, 2013). http://www.federalreserve.gov/pubs/feds/2013/201362/201362pap.pdf

69 percent used their loans: Morse, "Payday Lenders: Heroes or Villains?"

Eighty-five percent of borrowers: The Center for Financial Services Innovation surveyed payday borrowers and grouped them according to why individuals took out payday loans. The researchers found that about two-thirds of the loans were taken out to fill a single need. The four most common reasons were (1) to pay for an unexpected expense, (2) to handle a misaligned cash flow (e.g., when payments are due in the interim period between paychecks), (3) because the borrower's expenses regularly exceeded their income, and (4) for a planned purchase. Those who borrowed because of a misaligned cash flow or because their expenses regularly exceeded their income were the most likely to have taken out multiple loans (more than six) in the year prior to the survey. In a study that also looked at groupings of borrowers, Clarity Services, a credit reporting agency that focuses on the subprime market, used in-house data to segment payday loans into the following groups: emerging, lower income and credit disinterested, prior prime, and perpetually unstable. See Ranney and Cook, "Changing Patterns and Behaviors of Unsecured Short-Term Loan Consumers."

US Department of Defense: Department of Defense, "Report on Predatory Lending Practices Directed at Members of the Armed Forces and Their Dependents" (Washington, DC: US Department of Defense, August 9, 2006).

89 *contribute to cyclical borrowing:* Ibid.

negative implications for their careers: Ibid.

financial issues are the cause: Ibid.

Each state has different rules: For a summary of this information, see Pew Charitable Trusts, "State Payday Loan Regulation and Usage Rates."

Georgia and North Carolina: Morgan and Strain, "Payday Holiday."

A 2008 study examined: Ibid.

Compared with other states: Ibid.

90 *"plausibly inferior" alternatives:* Zinman, "Restricting Consumer Credit Access: Household Survey Evidence on Effects Around the Oregon Rate Cap."

Other states have placed: Pew Charitable Trusts, "How State Rate Limits Affect Payday Loan Prices" (Washington, DC: Pew, 2014). http://www .pewtrusts.org/en/research-and-analysis/fact-sheets/2014/04/10/how -state-rate-limits-affect-payday-loan-prices

payments in Colorado amount: For the number of states where payday loans are illegal, see Pew Charitable Trusts, "State Payday Loan Regulation and Usage Rates" (Washington, DC: Pew, July 11, 2012). http:// www.pewtrusts.org/en/multimedia/data-visualizations/2014/-/media /data%20visualizations/interactives/2014/state%20payday%20loan%20 regulation%20and%20usage%20rates/report/state_payday_loan _regulation_and_usage_rates.pdf

after the legislation: Ibid.

91 *Pressure on policymakers:* At the time of this writing, the CFPB had not yet released its new rules for payday lenders. The proposal it circulated for comment in March 2015 included a rule designed to prevent consumers who use short- and longer-term credit products like payday loans, auto-title loans, and certain high-cost installment loans from becoming

over-indebted by requiring borrowers to determine consumers' ability to repay before loans are made. Lenders would be required to make a good-faith, reasonable effort to verify borrowers' income, significant financial obligations, and borrowing history. The rules also aim to protect consumers from some of the costly consequences of using payday loans and related products by restricting lenders' ability to collect payment from consumers' bank accounts. Lenders would be required to provide written notice to consumers three days before each attempt to collect payment from a checking, savings, or prepaid-card account. Lenders would also be prohibited from making further withdrawals after two unsuccessful attempts, limiting the fees a borrower may incur from an outstanding loan.

93 *take advantage of this gap:* For an account of problematic debt-collection practices, see Jake Halpern, *Bad Paper: Chasing Debt from Wall Street to the Underworld* (New York: Farrar, Straus and Giroux, 2014).

97 *extremely difficult for regulators:* Ibid. A significant subset of these online lenders are tribal lenders, and there are debates as to whether the tribes' sovereignty exempts them from state laws.

99 *The FTC gets more complaints:* Ibid.

100 *received 88,190 complaints:* Ibid., p. 212.

    the CFPB's entire budget: Ibid.

    The company then demanded: Check Center does not sell its data to third-party collectors. It writes off the debt immediately — as soon as a customer's check for a loan is returned to the bank. Zweig estimates that about two-thirds of these customers pay off their loans eventually, and that most of these pay within the first thirty days. If they never pay back, they have a debt with Check Center and won't be able to get another loan there until they repay, but they can probably get another loan at another payday lender.

101 *the inevitable result:* Halpern, *Bad Paper,* p. 185.

    Halpern cites a source: Ibid., p. 184.

102 *I published a magazine article:* Lisa Servon, "What Good Are Payday Loans?" *The New Yorker,* February 13, 2014. http://www.newyorker.com/currency-tag/what-good-are-payday-loans

    Ariane insisted that I use: Ariane's name has been changed in this book, as has that of every other person I worked with or interviewed.

6. LIVING IN THE MINUS:
THE MILLENNIAL PERSPECTIVE

103 *NEETs, "not in education":* Robert Guest, "Generation Uphill," *The Economist,* January 23, 2016. http://www.economist.com/news/special -report/21688591-millennials-are-brainiest-best-educated-generation -ever-yet-their-elders-often

Making up more than: Council of Economic Advisers, "15 Economic Facts About Millennials" (Washington, DC: The White House, October 2014), p. 3. https://www.whitehouse.gov/sites/default/files/docs/millennials_ report.pdf

totals eighty-three million: US Census Bureau, "Millennials Outnumber Baby Boomers and Are Far More Diverse, Census Bureau Reports" (Washington, DC: US Census Bureau, June 25, 2015). https://www.census .gov/newsroom/press-releases/2015/cb15-113.html

When asked to describe: Larissa Faw, "Why Millennials Are Spending More Than They Earn, and Parents Are Footing the Bill," *Forbes,* May 18, 2012. http://www.forbes.com/sites/larissafaw/2012/05/18/why -millennials-are-spending-more-than-they-earn/

22 percent chose "stress": Fidelity Investments, "Millennial Money Study: Facts, Figures, and Findings" (Smithfield, RI: Fidelity, 2014). https:// www.fidelity.com/bin-public/060_www_fidelity_com/documents /fidelity/millennial-money-study.pdf

105 *Headlines like "Why Millennials":* Catherine Collinson, "Millennial Workers: An Emerging Generation of Super Savers" (Baltimore, MD: Transamerica Center for Retirement Studies, July 2014); Northwestern Mutual Life Insurance Company, "2015 Northwestern Mutual Planning and Progress Media Study: Millennials and Money" (Milwaukee, WI: Northwestern Mutual, April 2015). https://www.northwesternmu tual.com/~/media/nmcom/files/studies%20and%20resources/2015%20 planning%20and%20progress%20-%20millennials%20and%20money .ashx?la=en

106 *But research shows that:* Northwestern Mutual Life Insurance Company, "Millennials and Money: Part Young Idealists, Part Old Souls" (Milwaukee, WI: Northwestern Mutual, PR Newswire, April 7, 2015). https:// www.northwesternmutual.com/news-room/122886

A 2015 study found that: Fidelity Investments, "Millennial Money Study."

39 percent of millennials: Institute for Women's Policy Research, "The Status of Women in the States: 2015 Employment and Earnings" (Washington, DC: IWPR, March 2015), p. 10. http://statusofwomendata.org /app/uploads/2015/02/EE-CHAPTER-FINAL.pdf

about eighty-five cents: Sixty-nine percent of millennials have savings accounts, but most have less than five thousand dollars saved. Hadley Malcolm, "Millennials Want to Save, Many Can't," *USA Today,* November 19, 2014. http://www.usatoday.com/story/money/personal finance/2014/11/19/millennial-money-habits-survey/19169671/

Most millennials have savings: Pew Research Center, "Millennials: A Portrait of Generation Next: Confident. Connected. Open to Change" (Washington, DC: Pew, February 2010). http://www.pewsocialtrends .org/files/2010/10/millennials-confident-connected-open-to-change.pdf

More than three-quarters: Anya Kamenetz, *Generation Debt* (New York: Riverhead, 2006), p. 5.

107 *But since the 1980s, college:* Debt load equals total amount of debt owed, in this case student loan debt.

increased by 400 percent: Kamenetz, *Generation Debt,* p. 50.

Millennials are more than twice: The Nielsen Company, "Millennials in 2015: Financial Deep Dive" (New York: Nielsen, October 2015). http:// www.nielsen.com/us/en/insights/reports/2015/millennials-in-2015 -financial-deep-dive.html

more than a quarter: Amanda Reaume, "The Millennial Debt Sentence: Will They Ever Escape?" Credit.com blog, October 29, 2014. http://blog .credit.com/2014/10/the-millennial-debt-sentence-will-they-ever -escape-99964/

108 *Only 41 percent were:* Pew Research Center, "Millennials: A Portrait of Generation Next."

A 2014 survey found: Danny Rubin, Jenny Goudreau, and Skye Gould, "Exclusive Survey Shows How Hard It Is for Millennials to Find Good Jobs," *Business Insider,* June 18, 2014. http://www.businessinsider.com /survey-on-millennials-and-first-jobs-2014-6

Forbes *reported that 44 percent:* Ashley Stahl, "The 5.4 Percent Unemployment Rate Means Nothing for Millennials," *Forbes,* May 11, 2015. http://

www.forbes.com/sites/ashleystahl/2015/05/11/the-5-4-unemployment
-rate-means-nothing-for-millennials/

109   *"The Clark University Poll"*: Jeffrey Jensen Arnett and Joseph Schwab,
       "The Clark University Poll of Parents of Emerging Adults" (Worcester,
       MA:ClarkUniversity,September2013).http://www.clarku.edu/clark-poll
       -emerging-adults/pdfs/clark-university-poll-parents-emerging-adults
       .pdf

   This poll offers insights into the developmental life stage between ages
twenty-one and twenty-nine, which the poll director and Clark psychology professor Jeffrey Jensen Arnett coined "emerging adulthood." The
polls of emerging adults, for which findings were produced in 2012 and
2015, consider a range of topics, including parental financial support, financial challenges, careers, work-life balance, communication, and more.

   More than a third of: US Chamber of Commerce Foundation, "Millennial General Research Review" (Washington, DC: US Chamber of
Commerce Foundation, 2012). http://www.uschamberfoundation.org
/millennial-generation-research-review

   Parents were concerned: Specifically, about one in five (19 percent) is
"very concerned," and one in three (31 percent) is "somewhat concerned."

   how long their child was taking: Arnett and Schwab, "Clark University
Poll."

110   *Seventy percent said they:* Isaac Saurez, "Report Shows Millennials Turn
       to Payday Loans," Loans.org, June 21, 2013. http://loans.org/payday
       /news/report-millennials-turn-cash-advance-92906

   Half of all millennials: US Chamber of Commerce Foundation, "Millennial General Research Review."

   9 percent higher: Josh Zumbrun, "Younger Generation Faces a Savings Deficit," *Wall Street Journal,* November 9, 2014. http://www.wsj.com/articles
/savings-turn-negative-for-younger-generation-1415572405

   college graduates who enter: US Chamber of Commerce Foundation,
"Millennial General Research Review."

111   *Nearly one in four trusts:* Fidelity Investments, "Millennial Money
       Study."

   A recent Time *magazine:* Dan Kadlec, "Why Millennials Would Choose

a Root Canal over Listening to a Banker," *Time,* March 28, 2014. http://
time.com/40909/why-millennials-would-choose-a-root-canal-over
-listening-to-a-banker/

All four of the largest banks: Viacom Media Networks, "Millennial Disruption Index," *Scratch,* 2014. http://www.millennialdisruptionindex
.com

Eighty-three percent of millennials: Saurez, "Report Shows Millennials
Turn to Payday Loans."

112 *A whopping 94 percent:* Jackson Mueller, "Millennials: A New Approach
to Handling Money," *Newsweek,* February 9, 2015. http://www.news
week.com/millennials-new-approach-handling-money-308098

74 percent say that: Independent Community Bankers of America, "The
2014 ICBA American Millennials and Community Banking Study,"
white paper (Washington, DC: ICBA, October 2014). https://www.icba
.org/files/ICBASites/PDFs/ICBAMillennialsandCommunityBanking
StudyWhitePaper.pdf

Nearly two-thirds of this: eMarketer, "Millennials Prefer to Manage Money Themselves," eMarketer.com, April 1, 2015. http://www
.emarketer.com/Article/Millennials-Prefer-Manage-Money-Them
selves/1012292

And nearly three-quarters: Viacom Media Networks, "The Millennial
Disruption Index."

The Millennial Disruption Index: Ibid.

Four out of five millennials: Mueller, "Millennials: A New Approach to
Handling Money."

113 *over half of millennials:* Fair Isaac Corporation, "Millennial Banking Insights and Opportunities" (San Jose, CA: FICO, 2014). http://www.fico
.com/millennial-quiz/pdf/fico-millennial-insight-report.pdf

In the quarter ending: PayPal, "Q2 2015 Fact Sheet" (San Jose, CA: Pay-
Pal, 2015). https://stories.paypal-corp.com/uploads/4/8/9/8/48984695
/paypal_q2_2015_fastfacts_final.pdf

P2P platforms act as: Federal Reserve Bank of Cleveland, "Peer-to-Peer
Lending Is Poised to Grow" (Cleveland: Cleveland Fed, August 14, 2014).
https://www.clevelandfed.org/newsroom-and-events/publications
/economic-trends/2014-economic-trends/et-20140814-peer-to-peer
-lending-is-poised-to-grow.aspx

Their average interest rates: These loans are not without their problems, as evidenced in Michael Corkery, "Pitfalls for the Unwary Borrower out on the Frontiers of Banking," *New York Times,* September 13, 2015. http://www.nytimes.com/2015/09/14/business/dealbook/pitfalls-for-the-unwary-borrower-out-on-the-frontiers-of-banking.html

"the convenience of transacting": PricewaterhouseCoopers, "Peer Pressure: How Peer-to-Peer Lending Platforms Are Transforming the Consumer Lending Industry" (London: PricewaterhouseCoopers LLP, February 2015). http://www.pwc.com/us/en/consumer-finance/publications/assets/peer-to-peer-lending.pdf

P2P lending has grown: Federal Reserve Bank of Cleveland, "Peer-to-Peer Lending Is Poised to Grow."

115   *Mint.com launched in 2007:* Mandi Woodruff, "How Mint.com Turned Two Million Users into a Living Snapshot of the Economic Recovery," *Business Insider,* July 18, 2013. http://www.businessinsider.com/mintcom-uses-big-data-to-track-consumer-spending-2013-7#ixzz3geWRXKfv

Its founder, Jake Fuentes: Tara Seigel Bernand, "Make a Resolution to Budget? Here Are Some Apps to Help," *New York Times,* January 4, 2014. http://www.nytimes.com/2014/01/04/your-money/household-budgeting/review-apps-to-track-income-and-expenses.html?_r=1

118   *A 2013 online survey found:* Results of an online poll conducted by Harris Interactive on behalf of Think Finance: "Millennials Demand Better Fees and Convenience from Financial Services Providers — In Tough Economic Environment, Many Young Americans Use Alternative Financial Services to Bridge Financial Gaps" (June 11, 2013). http://www.harrisinteractive.com/vault/Harris-ThinkFinance-Survey-Release6-11-13.pdf

one in four had used: Think Finance, "Millennials Use Alternative Financial Services Regardless of Their Income Level — Think Finance Survey Finds Young Americans Are Satisfied with Emergency Cash Products" (Fort Worth, TX: Think Finance, May 17, 2012). http://www.thinkfinance.com/press/news-events/2012-05-17.php

a Forbes *magazine article:* J. Maureen Henderson, "The Surprising and Smart Reason Millennials Love Payday Loans and Prepaid Debit Cards," *Forbes,* February 22, 2014.

Sixty-three percent of respondents: Think Finance, "Millennials Use Alternative Financial Services Regardless of Their Income Level"; Henderson, "The Surprising and Smart Reason Millennials Love Payday Loans and Prepaid Debit Cards."

7. BORROWING AND SAVING UNDER THE RADAR

126 *Ardener described how:* Shirley Ardener, "Microcredit, Money Transfers, Women, and the Cameroon Diaspora," *Afrika Focus,* vol. 23, no. 2 (2010): 11–24.

Boston-based Ethiopian: Viviana A. Rotman Zelizer, *The Social Meaning of Money: Pin Money, Paychecks, Poor Relief, and Other Currencies* (New York: Basic Books, 1994).

127 *Six percent of the US:* Asli Demirgüç-Kunt and Leora F. Klapper, "Measuring Financial Inclusion: The Global Findex Database," World Bank Policy Research Working Paper No. 6025 (Washington, DC: World Bank, 2012).

The sociologist Viviana Zelizer: Viviana A. Rotman Zelizer, *Economic Lives: How Culture Shapes the Economy* (Princeton, NJ: Princeton University Press, 2011).

defines the "underground economy": Sudhir Alladi Venkatesh, *Off the Books* (Cambridge, MA: Harvard University Press, 2006), p. 8.

128 *Venkatesh argues that:* Ibid., p. xvii.

"wove together the social fabric": Ibid., p. 5.

129 *researchers have found:* Carol B. Stack, *All Our Kin* (New York: Basic Books, 1975); Regine O. Jackson, Darrick Hamilton, and William Darity Jr., "Low Wealth and Economic Insecurity Among Middle-Class Blacks in Boston," Community Development Issue Brief No. 3 (Boston: Federal Reserve Bank of Boston, 2015). http://www.bostonfed.org/commdev/issue-briefs/2015/cdbrief32015.htm; Ngina Chiteji and Darrick Hamilton, "Family Connections and the Black-White Wealth Gap Among the Middle Class," *Review of Black Political Economy,* vol. 30, no. 1 (2002): 9–27; Ngina Chiteji and Darrick Hamilton, "Kin Networks and Asset Accumulation," in *Inclusion in the American Dream: Assets, Poverty, and Public Policy,* edited by Michael Sherraden (New York: Oxford University Press, 2005).

132 *"different monies were used":* Zelizer, *The Social Meaning of Money.*

words for different kinds: Ibid., p. 24.

133 *"The earmarking of money":* Ibid., p. 25.

137 *the United States has a savings rate:* Organization for Economic Cooperation and Development, "Household Savings Forecast (Indicator)" (Paris:
OECD, 2015). http://dx.dol.org/10.1787/eo-data-en

savings in our country have dropped: Ibid.

1,725 square feet in 1983: Les Christie, "America's Homes Are Bigger Than
Ever," *CNNMoney,* June 5, 2014. http://money.cnn.com/2014/06/04
/real_estate/american-home-size/

138 *This pooling of information:* Giuseppe Bertola, Richard Disney, and
Charles Benedict Grant, *The Economics of Consumer Credit* (Cambridge,
MA: MIT Press, 2006).

"predict individual repayment": Ibid., p. 22.

These informal practices are not: Sudhanshu Handa and Claremont
Kirton, "The Economics of Rotating Savings and Credit Associations:
Evidence from the Jamaican 'Partner,'" *Journal of Development Economics,* vol. 60, no. 1 (1999): 173–94; Sowmya Varadharajan, "Explaining Participation in Rotating Savings and Credit Associations (ROSCAs): Evidence from Indonesia" (Ithaca, NY: Cornell University, 2004).

141 *almost less than one in ten:* PricewaterhouseCoopers, "The Sharing Economy," Consumer Intelligence Series, pwc.com/CISsharing, April 2015.

the sharing economy: Havas Worldwide, "The New Consumer and the
Sharing Economy," Prosumer Report (New York: Havas, 2014).

8. INSIDE THE INNOVATORS

143 *This moment is notable:* Brett King, *Breaking Banks: The Innovators,
Rogues, and Strategists Rebooting Banking* (Singapore: John Wiley &
Sons, 2014), p. xv.

Creative destruction, a term: Joseph Alois Schumpeter, *The Theory of
Economic Development: An Inquiry into Profits, Capital, Credit, Interest,
and the Business Cycle* (London: Transaction Publishers, 1934).

144 *Dave Birch, a director at:* King, *Breaking Banks,* p. 42.

Mobile phones have already: "The Future of Money," *60 Minutes,* CBS
News, November 22, 2015. http://www.cbsnews.com/news/future-of
-money-kenya-m-pesa-60-minutes/

146   *Smartphone use grew:* Personal correspondence with Mike Mondelli, April 8, 2016.

163   *interest rate of 36 percent:* There's a broader movement supporting the 36 percent rate. It references the 36 percent exception to the usury rate that Russell Sage advocated for in the 1920s and that led to the Uniform Small Loan Law. Even though it seems fairly arbitrary — why not 30 percent, or 42 percent? — it's a kind of policy touchstone that consumer advocates have once again begun to rally around. Voters support a 36 percent cap, as do several branches of government.

9. REJECTING THE NEW NORMAL

166   *Center for Financial Services Innovation:* Consumer Financial Protection Bureau, "Measuring Financial Well-Being: A Guide to Using the CFPB Financial Well-Being Scale" (Washington, DC: CFPB, December 2015). http://files.consumerfinance.gov/f/201512_cfpb_financial-well-being -user-guide-scale.pdf

Other research supports these conclusions. See Ivo Vlaev and Antony Elliott, "Financial Well-Being Components," *Social Indicators Research,* vol. 118, no. 3 (2014): 1103–23.

"financial health is achieved": Aliza Gutman et al., "Understanding and Improving Consumer Financial Health in America" (Chicago: CFSI, March 24, 2015). http://www.cfsinnovation.com/Document-Library /Understanding-Consumer-Financial-Health

Consumer Financial Protection Bureau: Susan Burhouse et al., "2013 National Survey of Unbanked and Underbanked Households" (Washington, DC: FDIC, October 2014). https://www.fdic.gov/householdsurvey/2013 report.pdf

57 percent of Americans: For more on this idea and why it is so critical, particularly in the wake of welfare reform, see Kathryn J. Edin and H. Luke Shaefer, *$2.00 a Day: Living on Almost Nothing in America* (New York: Houghton Mifflin Harcourt, 2015).

167   *a strong safety net:* Michael S. Barr, Sendhil Mullainathan, and Eldar Shafir, "Behaviorally Informed Regulation," in *No Slack: The Financial Lives of Low-Income Americans,* edited by Michael S. Barr (Washington, DC: Brookings Institution Press, 2012).

169   *"choice architecture"*: Richard H. Thaler and Cass R. Sunstein, *Nudge: Improving Decisions About Health, Wealth, and Happiness* (New Haven, CT: Yale University Press, 2008).

     simply changing the default option: John Beshears et al., "The Importance of Default Options for Retirement Savings Outcomes: Evidence from the United States," NBER Working Paper No. 12009 (Cambridge, MA: National Bureau of Economic Research, February 2006).

     how to "nudge" people: Barr, *No Slack;* Thaler and Sunstein, *Nudge.*

170   *"favoring bank profitability"*: Mehrsa Baradaran, *How the Other Half Banks: Exclusion, Exploitation, and the Threat to Democracy* (Cambridge, MA: Harvard University Press, 2015), p. 7.

171   *enable them to borrow:* International Monetary Fund, "Big Banks Benefit from Government Subsidies," *IMF Survey Magazine,* March 31, 2014. http://www.imf.org/external/pubs/ft/survey/so/2014/POL033114A.htm

172   *through the postal service:* Mehrsa Baradaran endorses this idea in *How the Other Half Banks.*

     "the most successful experiment": Ibid., p. 207.

173   *Financial-information boxes:* Some studies show that consumers are using nutrition labels to make healthier food choices. Programs like the Department of Energy and the Environmental Protection Agency's Energy Star have been highly successful in changing consumers' buying patterns. The Affordable Care Act included a provision that requires all health plans to provide a uniform summary, in plain language, of coverage for all enrollees and applicants. According to a recent Kaiser Family Foundation poll, this is among the most popular provisions of the law. John Kozup and Jeanne M. Hogarth, "Financial Literacy, Public Policy, and Consumers' Self-Protection—More Questions, Fewer Answers," *Journal of Consumer Affairs,* vol. 42 (2008): 127–36; Henry J. Kaiser Family Foundation, "Pulling It Together: The Most Popular Provision in the ACA?" (Washington, DC: Henry J. Kaiser Family Foundation, November 29, 2011). http://kff.org/health-costs/perspective/pulling-it-together-the-most-popular-provision/

174   *Some progress has already:* Twenty-eight financial institutions, including the four largest banks, have adopted a simple checking-account disclosure box created by the Pew Charitable Trusts.

     making comparisons difficult: Barr, *No Slack,* p. 259.

Consumer Financial Protection Bureau: The CFPB created "Know Before You Owe" mortgage disclosure forms and is currently prototyping financial disclosure boxes for prepaid debit and credit cards.

the New York City: New York City Department of Health, "What to Expect When You're Inspected: A Guide for Food Service Operators" (New York: NYDOH, December 2010). http://www.nyc.gov/html/doh/down loads/pdf/rii/blue-book.pdf

Michael Barr recommends: Barr, *No Slack.*

175   *A recent study conducted:* Brett Theodos et al., "An Evaluation of the Impacts and Implementation Approaches of Financial Coaching Programs" (Washington, DC: Urban Institute, October 2015). http://www.urban .org/research/publication/evaluation-impacts-and-implementation -approaches-financial-coaching-programs

This kind of coaching will: Laura Choi et al., *What It's Worth: Strengthening the Financial Future of Families, Communities, and the Nation* (San Francisco: Federal Reserve Bank of San Francisco and CFED, 2015).

as JoAnn Barefoot puts it: UK Financial Conduct Authority, "Regulatory Sandbox" (London: UK FCA, November 2015). http://www.fca.org.uk /static/documents/regulatory-sandbox.pdf

"strangled in the cradle": JoAnn Barefoot, "Disrupting Consumer Financial Services," *Forbes,* September 10, 2014. http://www.forbes.com/sites /realspin/2014/09/10/disrupting-consumer-financial-services/

176   *"regulatory sandbox":* UK Financial Conduct Authority, "Regulatory Sandbox."

The sandbox can also: Ibid.

    Research from other industries suggests that eliminating this uncertainty, which the sandbox would do, can reduce by one-third the time needed to develop and introduce a new product, which also contributes to reduced cost to the developer.

potential to improve consumers': Ibid.

to manage regulatory risk: Ibid.

Paul Krugman argued: Paul Krugman, "Making Banking Boring," *New York Times,* April 9, 2009. http://www.nytimes.com/2009/04/10/opinion /10krugman.html?_r=0

BIBLIOGRAPHY

Akasha, Nan. "Money Archetypes and Guilt and Shame." Nan Akasha blog, May 29, 2012.

Akerlof, George A., and Robert Shiller. *Phishing for Phools: The Economics of Manipulation and Deception.* Princeton, NJ: Princeton University Press, 2015.

Ardener, Shirley. "Microcredit, Money Transfers, Women, and the Cameroon Diaspora." *Afrika Focus,* vol. 23, no. 2 (2010): 11–24.

Arnett, Jeffrey J., and Joseph Schwab. "The Clark University Poll of Parents of Emerging Adults." Worcester, MA: Clark University, September 2013.

Associated Press. "Citigroup Ordered to Refund $700 Million in Credit Card Case." *New York Times,* July 21, 2015.

Avery, Robert B., Kenneth B. Brevoort, and Glenn B. Canner. "Higher-Priced Home Lending and the 2005 HDMA Data." *Federal Reserve Board Bulletin,* September 18, 2006, revised.

Bakker, Trevor, Nicole Kelly, Jesse Leary, and Éva Nagypál. "Data Point: Checking Account Overdraft." Washington, DC: Consumer Financial Protection Bureau, 2014.

Baradaran, Mehrsa. *How the Other Half Banks: Exclusion, Exploitation, and the Threat to Democracy.* Cambridge, MA: Harvard University Press, 2015.

Barefoot, JoAnn. "Disrupting Consumer Financial Services," *Forbes,* September 10, 2014.

Barr, Michael S., ed. *No Slack: The Financial Lives of Low-Income Americans.* Washington, DC: Brookings Institution, 2012.

Barr, Michael S., Sendhil Mullainathan, and Eldar Shafir. "Behaviorally Informed Regulation." In *No Slack: The Financial Lives of Low-Income Americans,* edited by Michael S. Barr. Washington, DC: Brookings Institution, 2012.

Barrington, Richard. "Bank Fees Survey Mid-2014: Fees Hit New Highs." Moneyrates.com, August 25, 2014.

Bell, Claes. "Checking Account Fees Rise but Less Steeply." Bankrate.com, no date.

———. "Checking Fees Rise to Record Highs in 2012." Bankrate.com, no date.

Bertola, Giuseppe, Richard Disney, and Charles Benedict Grant. *The Economics of Consumer Credit*. Cambridge, MA: MIT Press, 2006.

Beshears, John, James J. Choi, David Laibson, and Brigitte C. Madrian. "The Importance of Default Options for Retirement Savings Outcomes: Evidence from the United States." NBER Working Paper No. 12009. Cambridge, MA: National Bureau of Economic Research, January 2006.

Black, Sandra E., and Donald P. Morgan. "Meet the New Borrowers." *Current Issues in Economics and Finance, Federal Reserve Bank of New York,* vol. 5, no. 3 (February 1999).

Boak, Josh. "One in Four US Renters Spends Half Their Pay on Rent and Utilities." *Business Insider,* May 1, 2015.

Board of Governors of the Federal Reserve System. "Report on the Economic Well-Being of US Households in 2014." Washington, DC: Board of Governors of the Federal Reserve System, May 2015.

———. "Report to Congress on the Profitability of Credit Card Operations of Depository Institutions." Washington, DC: Board of Governors of the Federal Reserve System, June 2014.

———. "What You Need to Know: New Overdraft Rules for Debit and ATM Cards." Washington, DC: Board of Governors of the Federal Reserve System, 2010.

Boshara, Ray. "Policy Perspectives on Fostering Consumer Financial Health." Paper presented at Emerge Conference, Los Angeles, 2014.

Brownstein, Ronald. "Meet the New Middle Class: Who They Are, What They Want, and What They Fear." *The Atlantic,* April 25, 2013.

Bruce, Laura. "Key Finds of Fall 2001 Checking Account Pricing Study." Bankrate.com, September 28, 2001.

Burhouse, Susan, Karyen Chu, Ryan Goodstein, Joyce Northwood, Yazmin Osaki, and Dhruv Sharma. "2013 FDIC National Survey of Unbanked and Underbanked Households." Washington, DC: FDIC.

Calum, Paul S. "The Impact of Geographic Deregulation on Small Banks." *Business Review,* November/December 1994.

Campbell, Dennis, Asis Martinez-Jerez, and Peter Tufano. "Bouncing out of the Banking System: An Empirical Analysis of Involuntary Bank Account Closures." Boston, MA: The Federal Reserve Bank of Boston, June 6, 2008.

Carrell, Scott E., and Jonathan Zinman. "In Harm's Way? Payday Loan Access and Military Personnel Performance." *Review of Financial Studies,* vol. 27, no. 9 (May 28, 2014).

Choi, Laura, David Erickson, Kate Griffin, Andrea Levere, and Ellen Seidman, eds. *What It's Worth: Strengthening the Financial Future of Families, Communities, and the Nation.* San Francisco: Federal Reserve Bank of San Francisco and CFED.

Clements, Nick. "Bad Credit? Banks Want to Give You Credit Cards." *Forbes,* May 20, 2015.

Collinson, Catherine. "Millennial Workers: An Emerging Generation of Super Savers." Baltimore, MD: Transamerica Center for Retirement Studies.

Confessore, Nicholas, Sarah Young, and Karen Yourish. "Small Pool of Rich Donors Dominates Election Giving." *New York Times,* August 1, 2015.

Consumer Financial Protection Bureau. "CFPB Spotlights Concerns with Medical Debt Collection and Reporting." Press release, December 11, 2014.

———. "CFPB Study of Overdraft Programs." Washington, DC: CFPB, June 2013.

———. "Consumer Credit Reports: A Study of Medical and Nonmedical Collections." Washington, DC: CFPB, December 2014.

———. "Measuring Financial Well-Being: A Guide to Using the CFPB Financial Well-Being Scale." Washington, DC: CFPB, December 2015.

Cooper, David, and Doug Hall. "Raising the Federal Minimum Wage to $10.10 Would Give Working Families, and the Overall Economy, a Much-Needed Boost." Washington, DC: Economic Policy Institute, March 13, 2013.

Corkery, Michael. "Pitfalls for the Unwary Borrower out on the Frontiers of Banking." *New York Times,* September 13, 2015.

The Data Team. "American House Prices: Realty Check." *The Economist,* November 3, 2015.

Day, Kathleen. "Bankruptcy Bill Passes; Bush Expected to Sign." *Washington Post,* April 15, 2005.

Demirgüç-Kunt, Asli, and Leora F. Klapper. "Measuring Financial Inclusion: The Global Findex Database." World Bank Policy Research Working Paper No. 6025. Washington, DC: World Bank, 2012.

Dilworth, Kelly. "Average Credit Card Interest Rates Rise to 15.07 Percent." CreditCards.com, 2014.

Dougherty, Carter. "Banks Face Hit from CFPB on $30 Billion in Overdraft Fees." *Bloomberg Businessweek,* August 1, 2014.

Drum, Kevin. "Chart of the Day: Even the Rich Think the Middle Class Is Getting Screwed." *Mother Jones,* March 15, 2015.

Durkin, Thomas A. "Credit Cards: Use and Consumer Attitudes, 1970–2000." *Federal Reserve Bulletin,* September 2000.

Edin, Kathryn J., and H. Luke Shaefer. *$2.00 a Day: Living on Almost Nothing in America.* New York: Houghton Mifflin Harcourt, 2015.

El Issa, Erin. "American Household Credit Card Debt Study." nerdwallet.com, 2015.

Elliehausen, Gregory. "An Analysis of Consumers' Use of Payday Loans." *Financial Services Research Program Monograph,* no. 41 (January 2009).

Ellis, Blake. "Nine Most Annoying Bank Fees." *CNN Money,* June 16, 2011.

eMarketer. "Millennials Prefer to Manage Money Themselves." eMarketer .com, April 1, 2015.

Emmons, W. R., and B. J. Noeth. "Economic Vulnerability and Financial Fragility." *Federal Reserve Bank of St. Louis Review,* vol. 95, no. 5 (2013).

Eveleth, Rose. "Forty Years Ago, Women Had a Hard Time Getting Credit Cards." *Smithsonian Magazine,* January 8, 2014.

Fair Isaac Corporation. "Millennial Banking Insights and Opportunities." San Jose, CA: Fair Isaac, 2014.

Faw, Larissa. "Why Millennials Are Spending More Than They Earn, and Parents Are Footing the Bill." *Forbes,* May 18, 2012.

Federal Deposit Insurance Corporation. "The FDIC's Small-Dollar Loan Pilot Program: A Case Study After One Year." *FDIC Quarterly,* vol. 3, no. 2 (2009).

———. "2013 FDIC National Survey of Unbanked and Underbanked Households." Washington, DC: FDIC, October 2014.

Federal Reserve. "Changes in US Family Finances from 2010 to 2013: Evidence from the Survey of Consumer Finances." *Federal Reserve Bulletin,* vol. 100, no. 4 (September 2014).

———. "Report to the Congress on the Profitability of Credit Card Operations of Depository Institutions." Washington, DC: Federal Reserve, 2012.

Federal Reserve Bank of Cleveland. "Peer-to-Peer Lending Is Poised to Grow." Cleveland: Federal Reserve Bank of Cleveland, August 14, 2014.

Fidelity Investments. "Millennial Money Study: Facts, Figures, and Findings." Smithfield, RI: Fidelity, 2014.

Finkle, Victoria. "Is Dodd-Frank Really Killing Community Banks?" *American Banker,* August 18, 2015.

Foust, Dean, and Aaron Pressman. "Credit Scores: Not So Magic Numbers." *Bloomberg Business,* February 6, 2008.

Frellick, Marcia. "The Rise and Fall of the Credit Card Magnetic Stripe." Credit Cards.com, June 14, 2011.

FTI Consulting. "Allstate/National Journal Heartland Monitor XVI Key Findings." Memorandum. Washington, DC: FTI Consulting, April 15, 2013.

Fulford, Scott L. "How Important Is Variability in Consumer Credit Limits?" Federal Reserve Bank of Boston Working Paper No. 14-8. Boston: Federal Reserve Bank of Boston, May 2014.

Fusaro, Marc Anthony, and Patricia J. Cirillo. "Do Payday Loans Trap Consumers in a Cycle of Debt?" *Social Science Research Network*, November 16, 2011.

Garcia, Jose. "Borrowing to Make Ends Meet: The Rapid Growth of Credit Card Debt in America." Washington, DC: Demos, 2007.

GlobeScan. "Seven Years on from the Financial Crisis, Trust in Banks Remains at All-Time Low." Toronto, Canada: GlobeScan, 2015.

Gordon, Taylor. "Eight Major American Banks That Got Caught Discriminating Against Black People." *Atlanta Black Star,* March 3, 2015.

Gould, Elise, and Tanyell Cooke. "High-Quality Child Care Is Out of Reach for Working Families." Washington, DC: Economic Policy Institute, October 6, 2015.

Guest, Robert. "Generation Uphill." *The Economist,* January 23, 2016.

Hacker, Andrew. "The Wrong Way to Teach Math." *New York Times,* February 27, 2016.

Hacker, Jacob. *The Great Risk Shift: The New Economic Insecurity and the Decline of the American Dream.* Oxford, UK: Oxford University Press, 2008.

Halpern, Jake. *Bad Paper: Chasing Debt from Wall Street to the Underworld.* New York: Farrar, Straus and Giroux, 2014.

Hamilton, Darrick, and William Darity Jr. "Can 'Baby Bonds' Eliminate the Racial Wealth Gap in Putative Post-Racial America?" *Review of Black Political Economy,* no. 37 (2010): 207–16.

Harvard Joint Center for Housing Studies. "Record Number of American Renters Feel the Strain of Housing Cost Burdens." Interactive map. http://harvard-cga.maps.arcgis.com/apps/MapSeries/

Havas Worldwide. "The New Consumer and the Sharing Economy: Prosumer Report." New York: Havas, 2014.

Henderson, J. Maureen. "The Surprising and Smart Reason Millennials Love Payday Loans and Prepaid Debit Cards." *Forbes,* February 22, 2014.

The Henry J. Kaiser Family Foundation. "Pulling It Together: The Most Popular Provision in the ACA?" Washington, DC: The Henry J. Kaiser Family Foundation, 2011.

Himmelstein, David, Deborah Thorne, Elizabeth Warren, and Steffie Woolhandler. "Medical Bankruptcy in the United States, 2007: Results of a National Study." *American Journal of Medicine,* vol. 22, no. 9 (2009).

Huang, Daniel. "New Rules Will Change How Bank Uses Information from Reporting Agency." *Wall Street Journal,* January 27, 2015.

Independent Community Bankers of America. "The 2014 ICBA American Millennials and Community Banking Study." Washington, DC: ICBA, October 2014.

IndexCreditCards. "Credit Card Late Fees Average $34.09, Over-the-Limit Fees Average $36.53." indexcreditcards.com, October 6, 2009.

Institute for Women's Policy Research. "The Status of Women in the States: 2015 Employment and Earnings." Washington, DC: IWPR, March 2015.

Jakabovics, A., et al. "Projecting Trends in Severely Cost-Burdened Renters." Cambridge, MA: Enterprise Community Partners and Harvard Joint Center for Housing Studies, 2015.

James, Stephen. "The Ancient Evil of Usury." *Sacramento News and Review,* July 19, 2001.

Johnson, Andrew R. "Workplace Loans Gain in Popularity." *Wall Street Journal,* December 15, 2013.

Jones, Janelle, and John Schmitt. "Update on Low-Wage Workers." CEPR blog, 2014.

Kadlec, Dan. "Why Millennials Would Choose a Root Canal over Listening to a Banker." *Time,* March 28, 2014.

Kamenetz, Anya. *Generation Debt.* New York: Riverhead, 2006.

Karlan, Dean, and Jonathan Zinman. "Expanding Credit Access: Using Randomized Supply Decisions to Estimate the Impacts." Working paper, September 2008.

Kaufman, Alex. "Payday Lending Regulation." Finance and Economics Discussion Series. Washington, DC: Federal Reserve Board, Divisions of Research and Statistics and Monetary Affairs, August 15, 2013.

King, Brett. *Breaking Banks: The Innovators, Rogues, and Strategists Rebooting Banking.* New York: John Wiley & Sons, 2014.

Kochhar, Rakesh, Richard Fry, and Paul Taylor. "Wealth Gaps Rise to Record Highs Between Blacks, Whites, and Hispanics." Washington, DC: Pew Research Center, July 2011.

Kotkin, Joel. "The US Middle Class Is Turning Proletarian." *Forbes,* February 16, 2014.

Kozup, John, and Jeanne M. Hogarth. "Financial Literacy, Public Policy, and Consumers' Self-Protection — More Questions, Fewer Answers." *Journal of Consumer Affairs,* no. 42 (2008): 127–36.

Krugman, Paul. "Making Banking Boring." *New York Times,* April 10, 2009.

Lam, Bourree. "US Housing Costs: Up, Up, Up, Up." *The Atlantic,* August 22, 2014.

LaMontagne, Christina. "NerdWallet Health Study: Medical Debt Crisis Worsening Despite Policy Advances." nerdwallet.com, 2014.

Lepore, Jill. "The Warren Brief." *The New Yorker,* April 21, 2014.

Madigan, Kathleen. "The High Share of Part-Time Workers Helps Explain Weak Wage Growth." *Wall Street Journal,* May 8, 2015.

Malcolm, Hadley. "Millennials Want to Save, Many Can't." *USA Today,* November 19, 2014.

Marte, Jonnelle. "The Cities Where Americans Are Most Likely to Spend More Than Half of Their Paycheck on Rent." *Washington Post,* July 15, 2015.

Matthews, Christopher. "Nearly Half of America Lives Paycheck-to-Paycheck." *Time,* January 30, 2014.

McKendry, Ian. "The ChexSystems Probe Could Benefit the Unbanked." *American Banker,* April 27.

Melzer, Brian. "The Real Costs of Credit Access: Evidence from the Payday Lending Market." Working paper, November 15, 2007.

Menin, Julie. "Bad Alternative to Banks." Letter to the editor. *New York Times,* November 14, 2014.

Meyerson, Harold. "The Forty-Year Slump: The State of Work in the Age of Uncertainty." *American Prospect,* November 12, 2013.

Miller, Bruce. "Credit: Where We Are and Where We're Going." Paper presented at FiSCA at 25 Conference, Chicago, October 2012.

——. "Mergers and Acquisitions Activity in the Alternative Financial-Services Industry: The Current Environment and Thoughts on the Future." Paper presented at FiSCA at 25 Conference, Chicago, October 2012.

Mishel, Lawrence. "Low-Wage Workers Have Far More Education Than They Did in 1968, Yet They Make Far Less." Washington, DC: Economic Policy Institute, 2014.

——. "The Wedges Between Productivity and Median Compensation Growth." Washington, DC: Economic Policy Institute, 2012.

Morduch, Jonathan, and Rachel Schneider. "Spikes and Dips: How Income Uncertainty Affects Households." *US Financial Diaries*, October 2013.

Morgan, Donald, and Michael R. Strain. "Payday Holiday: How Households Fare After Payday Credit Bans." Federal Reserve Bank of New York Staff Report No. 309. New York: Federal Reserve Bank of New York, February 2008.

Morgan-Cross, Colin, and Marieka Klawitter. "Effects of State Payday Loan Price Caps and Regulation." Seattle: University of Washington, Evans School of Public Affairs, 2011.

Morisi, Teresa L. "Commercial Banking Transformed by Computer Technology." *Monthly Labor Review,* August 30, 1996.

Morse, Adair. "Payday Lenders: Heroes or Villains?" *Journal of Financial Economics,* vol. 102, no. 1 (October 2011).

Mottola, G. R. "In Our Best Interest: Women, Financial Literacy, and Credit Card Behavior." Washington, DC: FINRA Investor Education Foundation, April 2012.

Mueller, Jackson. "Millennials: A New Approach to Handling Money." *Newsweek,* February 9, 2015.

Mullainathan, Sendhil, and Eldar Shafir. *Scarcity: The New Science of Having Less and How It Defines Our Lives.* New York: Times Books, 2013.

New York City Department of Health. "What to Expect When You're Inspected: A Guide for Food-Service Operators." New York: NYC Dept. of Health, December 2010.

Nielsen Company. "Millennials in 2015: Financial Deep Dive." nielsen.com, October 2015.

Noah, Timothy. *The Great Divergence: America's Growing Inequality Crisis and What We Can Do About It.* New York: Bloomsbury Press, 2012.

Northwestern Mutual. "Millennials and Money: Part Young Idealists, Part Old Souls." Milwaukee: Northwestern Mutual, 2015.

———. "2015 Northwestern Mutual Planning and Progress Media Study: Millennials and Money." Milwaukee: Northwestern Mutual, 2015.

Olen, Helaine. "The Semi-Retirement Myth." *Slate,* March 2, 2015.

Organization for Economic Cooperation and Development. "Household Savings Forecast (Indicator)." Paris: OECD, 2005.

Orman, Suze. "IOU 101." *O, The Oprah Magazine,* July 2008.

Packman, Carl. *Loan Sharks: The Rise and Rise of Payday Lending.* Cambridge, UK: Searching Finance Books, 2012.

Parramore, Lynn Stuart. "Dear Middle Class: Welcome to Poverty." *Salon,* January 8, 2014.

Patton, Mike. "US Health Care Costs Rise Faster Than Inflation." *Forbes,* June 29, 2015.

PayPal. "Q2 2015 Fact Sheet." San Jose, CA: PayPal, 2015.

Peterson, Christopher Lewis, and Steve Graves. "Usury Law and the Christian Right: Faith-Based Political Power and the Geography of American Payday Loan Regulation." *Catholic University Law Review,* vol. 57, no. 3 (2008).

Pew Charitable Trusts. "Checks and Balances: 2014 Update." Washington, DC: Pew, 2014.

———. "Hidden Risks: The Case for Safe Checking Accounts." Washington, DC: Pew, 2011.

———. "How State Rate Limits Affect Payday Loan Prices." Washington, DC: Pew, April 10, 2014.

———. "Overdrawn: Persistent Confusion and Concern About Bank Overdraft Practices." Washington, DC: Pew, 2014.

———. "Payday Lending in America: Policy Solutions." Payday Lending in America Series No. 3. Washington, DC: Pew, October 2013.

———. "State Payday Loan Regulation and Usage Rates." Washington, DC: Pew, July 11, 2012.

Pew Research Center. "Millennials: A Portrait of Generation Next: Confident. Connected. Open to Change." Washington, DC: Pew Research Center, February 2010.

——. "Most Say Government Policies Since Recession Have Done Little to Help Middle Class, Poor." Washington, DC: Pew Research Center, 2015.

Philadelphia Media Network. "History of Credit Scores." philly.com, May 8, 2008.

Phillips, Sandra. "The Subprime Mortgage Calamity and the African American Woman." *Review of Black Political Economy* (June 2012).

Rampell, Catherine. "In Hard Economy for All Ages, Older Isn't Better . . . It's Brutal." *New York Times,* February 2, 2013.

Raphael, T. J. "The American Middle Class Is Shrinking." *Public Radio International,* December 13, 2015.

Reaume, Amanda. "The Millennial Debt Sentence: Will They Ever Escape?" Credit.com blog, October 29, 2014.

Remolona, Eli M., and Kurt C. Wulfekuhler. "Finance Companies, Bank Competition, and Niche Markets." *Quarterly Review, Federal Reserve Bank of New York* (Summer 1992).

Ross, Allison. "Checking Account Fees Surge to New Highs." Bankrate.com, 2014.

Rubin, Danny, Jenny Goudreau, and Skye Gould. "Exclusive Survey Shows How Hard It Is for Millennials to Find Good Jobs." *Business Insider,* June 18, 2014.

Ruetschlin, Catherine, and Dedrick Asante-Muhammad. "The Challenge of Credit Card Debt for the African American Middle Class." Washington, DC: Demos and NAACP, December 2013.

Ryan, Andrea, Gunnar Trumbull, and Peter Tufano. "A Brief Postwar History of US Consumer Finance." Harvard Business School Working Paper 11-058. Cambridge, MA: HBS, 2010.

Said, Hashem. "High Price Paid by Americans with Onerous Medical Debt." *Al Jazeera America,* June 5, 2015.

Santucci, Larry. "A Tale of Two Vintages: Credit Limit Management Before and After the CARD Act and Great Recession." Federal Reserve Bank of Philadelphia, Payment Cards Center, Discussion Paper 15-01. Philadelphia: Federal Reserve Bank of Philadelphia, February 2015.

Saunders, Lauren K. "Why 36 Percent?: The History, Use, and Purpose of the 36 Percent Interest Rate Cap." Washington, DC: National Consumer Law Center, April 2013.

Saurez, Isaac. "Report Shows Millennials Turn to Payday Loans." Loans.org, June 21, 2013.

Schectman, Joel. "The South Bronx Is a Banking Wasteland." *New York Daily News,* March 10, 2009.

Schumpeter, Joseph Alois. *The Theory of Economic Development: An Inquiry into Profits, Capital, Credit, Interest, and the Business Cycle.* London: Transaction Publishers, 1934.

Seigel Bernand, Tara. "Make a Resolution to Budget? Here Are Some Apps to Help." *New York Times,* January 3, 2014.

Servon, Lisa. "What Good Are Payday Loans?" *The New Yorker,* February 13, 2014.

Shin, Laura. "Why McDonald's Employee Budget Has Everyone up in Arms." *Forbes,* July 18, 2013.

Silver-Greenberg, Jessica. "Major Banks Aid in Payday Loans Banned by States." *New York Times,* February 23, 2013.

———. "Over a Million Denied Bank Accounts for Past Errors. *New York Times,* July 30, 2013.

Silver-Greenberg, Jessica, and Michael Corkery. "Bank Tool Is Expanding Unbanked Households, Regulators Say." *New York Times,* June 15, 2014.

Silver-Greenberg, Jessica, and Robert Gebeloff. "Arbitration Everywhere, Stacking the Deck of Justice." *New York Times,* October 31, 2015.

Skiba, Paige, and Jeremy Tobacman. "Do Payday Loans Cause Bankruptcy?" Working paper, February 19, 2008.

Sommeiller, Estelle, and Mark Price. "The Increasingly Unequal States of America: Income Inequality by State, 1917 to 2012." Washington, DC: Economic Policy Institute, 2015.

Stack, Carol B. *All Our Kin.* New York: Basic Books, 1975.

Stahl, Ashley. "The 5.4 Percent Unemployment Rate Means Nothing for Millennials." *Forbes,* May 11, 2015.

Standing, Guy. *A Precariat Charter: From Denizens to Citizens.* London: Bloomsbury, 2014.

Stango, Victor. "Some New Evidence on Competition in Payday Lending Markets." *Contemporary Economic Policy,* vol. 30, no. 2 (2012): 149–61.

Stempel, Jonathan. "US Agency Claims Darden Won't Hire 'Old White Guys' for Dining Chain." Reuters, February 12, 2015.

Sweetland Edwards, Haley. "The Middle Class Is Doing Worse Than You Think." *Time*, April 8, 2015.

Thaler, Richard H., and Cass R. Sunstein. *Nudge: Improving Decisions About Health, Wealth, and Happiness*. New Haven, CT: Yale University Press, 2008.

Theodos, Brett, Margaret Simms, Mark Treskon, Christina Plerhoples Stacy, Rachel Brash, Dina Emam, Rebecca Daniels, and Juan Collazos. "An Evaluation of the Impacts and Implementation Approaches of Financial Coaching Programs." Washington, DC: Urban Institute, October 2015.

Think Finance. "Millennials Demand Better Fees and Convenience from Financial Services Providers — In Tough Economic Environment, Many Young Americans Use Alternative Financial Services to Bridge Financial Gaps." Fort Worth, TX: Think Finance, June 14, 2013.

——. "Millennials Use Alternative Financial Services Regardless of Their Income Level — Think Finance Survey Finds Young Americans Are Satisfied with Emergency Cash Products." Fort Worth, TX: Think Finance, 2012.

Thomas Aquinas. *Summa Theologica*. Translated by the Fathers of the English Dominican Province. London: R. T. Washburne, Ltd., 1918; reprinted in Roy C. Cave and Herbert H. Coulson, *A Source Book for Medieval Economic History*. New York: Biblo and Tannen, 1965.

Timiraos, Nick. "Elevated Level of Part-Time Employment: Post-Recession Norm?" *Wall Street Journal*, November 12, 2014.

Tracy, Ryan. "Tally of US Banks Sinks to Record Low." *Wall Street Journal*, December 3, 2013.

Traub, Amy, and Catherine Ruetschlin. "The Plastic Safety Net: Findings from the 2012 National Survey on Credit Card Debt of Low- and Middle-Income Households." New York: Demos, May 22, 2012.

UK Financial Conduct Authority. "Regulatory Sandbox." London: FCA, November 2015.

US Census Bureau Newsroom. "Millennials Outnumber Baby Boomers and Are Far More Diverse, Census Bureau Reports." Washington, DC: US Census Bureau, 2015.

US Chamber of Commerce Foundation. "Millennial General Research Review." Washington, DC: US Chamber of Commerce Foundation, 2012.

US Department of Defense. "Report on Predatory Lending Practices Directed at Members of the Armed Forces and Their Dependents." Washington, DC: US Dept. of Defense, August 9, 2006.

US Department of Housing and Urban Development. "Affordable Housing." portal.hud.gov, no date.

US Department of Justice. "Justice Department Reaches $335 Million Settlement to Resolve Allegations of Lending Discrimination by Countrywide Financial Corporation." Press release, 2014.

US Department of Labor, Bureau of Labor Statistics. "The Employment Situation." Washington, DC: US Dept. of Labor, November 2015.

Valletta, Rob, and Leila Bengali. "What's Behind the Increase in Part-Time Work?" Federal Reserve Bank of San Francisco Economic Letter 2013–24. San Francisco: Federal Reserve Bank of San Francisco, August 26, 2013.

Veiga, Alex. "ATM Fees Keep Climbing, Survey Says." Associated Press, September 29, 2014.

Venkatesh, Sudhir Alladi. *Off the Books.* Cambridge, MA: Harvard University Press, 2006.

Viacom Media Networks. "Millennial Disruption Index." *Scratch,* 2014.

Vlaev, Ivo, and Antony Elliott. "Financial Well-Being Components." *Social Indicators Research,* vol. 118, no. 3 (2014).

Von Hoffman, Alexander. *House by House, Block by Block: The Rebirth of America's Urban Neighborhoods.* New York and Oxford, UK: Oxford University Press, 2004.

Wessler, Seth F. "Middle-Class Betrayal? Why Working Hard Is No Longer Enough in America." *NBC News,* 2015.

The White House Council of Economic Advisers. "Fifteen Economic Facts About Millennials." Washington, DC: The White House, October 2014.

Wilcox, Pamela, and John E. Eck. "Criminology of the Unpopular: Implications for Policy Aimed at Payday Lending Facilities." *Criminology and Public Policy,* vol. 10, no. 2 (2011): 473–82.

Williams, Fred O. "Measuring Average Credit Card Debt." CreditCards.com, 2015.

Wilson, Bart, David Findlay, James Meehan, Charissa Welford, and Karl Schurter. "An Experimental Analysis of the Demand for Payday Loans." Working paper, April 1, 2008.

Wolkowitz, Eva. "2013 Financially Underserved Market Size." Chicago: Center for Financial Services Inclusion, December 10, 2014.

Woodruff, Mandi. "How Mint.com Turned 2 Million Users into a Living Snapshot of the Economic Recovery." *Business Insider,* July 18, 2013.

Zelizer, Viviana A. *Economic Lives: How Culture Shapes the Economy.* Princeton, NJ: Princeton University Press, 2011.

——. *The Social Meaning of Money: Pin Money, Paychecks, Poor Relief, and Other Currencies.* New York: Basic Books, 1994.

Zinman, Jonathan. "Restricting Consumer Credit Access: Household Survey Evidence on Effects Around the Oregon Rate Cap." *Journal of Banking and Finance,* vol. 34, no. 3 (March 2010).

Zumbrun, Josh. "Younger Generation Faces a Savings Deficit." *Wall Street Journal,* November 9, 2014.

INDEX

direct deposit and withdrawal, 21,
    98–99, 215–16n91
disclosure statements, 19, 39, 173,
    226n174
discrimination, 41–45, 56–57, 65–66,
    67, 210n70
Dodd, Christopher, 38–39
Dodd-Frank Act (2010), 32, 39

EBT cards. See Electronic Benefits
    Transfer cards
ECOA. See Equal Credit Opportunity
    Act
economic security. See financial
    security
economy. See also financial crisis
    (2008)
    bank success and, 36
    financial sector and, 34–36
    free market and, 34–35, 170
    human capital and, 167–68
    productivity vs. wages, 51–52
    savings and loan crisis (1980s and
        1990s), 28
    shared, 139–41
    underground, 127–28
education, xiv, 48–50, 54–56, 60,
    107–9, 167–68, 177–78
Edwards, John, 40
Ehrenreich, Barbara, 156
Electronic Benefits Transfer (EBT)
    cards, 3, 11–12, 18
emergency funds, 48, 59, 80–81, 88,
    132, 213–15n88
emerging adults. See millennials
employment. See also entrepreneurs
    age and, 56
    benefits, xiv, 50, 55, 107
    creation of, 168
    credit scores and, 68
    education leading to, 107–8
    financial crisis (2008) and, 53, 55–57
    irregularity of, 52–53

part-time, 53, 56
    payday loans to preserve, 88
    as requirement of payday lenders,
        78–79
    unemployment, 50, 64, 73–74, 107–8
entrepreneurs, 14–16, 52–53, 133,
    148–49. See also innovations
Equal Credit Opportunity Act (ECOA,
    1974), 42, 65, 200n43
Equal Employment Opportunity
    Commission, 56
ethics, 34–35, 64–65

Fair Credit Reporting Act (1970),
    200n43
Fair Debt Collection Practices Act
    (1977), 93, 99
Fair Housing Act (1968), 42
Fairchild, Greg, 87
fair-lending laws, 42–44
family and friends
    stress from, 57, 105
    support to and from, xv, 57–59, 82,
        109–10, 139–40, 154, 219n109
Farrell, Lyn, 29–30
FCA. See Financial Conduct Authority
Federal Deposit and Insurance
    Corporation (FDIC), xvi–xvii,
    25
Federal Reserve, 17, 44, 75
Federal Trade Commission (FTC),
    99–100
fees. See also overdraft fees
    bank account, xiv–xvi, 16–17, 29, 98,
        111, 159
    check cashers, 7, 15, 18, 19, 21–22
    consumer expectations of, 19,
        194n19
    credit cards, 32–33, 68, 72
    debit resequencing and, 33–34, 159
    discrimination and, 44
    informal savings and loans, 125, 132
    late payment, 18, 68, 72